"Urgent and actionable, this passionate manifesto will be a welcome addition to any leader's desk."
  —*Publishers Weekly* (starred review)

"*Radical Respect* [is] presented with thoughtful clarity and sensitivity. . . . Scott's advice is rooted firmly in common sense,
with a nod to the realities of human nature."
  —*Booklist*

"This book tackles serious issues with clarity and humor to
highlight smart steps that we can all take to combat discrimination and promote fairness."
  —**Adam Grant, #1** *New York Times* **bestselling author of**
  Think Again **and host of the TED podcast** *WorkLife*

"Kim Scott does it again! There are so many books about loving
your work, but so few about how to love the people you work
with. This beautifully written, wise, and practical guide shows
us how both are possible. *Radical Respect* is for anyone who
has wondered whether it is possible to create a workplace that
supports both belonging and individuality."
  —**Angela Duckworth, author of** *Grit*

"It's about time someone tackled this thorny subject. Bravo! Many
workplaces get tangled up or ignore the issues when dealing with
bias and difference. Thank goodness for Kim Scott and her dose
of candor, offering us not just the words but the courage and
compassion required to deal with conflicting points of view. *Radical Respect* holds our hands, kicks our butts, and shows us how."
  —**Beth Comstock, author of** *Imagine It Forward* **and former
  vice chair of GE**

"In this powerful and perceptive book, Kim Scott offers a bold
vision—a workplace where respect and collaboration prevail

over domination and conformity. *Radical Respect* is a sparkling combination of moral courage and practical solutions. It belongs on the shelves—and in the hearts and minds—of leaders everywhere."

—**Daniel H. Pink, #1** *New York Times* **bestselling author of** *When* **and** *Drive*

"Packed with stories from Scott's career, *Radical Respect* offers a solutions-focused perspective on #MeToo, acknowledging that gender injustice doesn't exist in a vacuum and broadening the frame to consider diversity and inclusion writ large. Each of us has an important role in creating a fair and reasonable workplace. When we play that role and create the conditions for others to do the same, we can create real change today in the place where most of us spend most of our time—at work."

—**Darren Walker, president of the Ford Foundation**

"Many books describe how to create a better workplace. What makes *Radical Respect* exceptionally interesting and valuable is that Kim Scott vividly describes specific situations: experiences she went through herself or saw happen to people around her; actions she did—or didn't—take, both as an employee and as a boss; and conversations she regrets having or not having. From lessons she learned the hard way, Kim Scott presents a practical framework for how to make work more just."

—**Gretchen Rubin,** *New York Times* **bestselling author of** *The Happiness Project*

"*Radical Respect* left me optimistic that we *can* create just workplaces. Kim Scott carefully explains how bias, prejudice, and bullying undermine all organizations—even those with the best of intentions—and provides an actionable system for countering each. Her acknowledgment that none of us—herself included—are free of this behavior marks an important starting point for a difficult but necessary conversation."

—Henry Louis Gates Jr., Alphonse Fletcher University Professor and director of the Hutchins Center for African and African American Research, Harvard University

"If you've been wringing your hands or hiding your head in the sand about the issues of injustice in your workplace (yes, yours!), this is the book to read. You will learn how to recognize and eradicate the bias, bad behavior, and discrimination that is holding back your team and company from succeeding at the highest levels possible."

—Sarah Kunst, managing director of Cleo Capital

"In debates over workplace inequality, we don't talk enough about the 'how'—how to respond to a boss or coworker who acts unfairly, how exactly that person should change their behavior. *Radical Respect* helps answer the how. Kim Scott provides actionable, effective ways for fighting discrimination and harassment with engagement, collaboration, and respect."

—Sheryl Sandberg, former COO of Facebook and founder of LeanIn.org and OptionB.org

ALSO BY KIM SCOTT

Radical Candor: Be a Kick-Ass Boss
Without Losing Your Humanity

RADICAL RESPECT

How to Work Together Better

KIM SCOTT

ST. MARTIN'S GRIFFIN
NEW YORK

Published in the United States by St. Martin's Griffin, an imprint of
St. Martin's Publishing Group

www.stmartins.com

The Library of Congress has cataloged the hardcover edition as follows:

Names: Scott, Kim (Kim Malone), author.
Title: Just work : get sh*t done, fast & fair / Kim Scott.
Description: First edition. | New York : St. Martin's Press, 2021. | Includes
    bibliographical references and index.
Identifiers: LCCN 2020045306 | ISBN 9781250203489 (hardcover) |
    ISBN 9781250275707 (international, sold outside the U.S., subject to rights
    availability) | ISBN 9781250277718 (signed) | ISBN 9781250270740 (ebook)
Subjects: LCSH: Discrimination in employment. | Sex discrimination
    in employment. | Diversity in the workplace. | Organizational change. |
    Organizational behavior.
Classification: LCC HD4903 .S25 2021 | DDC 658.3008—dc23
LC record available at https://lccn.loc.gov/2020045306

ISBN 978-1-250-62376-8 (trade paperback)
ISBN 978-1-250-36750-1 (ebook)

Our books may be purchased in bulk for promotional, educational, or
business use. Please contact your local bookseller or the Macmillan
Corporate and Premium Sales Department at 1-800-221-7945,
extension 5442, or by email at MacmillanSpecialMarkets@macmillan.com.

Previously published as *Just Work*

First St. Martin's Griffin Edition: 2024

10 9 8 7 6 5 4 3 2

For my soulmate, love, and partner in all things, Andy Scott.
And for our children: you are inheriting a broken world.
Your father and I have worked to mend it, but we have much
further to go. I hope this book will give you some of the tools
you'll need to continue our work.

Difference must be not merely tolerated, but seen as a fund of necessary polarities between which our creativity can spark . . . Only then does the necessity for interdependency become unthreatening.

—Audre Lorde

Contents

**INTRODUCTION: WE CAN FIX PROBLEMS
ONLY WHEN WE ARE WILLING TO NOTICE THEM**   1

PART ONE: EVERYONE HAS A ROLE TO PLAY   7

1. A Framework for Success   9

2. How Leaders Can Foster a Culture of Respect   26

3. Be an Upstander, Not a Silent Bystander   63

4. What to Say When You Don't Know What to Say   91

5. Be Part of the Solution, Not Part of the Problem   127

**PART TWO: DON'T LET POWER SCREW
IT ALL UP**   155

6. Design Principles for Radical Respect   157

7. Apply Design Principles to Management Systems   173

8. Create Virtuous Cycles, Prevent Vicious Cycles   217

9. Speak Truth to Power Without Blowing Up Your Career   229

10. Reinforce a Culture of Consent   254

11. A Letter to My Younger Self and Her Boss   298

12. Put Some Wins on the Board   318

ACKNOWLEDGMENTS   331

NOTES   339

INDEX   357

Introduction

We Can Fix Problems Only When We Are Willing to Notice Them

When you write a book about feedback, or guidance as I prefer to call it, you're bound to get a lot of it. In 2017, I published a book called *Radical Candor: Be a Kick-Ass Boss Without Losing Your Humanity*. It advocated for caring personally and challenging directly at the same time, a combination of real compassion for the other person and a commitment to helping them succeed.

Hands down, the best feedback I got on the book came from Michelle,[1] who'd been a colleague for the better part of a decade. I liked and admired Michelle enormously and was thrilled when she invited me to give a talk about Radical Candor at the tech start-up where she was CEO.

When I finished giving the presentation, Michelle pulled me aside and said, "I'm excited to roll out Radical Candor here, Kim. I think it's going to help me build the kind of innovative culture we need to succeed. But I gotta tell you. As soon as I give anyone even the gentlest, most compassionate criticism, I get accused of being an angry Black woman."

I'd been in innumerable meetings with Michelle. I'd never once heard her raise her voice or even seem annoyed, let alone angry. She's one of the most even-keeled, cheerful people I've met. Calling her "angry" and following that up with "Black" and "woman" was no small indication that something other than an objective assessment was going on with the people who called her that.

Michelle's story made me realize I had not done much to dig into how bias, prejudice, and bullying get in the way of Radical Candor. These attitudes and behaviors destroy the trust that is foundational to the healthy exchange of different perspectives, they mar the quality of feedback, and therefore hurt our ability to do great work and build strong professional relationships. Michelle's feedback also made me realize I'd treated bias, prejudice, and bullying as though they were all the same thing, making it difficult to respond effectively. Different problems demand different solutions, after all.

My failure to consider all this had put Michelle in a jam when she implemented Radical Candor. Come to think of it, it had put me in a jam, too, though in different ways. Why had I not paused to think about this when writing my book?

I was certainly *aware* of the problems of bias, prejudice, and bullying and how they can give way to discrimination, harassment, and violence. I grew up in an upper-middle-class household in Memphis, Tennessee. Since I was a teenager, I'd been wrestling with being White[2] and Southern. Then I moved to New York and Silicon Valley and learned racism was unfortunately not just in the South. A tech CEO I coached was active in the BLM movement after the murder of Michael Brown in Ferguson, Missouri. But he didn't need to fly to Missouri to fight racism. There was plenty of that in California.

Bias, prejudice, bullying, discrimination, harassment, and physical assault weren't things that happened to "other people." I'd personally experienced all of these throughout my career. Given these experiences, how was it possible that I had written a book about management that barely touched on what causes the worst management train wrecks? Freud calls this kind of knowledge "knowing without knowing." Linsey McGoey and others call this *strategic ignorance*. Charles Mills has written about "epistemologies of ignorance."

Michelle's Radical Candor on *Radical Candor* helped me break through that kind of hazy knowing / not knowing so that I could analyze problems clearly enough to begin to develop a framework that might help me (and hopefully you, too) figure out what to do when we notice them. Too often in my career, I have not said or done anything about these problems either because I refused to notice them or because I didn't know what to say or do.

It wasn't Michelle's job to educate me, so I'm grateful to her for doing so. This book is my effort to pay it forward. It will offer a framework that helps us all recognize the different ways that bias, prejudice, and bullying interfere with our ability to work together and what to do to get back on track. It will also examine the ways they enter our management systems, creating even more intractable problems. It will also offer some design principles that will allow us to create better management systems.

The goal is not simply to describe the problems but to figure out what to *do* about fixing them. Awareness is the first step to change. But awareness without action quickly breeds despair. Unless we figure out the next step to take, we'll retreat into denial. Oedipus gouged his eyes out after he realized he'd committed crimes he was ashamed of. This violent depiction of the denial that comes before coming to grips with our own misdeeds, be they intentional or not, is a kind of denial complex. If we are willing to notice problems rather than retreating to denial we can fix them—a much better response than gouging our own eyes out.

This book doesn't promise to fix everything. What it offers are some practical, tactical suggestions that will help us start putting more wins on the board so that we can keep moving forward, so that we don't retreat back into denial.

You can use this book to figure out what you can do to improve your own situation and build a better culture where you work. Of course, your degrees of freedom are different depending on your role or roles—often, we are in two or more roles at once: leader, upstander/observer, person harmed, or person causing harm. Some key questions it addresses:

- What must leaders do to prevent bias, prejudice, and bullying from destroying respect and collaboration on their teams?
- How can we make sure we are upstanders and not silent bystanders when we observe bias, prejudice, and bullying affecting colleagues?
- When we are the person harmed by bias, prejudice, and bullying, how can we choose a response that will help us maintain personal agency?
- What can we do when we realize that we have caused harm? How can we come to grips with the fact that we *all* have our own biases and prejudices, and most of us bully others at least occasionally? If we want to do better in the future, we need to adopt a growth mindset about our own problematic attitudes and behaviors. As my son's baseball coach told his team, "You can't do right if you don't know what you're doing wrong."
- How can we design our management systems to minimize rather than reinforce these problems? When organizations layer power on top of bias, prejudice, and bullying, the result is discrimination, harassment, and physical violations. If leaders don't design management systems for justice, the result is predictable: systemic injustice. And if you are not a leader, how can you navigate your career so you minimize the damage that unfair, inequitable systems can do to you?

- How can we as individuals speak truth to power without blowing up our careers?

There are things each of us can *do*, today, to create a more respectful, collaborative working environment for ourselves and those around us. An equitable working environment in which we can all do the best work of our lives and build the best relationships of our careers is within our grasp.

Just Work, the original title of this book, just didn't work. People thought I was telling them to work all the time, or to return to the office, rather than to work more justly. Hence the new title: *Radical Respect*. I also revised the book based on feedback from people who read the hardcover, to make it shorter and more user-friendly.[3]

I hope this book will energize you to build the kind of working environment where you can love your work—and the people you work with. We must do better than merely tolerating one another if we are going to optimize for collaboration and honor individuality. We *can* work together better—joyfully, even.

Notes

1. When I tell a story in the first person, I'm describing something that happened to me. When I tell a story in the third person, it's either a composite of things I've seen firsthand told abstractly for clarity and efficiency, or it's a story that someone I know told me. Except when I use a first and last name, all names in this book have been changed. I am not naming names, because I want to focus on what we can learn from what happened and how we can apply the lessons to create more radically respectful workplaces everywhere. Also, I chose names that are common in the United States and do not reflect the cultural diversity of our country or our world. This is because when I chose a different set of names, it prompted others to start guessing who was who and to read the wrong things into certain stories.
2. I will capitalize both *Black* and *White* throughout this book. I'm persuaded to do this by the logic of Kwame Anthony Appiah, who argues that these are "both historically created racial identities—and avoid conventions that encourage us to forget this." In his article "The Case for Capitalizing the B in Black," he chose not to capitalize either. I choose to capitalize both, as to me capitalization implies the distinction is an arbitrary one, rather than something essential; you could call me a Tennessean since I grew up there or a Californian since I live there now; or you

could call me a Minnesotan since I was born there. But those descriptors are arbitrary and therefore artificial, not essential. Yet useful.

3. A diverse range of thinkers have influenced this book in significant ways, and their contributions are noted in the notes sections in the relevant chapters. The hardback version had footnotes for each chapter, but many readers felt they slowed them down, so I opted for this more user-friendly approach in the paperback.

PART ONE

EVERYONE HAS A ROLE TO PLAY

1

A Framework for Success

WHAT IS RADICAL RESPECT?

The word *respect* has two very different meanings. The first has to do with admiration for someone's abilities, qualities, or achievements. That kind of admiration has to be earned. But that's not what I'm talking about in this book.

The definition of respect I'm using here is a regard for the feelings, wishes, rights, and traditions of others. This kind of respect is something we owe to everyone; it is not something that needs to be "earned."

The kind of respect that is the birthright of every human being is crucial to a healthy culture. We don't have to respect a person's opinion on a particular topic—we can disagree, vehemently. We don't have to respect a particular action a person took—we can still disapprove and hold them account-able. But we do have to respect that person as a human being if we want to be able to work together productively while also leaving space to disagree and hold each other accountable when necessary.

Radical Respect happens in workplaces that do two things at the same time:

1. Optimize for collaboration, not coercion.
2. Honor individuality, don't demand conformity.

What makes it radical is that it is so fundamental, and yet it rarely occurs.

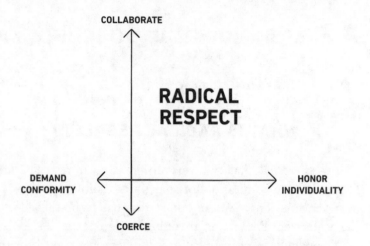

1. OPTIMIZE FOR COLLABORATION, NOT COERCION

Collaboration is essential to any great human accomplishment. Designing organizations that promote healthy collaboration requires proactive efforts to combat coercive behaviors from individuals and groups, such as arbitrary, ego-driven, fact-ignoring biased decision-making, bullying, harassment, and physical violations or violence. When we build management systems that put checks and balances on the power of leaders, they can be held accountable for their behavior *and* their results. Employees contribute ideas rather than being silenced. We help each other improve, and we achieve more than we could ever dream of achieving alone.

There is growing consensus that coercion, even by otherwise visionary leaders, neither gets the best results out of people nor generates the innovation necessary to thrive in the modern economy. Yes, most of us have the impulse to coerce when we can get away with it, and leaders often *can* get away with it unless checks and balances constrain them. When we design management systems carefully, we can mitigate the damage this can do.

2. HONOR INDIVIDUALITY, DON'T DEMAND CONFORMITY

If we want each person we're working with to bring their full potential to our collaborative efforts, we need to honor one another's individuality rather than demanding conformity. None of us (except actors) can do their best work while pretending to be somebody they aren't. Telling people to bring their best to work while discouraging them from being their true selves seems obviously doomed to fail. But we do that all the time, usually unconsciously. Too often, we look for "culture fit" rather than "culture add" when we hire, forcing employees to pretend to be someone they are not, making it difficult for our organizations to evolve, and excluding people who could make important contributions. Often we advertise that we admire people who "think different," but then we punish or ostracize outliers.

Successful collaboration requires diversity of thought *and* experience. Part of the benefit of collaboration is that "many hands make a light load." But the more important benefit is that diversity allows us to challenge each other because each of us has a different point of view, different life experiences. One person easily notices something that another person is oblivious to. But if that person is punished for speaking up, they will go silent and nobody will get the benefit of their observations in the future. When we challenge one another, we improve one another's work. That is why feedback at work is so vital to our individual and collective growth and success.

If we were all exact clones, we'd lose much of the benefit we get from working together. What is impossible for one person is simple for another. What is tedious drudgery for one person is a pleasure for another. We need one another.

WHAT GETS IN THE WAY
OF RADICAL RESPECT?

A "TOXONOMY"

Why is the combination of optimizing for collaboration and honoring individuality so rare that I dub it radical?

All too often, our biases cause us to expect conformity without even realizing what we are doing. And when you layer power and management systems on top of that, that expectation gets baked into who we hire, promote, and fire. Unconscious bias enables discrimination.

When we are at our worst, we seek to establish dominance or to bully others at work, rather than seeking to collaborate with them. And again when you layer management systems and power on top of those instincts, things go from bad to worse. Bullying escalates to harassment, physical violations, and violence.

These are universal human failings. "Progressive" organizations drift toward coercion and conformity as surely as do "conservative" ones. But these problems are not inevitable. Fighting the gravitational pull toward conformity and coercion requires much more than good intentions. We must act. Part of the solution is for leaders to consciously design norms and systems that keep us moving toward respect and collaboration. But leaders can't do this alone. We all have a role to play.

What can we do to make Radical Respect less rare? Let's start by naming the problems so we are more apt to notice them. As I learned when Michelle gave me some feedback on *Radical Candor*, we can't fix problems we refuse to notice.

What precisely do we mean when we talk about a "toxic" or "unfair" work environment? Those terms make the problem feel monolithic, insoluble. When you break a big problem down into its component parts, it's easier to find solutions. I'm not promising a quick fix; but by diagnosing more precisely what was unfair, we can figure out what to do about it and make our situation a little better.

This book offers a "toxonomy" that will help you notice the different problems that need fixing so you can match the right solution to the right problem. Throughout my career, I tended to lump a whole set of different problems into something I thought of as "BS." In so doing, I made it much harder to find solutions and much easier to feel cynical or helpless. I found that by forcing myself to be more precise—was it bias or actually discrimination; was it prejudice or bullying?—I put myself in a much better position to break free of my tendency to default to silence and easier to take some action to make things better. I also found that it was easier to build solidarity with people who were experiencing different but related things—racial bias rather than gender bias, for example. This simple toxonomy helped keep me oriented in disorienting situations. I hope it will help you, too.

BIAS   PREJUDICE   BULLYING   ⚡   DISCRIMINATION   HARASSMENT   PHYSICAL VIOLATIONS

Bias, prejudice, and bullying are big problems, and it can be hard to distinguish between them. When you lay power on top of them, things go from bad to worse. Bias and prejudice plus power creates the conditions for discrimination. Bullying plus power creates the conditions for harassment. Both positional and physical power create the conditions for physical violations and violence.

Throughout this book, I'll use this toxonomy to keep us focused on one problem at a time. Of course, these problems aren't mutually exclusive, and as with all dynamic situations, they can change over time. But the advantage of imposing order like this is that it can help us identify solutions rather than getting lost in the complexity of the problem.

DISAMBIGUATION

Let's look for a moment at the first half of the taxonomy. People often treat bias, prejudice, and bullying as though they are synonymous. For example, the term *microaggression* is useful in pointing out small injuries that add up to repetitive stress injury—a big problem that can keep you from doing your best work or living your happiest life. The problem is, there are three different reasons why people commit microaggressions: they can result from bias, prejudice, and bullying. As you'll learn in the pages that follow, each of these things requires a very different response.

To help parse the problem, let's start with some simple definitions.

Bias is "not meaning it." Bias is unconscious. It comes from the part of our minds that jumps to conclusions, often reflecting stereotypes that we don't believe if we stop to think.

Prejudice is "meaning it." It is a consciously held belief, often rationalizing flawed assumptions and stereotypes.

Bullying is "being mean." There may be no belief, conscious or unconscious, behind it. Often it is the instinctive use of in-group status or power to harm, humiliate, dominate, or coerce others.

Depending on one's perspective, these three problems carry different weight. For example, we are all biased, and bias usually doesn't come with bad intent. So it's tempting to dismiss bias as less severe than other infractions. That is certainly true from the perspective of the person who caused harm. However, it may be different from the perspective of the person harmed. Many people feel that bias is more harmful than prejudice or bullying because it happens much more often. Others have found prejudice or bullying looms larger in their experience. The point is that these are *all* problems that we need to solve, and comparing which one is "worse" than the other isn't helpful.

Often there's no belief, conscious or unconscious, behind bullying. But belief, be it conscious or unconscious, tends to guide our actions. So bias and prejudice tend to make bullying likelier. A person might bully with biased language, using words that wound, even if they don't consciously believe the implications of what they are saying. I worked with a woman who did not consciously believe that women were less courageous than men but who routinely called men she wanted to humiliate "p*$&ies." I've seen racist or homophobic slurs employed in an analogous way. When bullying is emboldened by conscious prejudice, it often becomes violent, as occurred in the Jim Crow South.

Here's a story that illustrates why it's important to distinguish between bias, prejudice, and bullying.

Mr. Safety Pin

I was just about to give a Radical Candor talk to the founders and executives of some of Silicon Valley's hottest start-ups. A couple of hundred men were at the conference. I was one of only a handful of women. Just as I was about to go onstage, one of these men ran up to me.

"I need a safety pin!" he hissed. He was clutching at his shirtfront—a button had popped off. Evidently, he assumed I was on the event staff. To prevent this very confusion, the conference organizers had given the event staff, most of whom were women a good twenty years younger than I was, bright yellow T-shirts. I was wearing an orange sweater. But all he could notice was his need and my gender.

I didn't know what to say. He was utterly certain that it was my job to fetch him a safety pin.

I wanted to believe that his assumption about me stemmed from unconscious bias. Not a federal offense. Most of us have made an incorrect assumption about another person's role based on some personal attribute. These moments are as embarrassing as they are common. It was a classic "Sorry, I don't work here" moment.

There was very little risk to me in challenging his assumptions. I was established in my career, and he couldn't harm me in any real way. Why didn't I say anything?

If I explained, "I need to prepare for my talk right now, so I can't help you out," there was some chance he might reply along the lines of, "Oh. You must be the Radical Candor lady. I don't believe in that soft, feminine leadership bullshit." Unlikely. But I've experienced that kind of prejudice, more than once. If my attempt at a courteous response prompted him to reveal a conscious prejudice against women, it would piss me off, and that would make it harder for me to focus on my talk.

Then, there was another possibility: bullying. What if I corrected him and he escalated, saying something like, "Hey, lady, no need to get your panties all in a wad"? Again, unlikely, but—alas—not impossible. Such things have been said to me, also more than once. Then I'd go onstage roiling mad. That would knock off my game.

There was another confounding factor here beyond gender: power. The man assumed he had a right to be rude to the people staffing the event. Perhaps when he realized I was a speaker, not a staffer, he would snap into polite mode. But talking to anyone the way he'd talked to me was not okay. And it was my job as a leader to remind him of this, to prevent him from treating the staff badly.

But I didn't feel like a leader. I felt like a target. All

this felt like too much for me to deal with in the moments before I walked onstage. So I said nothing, and the man stomped off, evidently wondering why I was refusing to do my job, muttering something about complaining to the event organizers about the unhelpful staff.

It was hard to know what to say because I didn't know whether it was bias, prejudice, or bullying behind his comment. Also, it was hard to know what my role was. Was I the person harmed since the comment was directed at me, the leader since I was the speaker, or an upstander for the staff? Or all three?

In retrospect, my silence was bad for everyone: bad for the staff because he was going to complain about them to their boss; bad for me because I hadn't lived in accordance with my own beliefs; and even bad for Mr. Safety Pin. By not pointing out his bias (if that's what was behind his request), I was making it likelier that he'd repeat his mistake.

The "flavor" of bias, prejudice, and bullying that I have experienced as a White woman in the workplace is obviously different from what a Black woman experiences. Indeed, the only Black woman at the conference had been secretary of state; all I'd had to do to earn my spot as a White woman was to be a director—a middle manager—at Google and Apple.

A colleague of mine who is a gay Black man and another who is a White Jewish lesbian and another who is a straight Latina executive also experience these attitudes and behaviors differently from each other, and differently from either Michelle or me. My husband, who is a straight White man, also has his own experiences with bias, prejudice, and bullying. And so on. We *all* have these experiences, sometimes as leaders, sometimes as upstanders, sometimes we are harmed by them, sometimes we cause harm.

My goal in pointing out the shared roots of our difficult experiences is to build solidarity between as many different people as possible.

HOW DO WE GET THESE PROBLEMS OUT OF THE WAY?

FRAMEWORKS FOR SUCCESS

To stay focused on solutions, this book will offer two frameworks. The first Radical Respect framework will help you figure out whether you are dealing with bias, prejudice, or bullying and what to do about each. The second framework, in the latter half of the book, will help you figure out what to do when power creates the conditions for discrimination, harassment, or physical violations.

Frameworks like these don't claim to fix everything; rather, they are a tool that helps us differentiate between different problems so that we can apply the right solutions.

For example, Michael Porter's Five Forces framework helps leaders identify the key strategic forces at play in their industry. The framework doesn't promise instant sustainable competitive advantage, but it can help you identify and manage the dynamics you are facing. It helps managers differentiate between pressures from competitors, new entrants, suppliers, customers, and substitute products. This seems obvious, but in the heat of the moment, it's easy to conflate different pressures from different sources or to blame everything on just one of the different problems you are facing.

Changing the attitudes and behaviors described in the toxonomy, many of which are deeply ingrained, will demand that you are patient and persistent with yourself and others. If you can extend yourself grace as you hold yourself accountable for missteps, you'll find it easier to extend grace to others when they mess up, as we are all bound to do.

The First Framework

The first Radical Respect framework will help you figure out how best to calibrate your response to bias, prejudice, or bullying, depending on which one you're dealing with.

BIAS: NOT MEANING IT
RESPOND WITH AN "I" STATEMENT

An "I" statement is a good way to respond to bias because it offers your perspective on a situation, giving the other person a new lens through which to understand what's happening.

Whether you are a leader, an observer, or the person harmed, you can use an "I" statement to help the person who said or did the biased thing to notice the mistake.

The easiest "I" statement is the simple factual correction. For example, when someone has made a false assumption about a person's role in an organization based on race or gender: "I am not the decider here, she is." Or, "I don't work here." In a case where a person has said something insensitive, saying something like, "I don't think you meant that the way it sounded to me," shows how it landed for you without attacking the other person. Or, "I don't think you'll

take me seriously when you call me 'honey.'" Or, "I don't think
calling her 'honey' sounds quite right." Or, "I am not sure why
you think I am angry; I am not even raising my voice." Or, "I don't
think they sound angry; they are not even raising their voice."

An "I" statement does not call the person out; it invites the
person in to understand your perspective. Starting with the word
I helps the person to consider things from your point of view—to
understand why what they said or did seemed biased to you.

An "I" statement is a generous response to someone else's
unconscious bias. It helps them learn. Another benefit of an "I"
statement is that it's a good way to figure out whether you're
dealing with bias or something worse. If people respond apologetically, it will confirm your diagnosis of unconscious bias. If
they double down or go on the attack, then you'll know you're
dealing with prejudice or bullying.

What can leaders do to make it likelier that people will be upstanders rather than silent bystanders and that people who are
harmed by bias don't get punished further when they point it out?

Good leaders figure out how to disrupt bias before bias disrupts their team's work. Chapter 2 will offer a three-step bias
disruption process, as well as other techniques leaders can use
to minimize the harm that bias can do.

PREJUDICE: MEANING IT
RESPOND WITH AN "IT" STATEMENT

Prejudice, unlike bias, is a conscious belief, usually incorporat-
ing an unfair and inaccurate stereotype. People of one race are
inferior or superior. One gender tends to be better or worse
leaders. People of a given generation are slower or faster on the
uptake, wiser or more foolish.

People don't change their prejudices simply because someone points them out with an "I" statement. Holding up a mirror tends not to work. When confronting prejudice, it's useful instead to draw a clear boundary: a person can believe whatever they want, but they can*not* impose their beliefs on others. People at work cannot do or say whatever they want.

An "it" statement can offer that boundary by appealing to the law, an HR policy, or common sense. For example, "it is against the law / an HR violation / ridiculous to refuse to hire the most qualified candidate because of their hairstyle"—or any other identity attribute.

Leaders need to create a space for conversation to explore a complicated issue. Each employee is free to believe what they want. Managers are not the thought police. But employees are not free to impose their beliefs on others. But where, exactly, is the line between each person's freedom to believe and freedom from other people's beliefs? I do not have a universal answer to this question. Different leaders are going to draw that line in different places. The most important thing is that you as a leader make it explicit where that line is on your team. Don't decide all alone—involve your team. Leaders are responsible for soliciting input from their teams in order to set and communicate clear expectations about the boundaries of acceptable behavior at work. Chapter 2 will go into more detail about how, exactly, to do this.

BULLYING: BEING MEAN
RESPOND WITH A "YOU" STATEMENT (OR QUESTION)

Workplace bullying is abusive conduct that is threatening, intimidating, or humiliating. It can often sabotage a person, preventing them from doing their best work. Most of us have been familiar with this kind of behavior since our school days, unfortunately. That is why I learned something important about how to respond from my kids.

One day, my children and their cousins described being bullied in school. I recommended they say, "I feel sad when you . . ." They did little to conceal how stupid they thought my advice was. I defended my position until my daughter said, banging her fist on the table in frustration, "*Mom!* They are *trying* to make me feel sad. Why would I tell them they succeeded?"

Bullies are *trying* to hurt someone or at the least to establish their dominance. Pointing out the pain they are inflicting with an "I" statement doesn't make them stop and may even encourage them to double down. And telling them where the boundaries are with an "it" statement will likely encourage them to push past the boundary. Bullies like to break the rules, so using an "it" statement to tell them what the rules are doesn't help.

A "you" response, as in "What's going on for you here?" or "You need to stop talking to me that way" works better. That's because the bully is trying to put you in a submissive role, to demand that you answer their questions or to shine a scrutinizing spotlight on you. A "you" response puts you in the active role, makes clear that you are not going to tolerate their abuse, and shines an uncomfortable spotlight on their behavior.

Here are some examples:

"What's going on for you here?" A man I know who was getting bullied for being gay in school found that this question often caused his tormentors to back off. He turned the tables so they were having to defend themselves, so the questions were about them, not him.

"Do you realize how you sound?" A Black woman executive explained that this could cause a person who didn't want to answer that question to back off.

"You need to stop now." My husband suggested this to my daughter. He explained that there can be a fine line between good-natured give-each-other-shit culture and cruel bullying, and this statement often got people back on the right side of that line.

"Where'd you get that shirt?" Dominatrix Kasia Urbaniak recommends responding with this kind of non sequitur to regain the upper hand when a person is bullying or harassing you. The point is to be the question asker, not the question answerer.

Of course, there's a limit to what you can do about bullying behavior, especially as an observer or as a person harmed. And there may be times when the people around you feel bullied, but you're not even aware of the impact you're having. Again, this is where leadership comes in.

A leader's job is to create three kinds of consequences for bullying: conversation, compensation, and career. Leaders need to learn how to shut down bullying when it happens in conversation; they need to make sure that people who engage consistently in bullying don't get good ratings or big bonuses, and need to resist the temptation to promote bullies, even if they seem to be high performing. There comes a moment in every team's history when the assholes begin to win; that is the moment when the team's culture begins to lose, and poor results will follow. Chapter 2 offers specific tactics leaders can employ to prevent this from happening.

In summary, an "I" statement invites the person to consider your perspective and is a good response to bias; an "it" statement establishes a clear boundary beyond which the other person should not go and is a good response to prejudice. With a "you" statement, you are taking an active stance and refusing to let the bully put you in the submissive role, so it can be an effective response to bullying, as long as you are not at risk of physical harm.

Do you want to charge into your next meeting and start flinging around "I," "it," or "you" statements? Probably not! In an ideal world, leaders would start the ball rolling. But this world is far from ideal. In the following chapters, I'll describe what each of us can do no matter what our role is to disrupt bias, prejudice, and bullying. As this kind of disruption becomes part of the culture, it will get easier to speak up in a way that improves our relationships and our results.

I hope this framework will make it easier to disentangle bias, prejudice, and bullying and to make it easier for you to think about how you might choose to respond differently to each. The next four chapters will go into detail about the different things you can do to apply this framework, depending on what role you play and how much power you have in a situation.

WHO IS RESPONSIBLE FOR RADICAL RESPECT?

ROLES AND RESPONSIBILITIES

Of course, an "I," "it," or a "you" statement lands differently coming from a leader than from the person harmed or an upstander. And your degrees of freedom will be different depending on your role.

This book is organized around the different things we can do to address each of these problems, depending on whether we are a leader, an observer, the person harmed, or the person who caused harm. At different moments, we all play all of these roles, and sometimes we play two or more of these roles at the same time. Even if you are not the "boss," you will be the leader in certain situations. And being the boss doesn't protect you from being the person harmed.

The first half of the book will focus on what we can do to limit the ways that bias, prejudice, and bullying damage us and our organizations. The second half will focus on what we can do to address discrimination, harassment, and physical violations.

Let's start by considering how leaders can use the first framework to prevent bias, prejudice, and bullying from harming the individuals on their teams and the results they are trying to achieve together.

BIAS
NOT MEANING IT

**BIAS
DISRUPTER**

"I" Statement

PREJUDICE
MEANING IT

**SPACE FOR
CONVERSATION**

"It" Statement

BULLYING
BEING MEAN

**CLEAR
CONSEQUENCES**

"You" Statement

2

How Leaders Can Foster a Culture of Respect

For me, the chief joy in being a leader is creating an environment where everyone can love their work *and* working together. That is what allows a team to achieve astounding results collectively and to do the best work of their lives individually. As a leader, you don't have to choose between collective results and each person's individuality. In fact, you can't get one without the other. The strength of the team is the individual, *and* the strength of the individual is the team. Bias, prejudice, and bullying will muck things up both for individuals and for your collective efforts.

PREVENT:
The Leader's Responsibility

To create a productive working environment, a leader's responsibility is to *prevent* bias, prejudice, and bullying from destroying a respectful team ethos. This can feel like trying to prevent the inevitable, given the prevalence of these attitudes and behaviors.

The solution is this: when these problems do occur despite your best efforts, respond in a way that makes them less likely to happen again. Some leaders act as though creating a fair and equitable working environment is a distraction from their "real" job: "to get shit done." But more and more leaders are beginning to understand that they will have trouble getting things done unless they first create a reasonable, inclusive working environment.

Bill Walsh, the former head coach of the San Francisco 49ers, explained in his book *The Score Takes Care of Itself* that his job was to win football games, but he couldn't win those games if he focused too much on the score. The score was a lagging indicator of what he was doing well or badly as a coach. He needed to back up and understand the leading indicators: behaving ethically, demanding high standards, holding people accountable, and teaching the players the right way to play. Note that good teamwork—caring about one's colleagues—goes hand in hand with holding people accountable. Bias, prejudice, and bullying cause unethical behavior, lower standards, prevent accountability, and harm collaboration. All of these things will prevent you from achieving your goals.

Of course, it's not your fault that bias, prejudice, and bullying are so common. But you're the boss, and so it *is* your problem. That's why leaders get paid the big bucks. Things that aren't a leader's fault are their problems. It's not your job to make the whole world just; but it is your job to make your little corner of the world as fair as possible. You can't do it by yourself or by executive order. You're going to need your team's help. And getting that help will require you to make it safe for them to challenge both you and each other.

This requires what psychologist Jennifer Freyd calls *institutional courage*. Institutional courage is a leadership commitment to seek the truth and to take action on behalf of those who trust or depend on the institution—even when it's unpleasant, diffi-

LEADERS &
BIAS PREJUDICE BULLYING ⚡ DISCRIMINATION HARASSMENT PHYSICAL VIOLATIONS

cult, and costly. Institutional courage requires proactive action (e.g., creating systems by which employees can raise concerns without fear of being punished) as well as responsive action (e.g., responding to reports of harm forthrightly, thoroughly, and fairly). These efforts can help prevent future incidents, allow people harmed to recover more quickly, increase trust between employees and leaders, and enhance the institution's overall reputation.

On the other hand, institutional betrayal (i.e., when an institution mistreats those who trust or depend on it) only compounds the harm to all involved. Some common forms of institutional betrayal are victim blaming, sweeping incidents under the rug, and the like. It can be tempting to engage in these behaviors to limit legal exposure. Ultimately, though, institutional betrayal harms people all over again and will harm your organization's reputation in the long run. Institutional betrayal is often cheaper in the short run but devastatingly expensive or even deadly to the institution in the long run.

To demonstrate institutional courage, it's not enough to demonstrate personal courage as a leader. You're human. Sometimes your courage and energy will falter or fail. Ditto for the people who work for you. And, you're only one person. You're not omnipresent. You need to develop systems that will hold you and others accountable.

Get started! Don't wait for reports of incidents and problems to come to you. Be proactive. The rest of this chapter will outline what you as a leader can do to prevent the toxic trio: bias, prejudice, and bullying.

BIAS

How can you teach your team to disrupt bias so that they can treat one another with respect, make more rational, impartial decisions, and collaborate in a way that makes the whole greater than the sum of its parts?

Much has been written about unconscious bias training: when it is helpful and when it can backfire. I'll say this: There are some trainings that are enormously helpful and others that aren't. The thing that most often goes wrong is that the training leaves people clear about the problem but unclear about how to fix it. This is a recipe for paralysis, or what I call "bummer liberalism." Luckily, there are plenty of things we can do to make things better.

The key thing for leaders to do is not to boil the ocean and try to educate their teams about *all* biases or bias as an abstraction. Rather, the idea is to teach a team to disrupt the biases relevant to the actual people in the room. Trying to be aware of every bias that might possibly be present is too much.

Also, there are very few absolutes. What might work for some or even many people won't work for others. The point is to listen when someone tells you that your use of language bothered them and to be both kind and clear when someone's language bothers you.

For example, it bugs me when people refer to adult women as "girls." But I don't speak for all women. Others don't mind. But if you're working with me, please don't persist in calling me a girl, justifying the choice of words by telling me that "other women prefer to be called 'girl.'" You're not talking to other women, you're talking to me.

Of course, if a person has a deeply ingrained habit of referring to women as "girls," I need to be patient and persistent, as long as I can tell they are trying to change that habit of speech when talking to me. They're not going to be able to change the habit after I tell them once. And of course I don't get to tell them what words to use when interacting with other women.

Yes, it would be nice if there were absolute "rules." But human communication has never followed predictable, rule-based patterns. And it evolves over time. Demanding absolutes gets in the way of learning, in the way of progress.

We need to adjust how we speak depending on whom we are talking to. Remember, being authentic doesn't mean ignoring the impact your words have on others. What matters in conversation is not how "most people" feel about a particular word, or what you've always said, or your good intentions. What matters is how what you are saying lands for *the specific person* you are speaking with. Good communication gets measured not at the speaker's mouth but at the listener's ear.

Creating a culture where people can educate each other about specific biases relevant to the people in the room will help your team disrupt bias before it disrupts your work and your relationships. As new people enter the room, everyone will learn new things. That can be fun. Learning new things is not only fun, though, it's also uncomfortable. The only way out is through.

HOW TO DISRUPT BIAS

If you want to help your team change unproductive, biased patterns of thought, one of the best things you can do is sit down with them and explain why you think doing so is essential to a collaborative, respectful working environment. But for this to work, you have to have an open conversation. Be willing to listen to the reasons why your team may be reluctant. People have painful experiences that make them reluctant to do this work. Talk about them. This is going to be uncomfortable. You can make it easier by reassuring people that they won't be punished for making good-faith mistakes or for correcting each other's mistakes. The only way out of this discomfort is through.

Entrepreneur and author Jason Mayden explains why it's important that teammates feel safe both to make mistakes and to point them out. He encourages people to "get beyond the fear of saying the wrong thing because you can't get to the right thing without first making some mistakes in between." At the same time, Mayden points out, "I should not hide my truth to make you feel comfortable in your bias."

Disrupting bias is not going to feel "comfortable." In fact, it's going to feel awkward at best and risky at worst. That's why starting with a conversation is important. Acknowledge how people feel. Don't say, "It's no big deal." Doing this *is* a big deal, and different people will be reluctant to do it for different reasons. It's also important not to confuse being uncomfortable with being unsafe. Don't minimize and don't exaggerate. Get it out on the table.

Once you've discussed the costs and benefits, odds are you all will decide that you don't want bias to skew your decision-making and your results. If you and your team reach that conclusion, there are three things you'll need to develop together to start disrupting bias:

- a shared vocabulary to make it easier to speak up
- a shared norm to take shame out of the game
- a shared commitment to build stamina

A Shared Vocabulary to Make It Easier to Speak Up

How can we get rid of unconscious bias, or at least minimize the harm it does? Becoming aware of something one is unaware of usually requires another person to point it out. But pointing bias out is something we too often avoid. We fear retribution, or being accused of virtue signaling. Or we just don't know what to say.

That's why it's helpful to have a shared vocabulary for pointing out bias. As disrupting bias becomes acceptable, people start to engage in this process more often, making it both lower stakes and expected, creating a virtuous cycle. On the other hand, if the usual response to bias is uncomfortable silence, bias and the disrespect that comes with it get reinforced, creating a vicious cycle. Let's avoid vicious cycles. Reassure your team that disrupting bias is not public criticism, it's a quick collaborative correction and a sign of shared accountability. You're all learning together.

Words matter. You are not the word dictator. Sit down with your team and get their suggestions for a common phrase that everyone can agree to use to point out bias. If everyone is speaking the same language to disrupt bias at work, upstanders and people harmed will find it much easier to speak up. People who said or did a biased thing will more quickly understand that this is a helpful correction, not a character assassination.

"I" statements invite everyone to consider the situation the way the speaker does. But the interruption doesn't have to be an "I" statement. Here are ideas that have been proposed in talks and workshops I've led:

"I don't think you meant that the way it sounded to me."
"Bias interruption."
"I'm throwing a flag on the field."
"Purple flag!"

"Yo, bias!"
"Bias alert."
"Ouch!"

If your team comes up with their own words or phrases, rather than having you dictate them, they're likelier to use them. However, you do need to offer some guidance. Bias disruption will backfire if the phrases chosen are themselves unconsciously biased.

It's not always easy to talk about disrupting bias with your team, and the conversation may be difficult. Some may feel that phrases like "Bias alert" or "Yo" trivialize the harm that bias does. Others may be irritated that you are "wasting so much time on this." And you may feel stuck in the middle.

Remind everyone of the goal: to disrupt bias without disrupting the meeting. You are holding up a mirror for each other because you care, not to attack people or indulge in self-righteous shaming. Remaining silent in the face of a colleague's bias in order to avoid their feelings of shame is neither kind nor respectful, assuming the colleague doesn't want to keep saying or doing the biased thing.

Once a catchphrase is agreed upon, make sure everyone practices using it until the whole team knows how to deploy it quickly and kindly, without drama. Make sure that it's not being weaponized. People should use it to invite others in, not to call them out.

A Shared Norm to Take Shame Out of the Game

It's important that the person whose bias has been disrupted is treated respectfully—and equally important that they respond with respect. But these are hard moments. Most people feel deeply ashamed when their biases are pointed out. Our fight-or-flight instincts may be activated. We rarely respond well in such a frame of mind. How can leaders help themselves and their employees learn to respond well when their biases are pointed out?

The solution is to work out a shared norm for responding that helps the person who said or did the biased thing get out of shame brain. What can help is to teach everyone what to say when someone else points their bias out.

If the person who said or did the biased thing understands why what they said or did was biased, they can say, "Thank you for pointing it out. I get it and I'll try not to say it again, but please point it out if I do." Addressing bias can be tricky because changing deeply ingrained habits of speech will take time and require both patience and persistence. One team was working on saying "you" instead of "you guys," and found it useful to have a jar into which people put a pebble when they made a mistake.

If the person doesn't understand or disagrees, they can say something like, "Thanks for pointing it out, but I don't get it. Can someone explain it to me after the meeting or send me an article to read?" This is hard. When I've been in that situation, I've felt doubly ashamed—I harmed someone and I'm ignorant. Having a norm to fall back on in such moments reassures me that I'm not so alone—it's a norm because it's not uncommon for us to harm each other without even being aware of it. And it reminds me that I want to be aware so I don't do it again.

The reason not to discuss it in the meeting is that bias happens so often that meetings would get derailed if these conversations happened every time it occurred. At the risk of repeating myself, the goal here is to disrupt the bias without disrupting the meeting.

Of course, at times the meeting *should* be disrupted. If someone on a promotion committee, for example, is objecting to someone's promotion for reasons that feel biased, then the promotion decision shouldn't be made without resolving the basis of the objection. If you don't do this, bias gives way to discrimination.

To make this norm a reality and not merely an aspiration, start with yourself. Disrupt your own biases whenever you notice them. Or ask the people on your team who are most comfortable challenging you to disrupt your biases in a meeting. Lead by example with your response. Thank them for pointing it out. Reaffirm that this is how you as a team will change destructive patterns of thought or speech.

A Shared Commitment to Build Stamina

If you've gone a while without disrupting any bias, it probably doesn't mean that your team magically eliminated bias. It means that either nobody noticed the bias or that they didn't feel comfortable pointing it out. So take a minute to recommit to the process.

Remind your team that when we ignore bias or fail to notice it, we reflect and reinforce it, even if we don't intend to. As Ruha Benjamin, author of *Race After Technology*, pointed out, we are pattern makers. We **can** change bad patterns and replace them with better ones. But only if we learn to recognize the bad patterns—our own biases.

Do your fair share of bias disrupting, but you can't be the only one. Your job is to lead by example—and to hold others accountable for doing their fair share of disrupting bias. The whole weight can't fall on your shoulders as the leader. Even less should it fall on the shoulders of the people who are harmed by the bias. If they are the only ones speaking up, they'll get tired of talking, and it will be harder for the team to listen. Hold folks accountable for upstanding. If you as the leader are consistently the only person who interrupts bias, point that out. Let everyone in the room know you expect them to notice and disrupt bias.

This is uncomfortable. But if you're doing your job as a leader, it is not unsafe. Remind your team there's a world of difference between what is uncomfortable and unsafe. People will make mistakes, others will point them out, and there will be emotions. But if you keep at it and build stamina, it will get easier. And if you don't disrupt bias, there also will be emotions—only they'll be repressed emotions that erupt destructively and usually at the worst possible moment, rather than healthy emotions that are part of learning and collaboration.

Experiment. One firm I work with is developing an emoji for Zoom meetings to be deployed when bias was observed. The hope is this new emoji will be used as often as the "raise hand" emoji. This will allow people who might be afraid to speak up to flag bias when they notice it. Other teams find a shared physical prop helps ease the burden of disrupting bias.

You may be wondering, *Is it really my job as a leader to deal with everyone's bias?* The short answer is yes. Here's a painful story from my career that shows what happens when a leader fails to disrupt bias.

It Is *a Big Deal*

I was leading a big team at Google when I heard Mitch, one of my reports, refer to the women on his team as "girls." For me, that is like fingernails on a chalkboard. Or the wrong answer on an SAT test. Men:Women, Boys:Girls. I'd had this conversation with dozens of men who'd worked for me, and I was tired of talking about it. I hoped one of the men from my team with whom I'd already had this conversation would give Mitch a heads-up. But I didn't explicitly hold anyone on my team accountable for doing so. Also, I felt a little intimidated by Mitch. He had been in the military, and I assumed (I only later learned how wrong/biased I was about this) that he'd disagree with me aggressively if confronted.

About a month into his tenure on my team, Mitch had a skip-level meeting with my boss, Sheryl Sandberg. It would be his first one-on-one meeting with her, and he was really excited. Unfortunately, within the first few minutes of the meeting, he made a reference to the "girls" on his team.

Ironically, I was at that moment finally meeting in my office with three men on my team. I'd hoped one of them would talk to Mitch about not calling women "girls." But as I had, they had defaulted to silence. A knock on the door revealed a very pale Mitch. There would be no need to enlist the men. Sheryl had told him *exactly* what she thought of his use of the word *girls*.

I immediately felt bad for having put him in that situation. It's a boss's job to tell a person when they are making mistakes that are going to get them into trouble. And I hadn't done my job. I rarely respond well when I feel guilty. I tried to make a joke of the whole thing. I turned to the other people on my team and said, "You can thank me now. You all thought I was a pain in the ass, but aren't you glad that you know not to call women 'girls'?"

Now Mitch looked mad. "Why didn't you tell *me*?"

I didn't have a good answer, so I did to Mitch what had been done to me too many times. I said, "Oh, come on, Mitch. It's no big deal."

"When you meet with your boss's boss for the first time and all you talk about is how you are an asshole for calling the women on your team 'girls,' I'd say it *is* a big deal."

He was right about that and understandably mad. It

was my job as his leader to have disrupted his bias. Part of the reason I failed was that I treated the whole thing as though I were the person harmed. And, to be fair, for years I had been referred to as a "girl," a "chick," or other words designed to diminish women. As a person harmed, I had every right to pick my battles. But if I wanted to lead effectively, I had to respond.

I learned something important that day. You may feel like the person harmed, and you may in fact have been harmed in the past, but if you are also the leader, you'd better act like one. It was my job to give Mitch that feedback, both for his sake and for the sake of the women on his team. I promised myself I wouldn't make that mistake again.

Having said all that, I'm now going to cut myself some slack and encourage you to cut yourself some slack if you've made similar mistakes. Being a leader is hard. Being a leader from a systemically disadvantaged[1] group is harder. We're all human, and we're all going to make mistakes. The purpose of sharing this story is to learn from it, not to induce self-flagellation. Mitch forgave me—we are still friends nearly fifteen years later. And the women on Mitch's team forgave me for allowing their boss to refer to them as "girls."

It is a big deal to have a boss who disrupts bias—and it's better for everyone.

PREJUDICE

What if the issue isn't unconscious bias but a very consciously held prejudice, reflecting a stereotype that you believe is inaccurate and unfair, and that people on your team find offensive? What can you as a leader do about that?

The first thing to do is to manage your own emotions. Prejudice can induce a strong response: incredulity, disgust, rage, impatience, avoidance. Take a deep breath.

You can't control what the people who work for you think. People on your team are free to believe whatever they want. But they are not free to impose those beliefs on others. Your job is to work with your team to identify and articulate where that line is—what is okay to say and do at work and what is not.

The trouble comes when you're the one charged with deciding when the murky line between "freedom to" and "freedom from" has been crossed. This is one of the toughest challenges you'll face as a leader.

It's a leader's job to create an environment where people can work with one another productively. Prejudice, a belief that some sort of false stereotype is actually "the truth," is inherently disrespectful. It gets in the way of a team's ability to collaborate, to honor one another's individuality, to communicate across differences.

Pointing out a prejudice probably isn't going to change it. When leaders teach their teams to hold up a mirror to a person's bias, they typically self-correct. But in the case of prejudice, if you hold up a mirror, the person is likely to say, "Yeah, that's me. Aren't I good-looking?" The person with the prejudiced belief doesn't acknowledge the prejudice; rather they think it's "the truth."

What, then, can a leader do when one person's prejudiced belief gets in the way of their ability to respect others on the team or even creates a hostile work environment?

I don't have The Answer to this question. But there is one thing you can do to improve your odds of arriving at a good outcome: create a space for conversation. When you spend a little time with your team talking about what is okay to say or do and not okay to say or do on your team, you'll build an important conflict-resolution muscle. You don't have to come up with a rationale that would satisfy a philosopher to figure out how to work better together. There are resources out there that can help. You can hire someone with experience to guide you through the conversation, or turn to articles mentioned in the endnotes.

Create a Space for Conversation

Leaders must set and communicate clear expectations about the boundaries of acceptable behavior at work. But how to do it? It's not practical or desirable to come up with a list of every image or word that can't be emblazoned on a shirt or a hat, a list of words that are not okay to say, beliefs that are not okay to express. Banning words, books, and ideas rarely works in the long run.

Instead, I'd again suggest starting a conversation with your direct reports about prejudice. A person has a right to believe whatever they want, but not to impose that belief on others. But where exactly is that line? This is a hard question to answer in the abstract. I recommend starting with a specific situation rather than abstract principles. Sit down with them and talk about some real shit shows that happened at other companies.

Or if you prefer a fictionalized example, you can use the one described in the next paragraph.

A Conversation Starter: What Would You Do?

Sometimes a person's belief is so blatantly prejudiced that it leaves you at a loss for words. Let's take the case of a company whose employee-engagement survey showed women at that company were less engaged than men. When the leadership had follow-up meetings with women to understand why, the women they spoke with hypothesized this was a result of bias they experienced. However, one employee, a man, asserted that the Big Five personality test "proved" that the problem was not gender bias but that women were genetically more neurotic than men. He went on to say that all efforts to improve the situation for women at the company were a waste of time and unfair to men. When people didn't listen to him, he wrote up his thoughts in a shared document and posted it on the intranet. When people challenged him, he removed them from the document. When his boss asked him to take the document off the intranet because many felt it was creating a hostile work environment for women and because many managers felt this document was creating a distraction that was hurting productivity, he leaked the document to the media. He then went on a popular podcast and claimed he was being "canceled."

What would you do if you had an employee who did

this? Sit down and review the scenario with your team.
Which of the following approaches seems best?

If you are willing to engage with this employee about
their belief, you could start with the following "it"
statement:

> "It is inaccurate to assert things like 'women are
> biologically more neurotic than men.' In this case,
> you're mixing up correlation with causation. The Big
> Five personality research tells us about correlation—say,
> which biological sex might be more associated with a
> given trait. That's not the same thing as causation—say,
> an attempt to chalk up a correlation to a biological cause.
> There are plenty of reasons why women might be likelier
> to experience so-called neurotic feelings like anxiety,
> worry, fear, and anger—this type of prejudice included—
> that have nothing to do with biology. Furthermore, it is
> a historical fact that doctors have used faux science to
> diagnose women as hysterical or crazy when they did
> not adapt to the norms their husbands or fathers tried to
> impose upon them."

Or, if you feel this is a conversation he should have
in private with the HR team and you are unwilling to
discuss his beliefs with him, you may want to take a
different approach. A different kind of "it" statement, also
appealing to common sense, could let him know whom to
have the conversation with, and how. For example:

> "It is a giant distraction from our work to assert that
> your interpretations of Big Five research are 'the truth.'
> I disagree with your interpretations. But it's not my job
> to discuss this with you. It's not your colleagues' job to

discuss this with you. People are stressed right now, and it's not a good use of time to have this conversation. If you have a criticism of the HR team's interpretation of the employee engagement data, please talk to them in private. The way you are approaching this is preventing you and many others at the company from getting their work done."

If you feel what he is doing violates an HR policy or a code of conduct, and you want to shut him down harder, you could use an "it" statement that appeals to company policy. This doesn't require anyone to discuss his beliefs with him, but it does let him know that he has stepped over a line. For example:

> "It is a violation of our code of conduct, which says that all employees should contribute to a respectful, safe, and inclusive working environment for other employees, for you to keep saying this."

If you want to make absolutely certain that he understands there will likely be consequences for him if he persists in proselytizing his prejudice, which can sometimes cross a line from prejudice to bullying, you can use an "it" statement that emphasizes consequences to him. For example:

> "It contributes to a hostile work environment for women when you say women are biologically programmed to be more neurotic than men. Furthermore, it is illegal

for management to fail to take action when one person contributes to a hostile work environment. So I am obligated by law to take disciplinary action."

If you are a senior leader at an organization, you can use this scenario or one like it to stress test the policies you've put in place. Do a "pre-mortem."

Give your team the basic facts of the case study you chose, whether it's the one above or another one. Then ask them how they would have handled a similar situation. Invite a bias buster in to have this conversation with you, especially if your team is homogeneous. The goal of these conversations is to come up with a shared understanding of what is okay and not okay to do or say in your workplace. If someone on your team wrote a memo like the one above, how would you handle it? What policy or set of guiding principles could you write now that would help you navigate a similar situation? Such principles might include things like "Communicate respectfully," or "When people tell you that your beliefs feel disrespectful, don't continue to discuss these beliefs with that person."

These conversations will take time, and they will elicit some emotion and even some heat. But avoiding these conversations will leave you and your team without the skills you need to figure out what to do when you're presented with a crisis of your own. If you have them now, before your team is in crisis, they will push you as a team to think as clearly about behavior as you do about performance. They will force you to create some explicit standards for behavior and to decide what the consequences ought to be for violating the standards you are setting forth. Then you can let employees know when they will get a warning and what is grounds for immediate dismissal. If you have these conversations when things are calm, *before* some painful public crisis erupts, you'll be better equipped to figure out what to do.

BULLYING

Bullying creates an atmosphere of fear that undermines a team's morale and ultimately their success. Unless managers intervene, bullying is likely to result in getting the bully more than their fair share of airtime, credit, head count, budget, or the like. If bullying gets rewarded, it's not surprising that some people are willing to do it. But it results in a misallocation of resources, which is inefficient. Bullying also creates a culture of fear, which hurts innovation and morale. Bullying may feel like a shortcut to the bully, but it hurts everyone else's ability to do their best work, so it does a lot more harm than good. It's a leader's job to stamp it out.

One of the things that makes preventing bullying so difficult is that we tend to be unaware when we are the one doing the bullying, but acutely aware when we are being bullied. According to a 2021 Workplace Bullying Institute survey, only 4 percent of people say they've bullied someone at work, but 49 percent say they have been bullied or witnessed bullying at work. It's easy to recognize when other people bully and hard to be aware of our own bullying.

Another thing that's tricky about bullying is that, as the leader, *you* are the one whose behavior is most likely to be experienced by others as bullying. Part 2 will cover the kinds of checks and balances leaders can put in place to make sure they get feedback when this happens.

It's a leader's job to create an environment in which bullying gets recognized and corrected. There are two important things you can do as a leader. You can create consequences for bullying, and you can shut down bloviating BS.

Create Consequences for Bullying

Unless leaders create real consequences for bullying, it does work for the bully, at the expense of others on the team. As a leader, you have three levers at your disposal:

- conversation consequences
- compensation consequences
- career consequences

CONVERSATION CONSEQUENCES

Your first response to bullying should be to pull the bully aside and give clear feedback. They might say they were unaware they were crossing a line or simply deny it. Or they may argue some version of "I'm doing what I have to do to get results. If others can't take it, they should find a new place to work."

Don't let them off the hook. Reiterate what you noticed and how it affects the team. Then explain that if the behavior continues, it will be noted in their performance review and may affect compensation and even their future at your company. If the person who engaged in bullying does it again, you must follow through with the consequences you outlined.

It's equally important to follow up with the people who were bullied to understand how they experienced the situation and to let them know you have their back.

COMPENSATION CONSEQUENCES

Never, ever give a raise or bonus to people who consistently bully their peers or employees. Compensation shows what a leader values. Behavior uncorrected is behavior accepted. Behavior rewarded is behavior requested.

In many companies, people who browbeat and demean others are allowed to continue doing so as long as they get results. They might be given feedback about the damage they're doing, but if their performance review and bonus are based on their numbers, not their behavior, their behavior won't change.

What is the result? No one wants to work with the bully, and valued employees quit. Over time, as the best people refuse to work with them, the bullies' performance suffers. But the process is so gradual that the bullies, and also their managers, don't make the connection between the bullying behavior and performance. After years of getting rewarded for their behavior, it suddenly may cease to work, and they are bewildered. They behaved exactly the same way that year as they did the year before. What changed? The punishment seems arbitrary to the person doing the bullying. Either way, the victims of the bullying are driven away, the person doing the bullying doesn't learn in time to change, and the manager is losing good people and getting poor results. Everyone suffers.

It's easy to say that people who mistreat their coworkers and employees shouldn't get raises or bonuses. But it's even better to create a performance management system that explicitly discourages bullying. I once spent some time working on the performance review system at a large tech company. Their process of evaluating employee performance was impressive, but what really struck me was its commitment to putting teamwork on par with results. Even if you hit all your performance goals, you'd still get a bad performance rating if you weren't a good team player, as measured by your peer reviews in a 360 review process. The manager couldn't determine unilaterally who was bullying and who wasn't; peer assessment had to be taken into account.

BIAS   PREJUDICE   ⌈ **LEADERS &** ⌉ ⚡ DISCRIMINATION   HARASSMENT   PHYSICAL VIOLATIONS
                ⌊ **BULLYING** ⌋

This was good for everyone, and it was good for results. It was good for leaders because it gave some teeth to their feedback about bullying. It was good for the people who would have been bullied if that kind of behavior had not had consequences. In many cases, it was even good for the people doing the bullying. Pushing them to develop knowledge and competence instead of trying to dominate or coerce their colleagues increased their self-assurance. And it was good for the company because it helped stamp out bullying and improved results.

Atlassian, an Australian enterprise software company, provides another great example of a performance management system that actively punishes bullying. The company explicitly designed their performance review system to create negative consequences for the "brilliant jerk," the bane of so many tech companies. At Atlassian, it's explicit that bullying will result in consequences, no matter how good a person's results are. Bullying can be flagged in a 360 review or observed by the person's manager.

CAREER CONSEQUENCES

Give feedback, encouragement, and goals for improvement to people prone to bullying behavior. If the behavior doesn't change, fire them. The long-term damage these people cause is not worth any quarterly result they may be delivering. And whatever you do, do not promote people with a track record of bullying, no matter how good their results. There comes a moment on too many teams when the jerks begin to win. That is the moment when the culture begins to lose.

It's Better to Have a Hole than an Asshole

I once worked with a particularly notorious bully. One
man I worked with commented, "Well, I have never had a
problem with him myself, but I've never met an executive
who is so universally hated by women." Here are a few
of the things I saw. Every interaction was an opportunity
for him to make women uncomfortable. His job required
frequent trips abroad. Driving from the airport, he'd point
out all the sex hotels along the way. He loved to start what
he leeringly called "catfights" between women at the office.
Once, he told me that he knew I secretly hated another
woman on his team. When I assured him that in fact I
liked and respected her, he began bad-mouthing her to
me, asking how I could be supportive of someone who'd
been promoted over me when she didn't deserve it. When I
disagreed again, he became visibly angry. Another time, he
stood onstage in front of a few thousand people, flanked
by his direct reports. He looked to his right, looked to his
left, then gave a lecherous smile and said, "Ooooh, the
ladies dressed up for me today!"

As is often the case, it wasn't only women he picked
on. It was anyone he deemed to be vulnerable. He once
walked into a man's office, put his phone on speaker, and
asked him to call a colleague and ask that colleague what
they thought of him without letting them know he was
listening to the call.

Even though the company prided itself on having a
good culture, this executive kept on getting promoted.
The message they wanted to put out was "You don't have

BIAS   PREJUDICE   [**LEADERS &**
                     BULLYING] ⚡ DISCRIMINATION   HARASSMENT   PHYSICAL VIOLATIONS

to pay the asshole tax here," but these promotions told a different story: bullying will get you ahead. People stopped trying to confront his behavior because it was getting *rewarded*. Which made more people think that they, too, had to behave like this executive to get ahead: abusive and domineering.

Why was this kind of behavior not punished? Why did he get promoted when he should have been penalized for his behavior? The usual reasons. His team was getting good results. There was pressure from Wall Street. It would be hard to replace him. There would be a "hole" on the leadership team if they got rid of him.

By the time the company fired this bullying executive, though, at least five top VPs had quit because of him, four of them women. And after he was gone, results improved. His behavior had been hurting performance. His team had gotten good results despite him, not because of him.

He got fired from his next job, too, for unethical behavior. Bullying and low moral standards often go hand in hand.

Shut Down Bloviating BS

We can all think of typical bullying behavior: finger-pointing, name-calling, and yelling, and ridiculing, threatening, and intimidating others. One particularly insidious form of bullying is what I call *bloviating BS*. This is what happens when one person, usually not the most informed person in the room, has the unearned confidence to make things up and take more than their fair share of the airtime in a meeting.

Frank Yeary, a senior finance executive at Citigroup who led his firm's early diversity and inclusion efforts, explained to me how he noticed this playing out in a way that was destructive. He remarked that though women tended to come to meetings better prepared than men, a few of the men did most of the talking, often speaking over the women. This was not only bad for the women's careers, he explained, it was bad for decision-making at the bank. The best-prepared people in the room were silenced by the bloviating BSers.

This kind of behavior can materially harm a team's success. Studies show that when one person does all the talking, it harms a team's performance. In studies of team effectiveness, Carnegie Mellon University professor Anita Woolley has found that "as long as everyone got a chance to talk, the team did well." But if only one person or a small subset of the team dominated conversations, the collective intelligence declined. The airtime didn't have to be perfectly equal in every meeting, but in the aggregate, it had to balance out.

Project Aristotle at Google also examined an enormous body of data about team performance and found that equal participation was a more significant predictor of team success than having one superstar on the team. I am not sure why so many leaders have an exaggerated faith that it's the "superstars" who determine a team's success and so give them all the oxygen in the room. Perhaps they read Ayn Rand at an impressionable age. But the data doesn't bear out this misconception.

Even if you disagree with my assertion that collaboration is more important than one person's efforts, one thing is clear: when a bloviating BSer who doesn't really know what they're talking about shuts everyone else down, it's no good. It hurts the team. And it also hurts the person who talks too much. Regardless of what's driving the bloviation (bullying, nervous energy, neurodiversity), the bottom line is that others

BIAS   PREJUDICE   [**LEADERS &**
BULLYING]   ⚡   DISCRIMINATION   HARASSMENT   PHYSICAL VIOLATIONS

won't appreciate it, as Dan Lyons explores in his book *STFU: The Power of Keeping Your Mouth Shut in an Endlessly Noisy World*. So if someone is talking too much, you do everyone a favor by sharing this feedback.

People who are from systemically advantaged groups or dominant in some way are much likelier to get away with or even be rewarded for bloviating BS. In a fascinating study, researchers asked men and women whether they were experts in sixteen distinct math topics, three of which were made-up. Men were much likelier to claim expertise in these made-up topics than women, as were the rich over the middle class. Also, people were likelier to challenge BS from those they perceived as their equals than from people with more power. So if you're a leader, you need to make sure you're creating the conditions for people to call BS on you.

Not getting called out on one's BS breeds a problematic overconfidence that harms collaboration. This can work in the BSer's favor in situations such as job interviews and grant applications. But that means that if you let it influence your decisions as a leader, you're hiring the BSer, not the expert, giving the grant to the BSer, not the expert. Allowing the BSer to hog airtime in a meeting means your decisions will be unduly influenced by a person who knows less than the others in the room. That's why it's your job as a leader to address it.

Not only does allowing bloviating BS to be rewarded harm decision-making, it's also unfair because people who are systemically disadvantaged can rarely get away with bloviating BS and so don't reap its rewards. The answer, though, is not to ensure that everyone gets rewarded for bloviation. The answer is to make sure no one does. There are some privileges that people from systemically advantaged groups have that should be extended to all and others that should be extended to none.

As a leader, it's your job to make sure that no one person dominates, especially not a BSer, and that everyone feels comfortable participating in meetings online or off- and also in the everyday back-and-forth of conversations at work.

Here are some things you can do to prevent bullying bloviation from ruining your team's ability to collaborate effectively:

- Give the quiet ones a voice
- Block bloviation
- Encourage people to track their airtime

GIVE THE QUIET ONES A VOICE

Jony Ive, the former chief design officer at Apple, said a leader's job is to "give the quiet ones a voice."

How can you do this? Annie Jean-Baptiste, who is the head of product inclusion at Google and an introvert, offers a simple suggestion. Ask them. She had a manager, Seth van der Swaagh, who noticed she was quiet during meetings. He asked her, "How many times have you had an idea and someone else said it, but you were afraid to speak up?" He then asked her, "Is it okay if sometimes I directly ask you in meetings if there are any thoughts you'd like to share?" By inviting Annie to speak up, he created a virtuous cycle. The more he asked her opinion, the more she spoke; the more she spoke, the more comfortable she became speaking. It was just like building a muscle: her voice got stronger over time. It is also helpful to send out the agenda beforehand so that introverts and others who often need to process information before they are on the spot have time to prepare what they want to say.

BLOCK BLOVIATION

If one person is doing all the talking, gently interrupt that person and say that you'd like to hear from everyone. When you ask a question, go around the room. Give everyone a set amount of time to answer if the same person is always giving long-winded answers. I once bought an hourglass (except it was a one-minute glass) for a conference room when I had one such person on my team.

When I taught at Apple University, an experienced professor taught me to block bloviation. He showed me how to body-block people who wouldn't shut up—literally, to walk over to them and stand in front of them. If they still didn't get the hint, the professor suggested, put your hand in the air in a "pause" gesture and say you'd like to hear from others in the room. When someone is speaking too loudly, walk toward them, even though it's usually instinctive to step away from someone who is yelling. Usually, they'll lower their voice.

ENCOURAGE PEOPLE TO TRACK THEIR AIRTIME

Share the research that shows why it's important that everyone on a team gets opportunities to contribute to conversation. (See notes.) Then measure what percentage of time everyone is talking. There are a number of airtime trackers folks can use to figure out what percentage of the time they spend talking. This is especially important for virtual meetings, which are even likelier than in-person meetings to be dominated by one person. If Zoom, Google Meet, and Microsoft Teams and other videoconferencing services offered a private airtime report to folks who spoke more than three times their "airtime" in a meeting, it would be a great service to both team effectiveness and inclusivity. Of course, you don't want to get too obsessed with measurement here. There may be a good reason why one person is talking a lot and another not at all in a particular meeting. But it would be useful to ask folks on your team to self-monitor.[2]

DON'T ALLOW BIAS, PREJUDICE, OR BULLYING TO CREATE FEEDBACK FAILS

This section focuses on advice for managers from systemically advantaged groups with direct reports from systemically disadvantaged groups because these are the feedback failures that most frequently do great harm.

Feedback is the atomic building block of management. A central part of a leader's job is to solicit feedback from everyone; to give specific, sincere praise and clear, kind criticism to everyone; and to encourage a culture of feedback. To state the obvious, you need to do this for both under- and overrepresented employees.

Bias, prejudice, and bullying inhibit leaders' ability to create a culture of feedback. Here are some things you can do to prevent this from happening on your team:

- Solicit feedback from *all* your direct reports; don't play favorites.
- Don't let bias, prejudice, and bullying taint feedback.
- Don't let bias cause you to become a micromanager.
- Don't let bias cause you to become an absentee manager.
- Beware of racist compliment syndrome and backhanded compliments.

SOLICIT FEEDBACK FROM *ALL* DIRECT REPORTS; DON'T PLAY FAVORITES

When your team knows that you are open to their feedback, that you respect them enough to listen to what they think and take action on it, you've fostered the kind of psychological safety so essential to successful collaboration.

Amy Edmondson, a Harvard Business School professor who studies the link between psychological safety and team outcomes, and I have written about the importance of soliciting feedback from each direct report to create a culture of psychological safety. And it is not enough to solicit feedback—you have to make your listening tangible by rewarding it and acting on it. Solicit feedback at the end of each one-on-one with your direct reports.

As a manager, it's also your job to create a culture of feedback. Make sure that people on your team solicit feedback from one another and give it.

In the story from the introduction, Michelle described how people would reject her feedback by invoking the "angry Black woman" stereotype. And this happened to her when she was the CEO. It must have been much worse earlier in her career. I found sexism more prevalent and difficult to deal with early in my career; she experienced the one-two punch of both sexism and racism.

So if you are a leader, make sure that you are having one-on-ones with each of your direct reports on a regular schedule and asking them for feedback at the end of each one. Try keeping a tally of how often you took action on feedback each of your direct reports gave you. Notice if you tend to ask for and take action on feedback from your direct reports from systemically advantaged groups more often than your direct reports from systemically disadvantaged groups. If there's a difference, ask yourself why. Is bias creeping in to whom you listen to? If so, correct that!

DON'T LET BIAS, PREJUDICE, OR
BULLYING TAINT YOUR FEEDBACK

How can you make sure that you don't give praise or criticism that is biased, prejudiced, or bullying? Unfortunately, you *are* going to make some mistakes. This is painful. As a White person, I dread the possibility of saying something that is racist. But if I let that dread get in the way of speaking openly with my colleagues who are Black, then I will do the racist thing. What I've found is that if I am open to feedback that I've made a mistake and am willing to hold myself accountable and to make amends, I can not only recover from these mistakes but learn something and grow. And set a great example for everyone else. Men I've talked with have said that they feel about gender the way I feel about race. No matter who you are and whom you're talking with, soliciting feedback is so important.

Remember, when you are a leader and you get feedback that you've given biased, prejudiced, or bullying feedback, you need to take a deep breath and take a step out of your leader role. You're now in the role of the person who caused harm. You need to practice your AAAAAC! skills. Acknowledge what you did wrong, make amends, accept the consequences, apologize, and change.

In 2014, Kieran Snyder wrote an article in *Fortune* called "The Abrasiveness Trap: High-Achieving Men and Women Are Described Differently in Reviews." And of course, it was worse for nonbinary employees. This article tore through several tech companies I was advising. It struck a nerve because so many women had experienced this form of bias. And when the bias made its way into performance reviews, it became discrimination.

HISTORICALLY ADVANTAGED LEADERS &
[BIAS   PREJUDICE   BULLYING] ⚡ DISCRIMINATION HARASSMENT PHYSICAL VIOLATIONS

DON'T LET BIAS CAUSE YOU TO BE A MICROMANAGER

When managers have biases or prejudices that leave them less confident that they can rely on employees from historically marginalized groups, they sometimes micromanage. This hurts both the morale and the performance of these employees. Often it's described as a form of bullying. For example, studies have shown that White managers in the United States micromanage and surveil Black employees two times more than they do White employees, due to bias or prejudiced beliefs.

DON'T LET BIAS CAUSE YOU TO BE AN ABSENTEE MANAGER

Sometimes the exact opposite happens. When managers have biases or prejudices that leave them afraid to give feedback to employees from systemically disadvantaged groups, they sometimes simply ignore these employees.

A clear explanation of expectations, reassurances that an employee can meet those expectations, and guidance when a candidate falls short are crucial in helping everyone do their best work, but especially people who are systemically disadvantaged.

In his book *Whistling Vivaldi*, Claude Steele describes how straightforward critical feedback from Tom Ostrom, Steele's PhD faculty adviser, helped him overcome the struggles he experienced as one of the few Black students in his program. *Whistling Vivaldi* references research that demonstrates that kind, clear development feedback helped Black students at other universities around the country to succeed. Similarly, Stanford sociologist Shelley Correll's research has shown that career success requires candid criticism—and that many women don't get that kind of candor from their bosses who are men.

How does this play out? A bank executive once described the

following scenario to me. He went to a meeting with a banker and an analyst. In the meeting, the analyst—a man—made a mistake. After the meeting, the banker explained to the analyst in no uncertain terms the mistake he'd made. The analyst never repeated the mistake. The following week, he went to a meeting with the same banker and a different analyst, this time a woman. This analyst made the same mistake the analyst the week before had made. But the banker didn't tell the analyst about it after the meeting. Not because he was a misogynist jerk hell-bent on destroying her career but because he was afraid if he did he'd be called sexist or an asshole or some such.

Why does this happen? David Thomas, the president of More-house College, calls this reluctance to engage across differences *protective hesitation*. Often this happens because the manager fears being seen as biased, sexist, or racist. A desire not to be *seen* as biased paradoxically leads the manager to do the biased thing: fail to give the same candid, helpful feedback to employees from system-ically disadvantaged groups that they give to everyone else. This is *really* unfortunate because it's precisely that kind of feedback that will most help these employees succeed and overcome the extra challenges they face as a result of bias, prejudice, and bullying.

Once, I was giving a Radical Candor talk to a group of CEOs. One of them said he would not give feedback to "certain" employees "because he didn't want to get into hot water with HR." In fact, HR reported to him. He was not so powerless that he could legitimately choose to avoid conversations in this way. When managers fail to give feedback to employees from historically marginalized groups, they give an unfair advantage to employees from systemically advantaged groups, compounding their advantage and contributing to discrimination. They are failing to fulfill their responsibilities as managers. These managers need training so they can learn to do better.

HISTORICALLY ADVANTAGED LEADERS &
| BIAS   PREJUDICE   BULLYING | ⚡ DISCRIMINATION   HARASSMENT   PHYSICAL VIOLATIONS

BEWARE OF RACIST COMPLIMENT
SYNDROME AND OTHER BACKHANDED PRAISE

Bias, prejudice, and bullying can turn praise into a punishment rather than a reward.

Have you ever gotten a compliment that revealed the other person's biased expectations? Think about the impact that had on you, and make sure you're not doing the same thing to others.

Sometimes this kind of compliment reveals bias; other times it is more insidious—it reveals a conscious prejudice or is a kind of bullying. In his memoir, civil rights attorney and presidential adviser Vernon Jordan tells of a searing incident that occurred during his summer job driving a retired White banker around Atlanta. While his employer napped after lunch, Jordan used the free time to read. "Vernon can read!" the banker exclaimed to his relatives, as if he were giving Jordan, a college student, a compliment. It's hard for me to imagine the banker didn't know that Jordan could read; my guess is he was just being an asshole, invoking an anachronistic stereotype that Black people were illiterate, while pretending to praise him.

Breeze Harper, PhD, who founded Critical Diversity Solutions and who was the bias buster for this book, described a problem that Black people have been pointing out for years, but that I had been unaware of: racist compliment syndrome. She is a Black woman, and when a White person praises her for something basic, for example, "You are so articulate," it's often a sign of covert racist beliefs about Black people. Some context: the people who said that to Breeze knew that she has an undergraduate degree from Dartmouth, a master's from Harvard, and a PhD from UC Davis. Why, then, did they seem surprised that she was articulate?

Be aware of that kind of mistake. But don't let it paralyze you or prevent you from speaking with people from systemically disadvantaged groups. Let it be a reminder to be open to feedback—which in all cases will make you a better leader.

Notes

1. Throughout this book, I'll use the phrases *systemically disadvantaged* and *historically marginalized*. To describe the opposite, I'll use the phrases *systemically advantaged* and *historically advantaged*. In the hardback, I used *overrepresented* and *underrepresented*, but after publication, I got feedback that these terms did not do enough to acknowledge either the systemic injustice or the history of trauma. I agreed with that feedback!
2. There are a number of tools, and no doubt new ones will be developed after this book is published. Some current ones are www.gong.io and www.macro.io.

RADICAL RESPECT FRAMEWORK FOR LEADERS

BIAS
NOT MEANING IT

BIAS
DISRUPTION

Shared Vocabulary, Shared
Norms, Shared Commitment

PREJUDICE
MEANING IT

SPACE FOR
CONVERSATION

People Shall Not Impose
Their Prejudices on Others

BULLYING
BEING MEAN

CLEAR
CONSEQUENCES

Conversation,
Compensation, Career

LEADERS HAVE A RESPONSIBILITY
TO PREVENT BIAS, PREJUDICE, AND BULLYING

3

Be an Upstander, Not a Silent Bystander

How to Intervene When You Notice Bias, Prejudice, or Bullying

The world did know and remained silent. And that is why I swore never to be silent whenever and wherever human beings endure suffering and humiliation. We must take sides. Neutrality helps the oppressor, never the victim. Silence encourages the tormentor, never the tormented. Sometimes we must interfere.

—Elie Wiesel

When you see something that is not right, not fair, not just, you must have the courage to stand up, to speak up and find a way to get in the way.

—John Lewis

A big part of why I wrote this book is to recognize the essential role of people who stand up to injustice. For every bad experience I've had as a woman in the workplace, I've had multiple good experiences with people who were there to help me navigate and offer support. I am so grateful to these friends, colleagues, employees, bosses, and even strangers. They are upstanders, and they far outnumber the people who cause harm. Upstanders fuel my optimism that we can solve the problem of workplace injustice.

INTERVENE: THE UPSTANDER'S RESPONSIBILITY

Upstanders are essential to a culture of Radical Respect. They help the targets of bias, prejudice, and bullying feel less alone and less gaslighted. They also provide clear feedback to the person who caused harm in a way that minimizes defensiveness and maximizes the odds that the offender will make amends. Upstanders lead by example, encouraging others to do the same. That creates a virtuous cycle.

Given my gratitude to upstanders, the last thing I want to do is to put them in harm's way with this chapter. You don't have to confront the person who is causing harm directly if the risks of doing so are too high. As an upstander, you can almost always show solidarity with the person who is being harmed, even if it's not safe for you to stand up to the offender directly. That acknowledgment—that "something is wrong here"—is invaluable. It helps the other person by letting them know you noticed what happened, they're not alone, and they're not imagining things. Being a good upstander doesn't always mean speaking truth to power, if that will just get the upstander into trouble without helping the person harmed.

THE UPSTANDER'S ADVANTAGES

Upstanders have several advantages that make them a logical line of defense against bias, prejudice, and bullying.

Strength in numbers. In a meeting of ten people, there may be one person causing harm, one person harmed, and one or no leaders. If just one or two of the other seven or eight become upstanders, the whole tenor of the meeting changes. Imagine what it would be like if four or five did. The person causing harm would almost certainly knock it off, without drama. We imagine that it's intervening that causes the disruption, when, in fact, it's not intervening that disrupts a team's ability to get things done, that leaves that productivity-killing, relationship-destroying elephant in the room.

Too often, though, we wait for someone else to step up, while everyone else is doing the same thing, so no one does anything. Sometimes the presence of others makes it less likely a bystander will intervene. Much has been written about this—the so-called bystander effect—and how the number of witnesses affects the likelihood of someone intervening. There's one clear lesson, though: don't wait for someone else to speak up! When you intervene, it's likelier others will, too.

Detachment. It's usually much easier for people to acknowledge that they have harmed someone when it is pointed out by a third party rather than by the person they harmed.

Solidarity across differences. Often, upstanders have different but related experiences they can bring to bear on a situation. For example, I work with Ernest Adams, a gay Black man; I am a straight White woman. While bias, prejudice, and bullying manifest very differently for each of us, the fact that we have both experienced all three at work makes the importance of upstanding clear for both of us. And there are times when it's easier for me as a straight White person to stand up to racism or homophobia he may be experiencing, and easier for him as a man to stand up to sexism I may be experiencing. Being upstanders for each other is often easier than having to stand up for ourselves. We both agree we need to encourage our systemically advantaged colleagues, who may have experienced less bias, prejudice, and bullying than either of us have, to do their fair share of upstanding. Part of that means letting them know what is happening for us.

Shared identity. If you share some attributes with a person whose bias, prejudice, or bullying you're addressing, the other person who caused harm may be more open to hearing about it from you than from someone who is different from them. Also, there may be less risk of retribution for you than for someone else. As a White person, I know it's safer for me to point out racial bias, prejudice, or bullying than it is for someone who's not White. As a straight person, it's safer for me to point out homophobia. I try to be proactive about remembering this, but sometimes I need a prod. I was working with a Black woman and a Latino man to help a majority White board of directors disrupt bias. They reminded me that it was going to be easier for this board to hear certain things from me, a White woman, than from either of them.

Share the load. Anyone who has to confront bias, prejudice, or bullying day after day, week after week, month after month, gets sick of it. Knowing that others notice what they notice and are willing to speak out is important to creating an inclusive working environment. Upstanding also reminds everyone in the workplace that making it compassionate and fair is *everyone's* job.

What follows is a story to help explain why an upstander's intervention benefits everyone—and why a failure to intervene harms everyone, including the silent bystanders.

The Baby Shower

Adriana's boss, Todd, walked into his staff meeting one morning complaining because he had to attend unconscious bias training that afternoon. "I don't believe that unconscious bias is a real thing," he declared.

It was an uncomfortable moment. The six men on Todd's team squirmed in their seats. Maybe they were subconsciously expecting Adriana, the only woman on the team, to challenge Todd. Todd was notorious not only for his bias but his prejudice and bullying as well. Sometimes he could exhibit all three at the same time. They all felt slimed by his bad behavior.

Adriana, though, had long ago decided it was her job to be a great software engineer, not to educate Todd about his attitudes and behaviors. She thought it would be easier for one of the guys on the team to say something to him, but she wasn't in the business of telling them what to do either.

A few weeks later, Todd did something that demonstrated why he didn't believe in unconscious bias: he was consciously prejudiced. One of the guys on the team, Ty, offered to buy a baby gift for Rajiv, who was going out on paternity leave. "Nah, Adriana will do it," Todd replied, gesturing toward her with his thumb. "Women are better at that sort of thing." Again, nobody said anything.

Well, Adriana thought, *he's saying the quiet part out loud*. (I would say that this was prejudice, one he was willing to share explicitly. Not unconscious bias.) But she was even less eager to challenge him about this than about the unconscious bias comment. She was in the middle of a critical project on a tight schedule. She didn't have time to collect money from thirty people, select a gift, buy it, and wrap it. But she did it anyway because it seemed faster

and less annoying than arguing with Todd. As a result, her
schedule slipped a bit, which slowed down the work of
four other people as well.

Meanwhile, her colleague Ty had just wrapped up a
big project and had a little slack in his schedule—that was
why he had offered to buy the gift in the first place. He
didn't say anything, but he knew how busy Adriana was,
and he was annoyed with Todd and with himself. The
whole thing was so stupid, and it woke him up a couple of
times in the middle of the night. He felt bad for Adriana,
and bad for his teammates whose work was delayed
because hers was. He felt weak for not pushing harder. He
was angry at Todd, but he was also angry at himself, and
that was worse.

And of course the baby gift was not the only instance
of this; Todd made several similar requests of her each
week—take the notes, plan the off-site, make a dinner
reservation for the team. He asked Adriana to do these
extra tasks even when she was working on a tight deadline
on a critical path project. These requests didn't just take
up time—they took up mental and emotional energy. As
a result, Adriana wasn't doing her best work, because she
was unnecessarily burdened at just the wrong time; her
peers who were dependent on her work weren't doing
their best work; Ty felt bad about himself and bad about
his boss, so he wasn't able to fully engage when his work
geared back up. Todd knew his team wasn't firing on all
cylinders but didn't know why and was full of more sound
and fury, which only made things worse. Ty knew it was
useless to confront Todd directly, but he wished he'd gone
to Adriana and told her he would buy the gift no matter
what Todd had said. And he wasn't even aware of all the
other office housework Adriana was doing.

These moments can sabotage an organization that could be running smoothly. When "office housework" tasks default to the person on the team with the least time to do it, that person's productivity takes a hit. And when one person's productivity takes a hit, the whole team's work suffers.

The kinds of bias, prejudice, or bullying that may be happening on your team may be very different from this story. Maybe they have nothing to do with gender. Maybe regional or racial or religious intolerance is what is tripping your team up. Maybe homophobia or transphobia is getting in the way of your team's ability to collaborate. No matter what kind of bias, prejudice, or bullying you observe, you can intervene by using an "I," "it," or "you" statement. And when you do, you can get things back on track with a minimum of disruption to the work at hand.

BIAS

Upstanders can hold up a mirror, inviting others to notice the bias they notice. Remember, you're calling people in, not calling them out. When you're offering critical feedback on any topic, but especially one as sensitive as bias, it's not effective to attack someone's personality, morality, or character. If you say or even imply something like, "You're a sexist/racist/homophobic turd ball from hell," it's not likely to motivate a person to examine their thinking. Can you imagine anyone who would respond sincerely, "Oh, thanks so much for letting me know. Now that I understand what the problem is, I will change"? Something as simple and direct as "I don't think you meant that the way it sounded" can be surprisingly effective, though.

Though many fear that confronting bias will harm their relationship with the person they're addressing, there are simple and productive approaches you can take that will *improve* your working relationships—and your team's ability to get things done. Here's an example of how that works.

A Seat at the Table

When Aileen Lee was a partner at the venture capital firm Kleiner Perkins, she and two other partners, Steve Anderson and Matt Murphy, attended a meeting with three senior executives at a Fortune 500 company. Steve, Matt, and Aileen arrived before the others and sat down in the middle of the table.

The executives they were meeting with, all older White men, took their seats opposite the Kleiner team. But they chose seats at the end of the table closest to Steve, leaving Aileen with nobody sitting across from her, subtly but unmistakably excluding her from the conversation. Bias often shows up in whom we choose to sit close to.

Aileen wasn't going to let this exclusion shut her out of the conversation. She had the expertise that would win her team the deal. However, when she spoke, the men on the other side of the table directed their questions at Aileen's colleagues, not at Aileen.

It happened once. It happened again. It happened a third time. Fortunately, one of Aileen's partners picked up on what was going on. "I think Aileen and I should switch seats," he said. They did, and the whole dynamic in the room changed.

Why did Aileen's partner choose to be an upstander? One, he cared about Aileen, and it bothered him that she was getting ignored. But also, he wanted to win the deal, and he knew they wouldn't if the other side didn't recognize Aileen's expertise. And finally, it was more efficient for him to say something than it would've been for her. If she had pointed it out, the response would likely have been more bias. (She might've been called "abrasive" or "oversensitive.") He knew they would be more open and less defensive to bias being pointed out by someone who was, as they were, a White man.

What happened? They won the deal. They worked well with that partner—better than they would have if the bias had been ignored. And Steve's working relationship with Aileen was better as a result. Interrupting the bias was constructive, not disruptive.

PREJUDICE

Let's go back to that baby shower moment and imagine a different ending, an ending in which an upstander intervened. When Todd said he didn't believe gender bias was a real thing, six other men and Adriana were present, all of whom were aware of—and made uncomfortable by—Todd's behavior, but nobody said a word.

What if, when Ty volunteered to buy the baby gift and Todd told him to let Adriana do it, one of those six other guys in the room had said, "It would be more efficient for Ty to do it. He has some slack time right now, and Adriana is on a tight deadline. Our deliverables depend on hers, so if her work suffers because she has to go buy a baby gift, our work does, too."

They might not have persuaded Todd that gender bias was a real thing, and it may not have convinced him that his prejudice about gender roles was wrong. But it might have prevented him from making Adriana find the time to buy the gift when it was more logical for Ty to do it. It would not have changed his beliefs, but it would have prevented him from imposing them on Adriana.

Here's an example of how an "it" statement from a colleague being a good upstander helped get me out of a tricky situation.

It Is Degrading to Be Asked to Pee in a Bucket

Once, a colleague, David, and I flew halfway around the world to negotiate a partnership with a company that had never had women employees; their beliefs prohibited women from working outside the home. I think they viewed me as an American, not really a woman at all—which worked okay until, after many cups of tea, I needed to use the bathroom. They didn't have a women's room. I suggested that, if nobody was in the men's room, perhaps I could use it. They explained that would violate their beliefs. One of the men motioned for me to follow him, led me to a mop closet, and pointed at a bucket.

I started to laugh, but one glance told me he wasn't joking. "It is degrading to ask me to pee in a bucket!" I said, and headed toward the men's room: I really needed to pee. But another man cut in front of me and blocked the door. Suddenly, what had seemed like a benign conflict had become quite tense.

Happily, David was an upstander. He reiterated what I'd said: "It is not okay to ask Kim to pee in a bucket when there's a bathroom right here." Then he proposed, "If Kim agrees, I suggest either she uses the facilities here, or Kim and I will drive back to the hotel and use the bathroom there." I am an efficiency freak: the idea of wasting a whole hour to go to the bathroom was something that would never have occurred to me. But, to my surprise, the men chose to wait while we drove to the hotel and back.

David was telling our hosts that it wasn't acceptable for them to impose their belief on me. He came up with a solution that inconvenienced not only us but them as well. It felt important to me that they bear some of the cost of their prejudice. It wasn't a perfect solution, but I could live with it. I certainly didn't have any better ideas, so I was grateful to David for his.

WHEN YOU MAY WANT TO
HAVE A DEEPER CONVERSATION

In the story above, neither David nor I wanted to have a debate with the people we were working with about gender roles. There will be moments when you, as an upstander, want to go beyond preventing people from imposing their prejudices on others and invite them to consider how their stereotyping beliefs are harming your team's efforts. Once you've established that the person cannot impose their beliefs on others, you can decide whether you want to engage with the person further. Is this a

"Good fences make good neighbors" situation or a "Let's sit down and break bread together" situation? If you decide it's the latter, don't go into it like a presidential debate, where there is a winner and a loser. Rather, think of it like a Rogerian argument.

In his book *Active Listening*, psychologist Carl Rogers proposed an approach to disagreement that helps us move away from coercive expectations that we can "make" a person believe what we believe and toward a productive, collaborative resolution that respects the other person's beliefs and individuality. The goal is to confirm that both people understand each other. Rather than pro/con, winner/loser debates, Rogerian arguments require both sides to be able to articulate each other's perspective and also to identify the points in one's own argument that can be amended or adjusted. To clarify your thinking, you listen to the other person and argue with yourself. Rhetorical scholars Sonja Foss and Cindy Griffin have developed a similar strategy for disagreement with respect called *invitational rhetoric*.

One way to apply active listening / invitational rhetoric to a debate at work that gets too intense is to switch roles, arguing for the position you disagree with and asking the person on the other side to do the same. This is a good way to make sure that egos don't get attached to ideas, to make sure that we are listening to each other and respecting each other. It also forces you to understand the conditions under which their belief could be reasonable. It makes you identify the unshared underlying assumptions that can produce two wildly different opinions on a subject in rational actors.

If you decide to have such a conversation with someone about what you consider to be a prejudiced belief, be aware that the odds are you won't convince the person to change their thinking. What, then, should be your goal in having a deeper conversation? Why engage? Here are some possible reasons.

To express yourself: Feeling free to express yourself is important psychologically. This is very different from wanting to change the other person's mind. Matthew Stevenson put it well in Eli Saslow's book *Rising Out of Hatred*: "It's our job to push the rock, not necessarily to move the rock."

To clarify your thinking: If your goal is to clarify and improve your own arguments rather than to change the other person's mind, the conversation will be far less frustrating.

To find common ground: A prejudiced belief, no matter how profoundly you disagree with it, does not constitute the whole person. Sometimes, if you manage to find something you agree on—the importance of family, the pain of meetings that last forever, or even the job itself—you may find it easier to work with the person. Take the friendship between Supreme Court justices Ruth Bader Ginsburg and Antonin Scalia as inspiration here. They disagreed with each other on many cases and were on different ends of the spectrum politically, but they were able to bond over their love of music and to work productively together.

I once gave a talk to a group that was pursuing a set of policies with which I vehemently disagree. In fact, I would argue their policies were prejudiced against women. However, I decided it was important to have a dialogue. As I engaged in the Q&A part of the talk, I had the sudden thought, *These people are not my enemies. I can disagree with them and still work with them.* After the talk, a woman approached me and asked me about my stance on the various policies we disagreed about. "Hm!" she said. "You don't seem evil." We had a little laugh. She had so rarely spoken with an actual person who shared my beliefs. It was an important human moment, even though neither one of us changed our minds.

BULLYING

The nature of bullying is to isolate the target, making them more vulnerable. The minute an upstander intervenes, showing solidarity, the bullying behavior has failed in its goal. Rather than being isolated, the target of the bullying has an ally, one who has demonstrated that bullying won't work and isn't acceptable.

Why then do we so often ignore bullying, thus allowing it to stand? Sometimes it may be a fear of the person doing the bullying that makes us hesitate to intervene; other times it is not fear but uncertainty about what might be the most effective response.

Right To Be, a nonprofit that develops training for upstanders, offers five different ways to intervene when you observe bullying:

- direct
- distract
- delegate
- delay
- document

Direct

Challenge the person doing the bullying in the moment. Try a "you" statement, as noted in chapter 1. Here are some examples:

"What's going on for you here?"
"Do you realize how you sound?"

"Do you know how what you said sounds?"

"You're being inappropriate (disrespectful, etc.)."

"Yo, not okay."

"You need to leave them alone now."

"What you're saying is biased (prejudiced, offensive, etc.)."

Remember: If you're a leader, you need to take the direct approach. The rest of the *D*s are for upstanders who are not leaders and for whom the direct approach may feel too risky.

Distract

While it may be more satisfying to confront bullying directly, sometimes the direct approach makes things worse for the person being bullied, might escalate the situation, or might put the upstander in harm's way. In these cases, the best thing to do might be to create a distraction.

There's a famous YouTube video called "Snack Man," where an upstander, witnessing a woman trying to get away from a man who followed her into a New York City subway car, steps between the two and creates a distraction by munching on potato chips. It was a surprisingly effective intervention.

Once, I was an intern on a trading floor and one of the traders started screaming at me in a hyperaggressive, bullying way. Another colleague chucked a squishy ball at his head. The yeller quit screaming at me and started playing catch with the upstander. Thirty years later, I still feel grateful.

Sometimes this is just a deft change of subject. I worked with a man prone to tell stories about his wife in a way that was not only belittling to her but to all the women in the room. Any time I opened my mouth in a meeting, he'd start talking about how his wife talked too much. Usually, I was the only woman, and I chose to ignore it. But once, we were meeting with a client who was also a woman, and he started in on one of his stories. Just as I was trying to figure out how to shut him up, another colleague, a man, said, "Hey, I heard you broke a speed record biking this weekend."

Here are some other strategies.

Delegate

By *delegate*, I don't mean ask someone "below" you in a hierarchy to do the work; I mean get help from another person who is in a better position to intervene, or build solidarity with others. You can delegate up, down, or sideways.

A student on a flight did this. One passenger, a middle-aged man in a suit, was bullying the flight attendant, saying he was going to get her fired because they'd run out of chicken. The student, worried any intervention from her wouldn't be taken seriously, tapped the shoulder of another middle-aged man in a suit sitting next to her and gestured to the altercation with her eyes. When the flight attendant got to their aisle, the passenger sitting next to the student said to the flight attendant that she had offered him some of the best service he'd ever had on a flight. He gave her his business card (some people still use them!) and said he'd be happy to give her a stellar review anytime. This man had a voice that boomed even louder than Chicken Man's. Other passengers took the cue and also stood up and gave her their contact information, too. The bully chilled out about his chicken.

Delay

Sometimes uncertainty about the risk of retribution may make you reluctant to intervene on the spot. But you can still check in with the person who got bullied later.

Once, at a sales conference, a woman I worked with commented in front of thousands of people about the "rock star thighs" of a man on the team. I didn't feel it would be productive to confront her directly in front of all those people. I would just call attention to the incident and make it more embarrassing for him.

That didn't mean I had to ignore what had happened either. After the conference, I made sure to find the man who'd been singled out and tell him that I'd felt her remark was out of line. He expressed gratitude, saying that her comment had, indeed, upset him. But nobody else had mentioned it, so he'd wondered if he was overreacting. I knew how he felt.

In retrospect, I wish I'd talked to her directly after as well. However, I understand why I didn't. She was much more senior than I was and known to be very political. While it might have been brave of me to speak truth to power, it also probably would not have changed things. I was at a vulnerable spot in my career; she did not have to listen to me. It would have been better if someone with more authority than I had, someone at her same level in the organization, had been willing to be the upstander.

Document

Your ability to document bad behavior can be an invaluable service to people harmed by bullying—whether because they want to report an episode (and third-party evidence helps) or simply because it is comforting to get a reality check that what happened to them was wrong. An upstander can take notes or even video what is happening during an incident in a way that the person harmed can't. If you document, remember, the document belongs to the person harmed, not to you. Don't go posting it on social media.

In summary, when you notice behavior that seems simply mean, you have several options for how to intervene. If you're not sure what to do, run through the five Ds and choose to do *something*. Direct. Distract. Delegate. Delay. Document.

BIAS   PREJUDICE   [UPSTANDERS & BULLYING]   ⚡ DISCRIMINATION   HARASSMENT   PHYSICAL VIOLATIONS

NO MATTER WHICH PROBLEM IT IS . . .

KEEP THESE THINGS IN MIND

Whether you're intervening in bias, prejudice, or bullying, there are several important things for upstanders to keep in mind.

- Beware of self-righteous shaming
- When upstanders intervene productively, everybody wins

BEWARE OF SELF-RIGHTEOUS SHAMING

It's the responsibility of upstanders to intervene when they notice bias, prejudice, or bullying. But attempting to *coerce* people into changing their attitudes or behavior by indulging in self-righteous shaming isn't going to work. Remember, Radical Respect optimizes for collaboration, it doesn't seek to coerce through force or shame.

Self-righteous shaming is an act of vengeance, not repair. Ultimately—insofar as we know at some level that it won't work—it is an act of despair. Given how addictive the rush of shaming others is and how social media tends to facilitate this kind of communication, self-righteous shaming is on the rise like a sickening virus, and it is spilling over from social networks into today's workplaces.

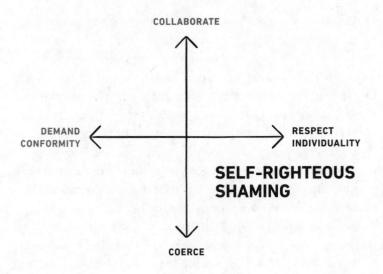

Often, we believe—incorrectly—that our *intentions* in shaming are good. But are we trying to fix a problem, or are we trying to make ourselves look or feel good?

Sometimes we are trying to defend a vulnerable individual or a group of people who are being disrespected. There is a big difference between standing up to a system that is unfair and standing up for someone we believe is weaker than we are. When we stand up to a system or person that is unfair, we're trying to make things better. But too often when we stand up for a person who has been treated unfairly, we wind up belittling them, aggrandizing ourselves, and going on the attack in a way that doesn't help anyone.

Other times we have been shamed ourselves, and so it feels legitimate to fight fire with fire. Turnabout is fair play, right? Not really. Fighting bias, prejudice, or bullying with bias, prejudice, or bullying just adds more of what we are trying to get rid of to the world.

UPSTANDERS &
BIAS PREJUDICE BULLYING ⚡ DISCRIMINATION HARASSMENT PHYSICAL VIOLATIONS

Or perhaps we're just communicating in bad faith in hopes of gaining something, often applause from an audience. Or we are just fed up with a broken system that isn't working for us, so we lash out at a person rather than trying to fix the system. Or perhaps the people we are shaming are more powerful than we are, so we assume they somehow deserve it or can take it.

Self-righteous shaming happens on the right and on the left. If you're on the left, you're probably thinking about how it applies to people on the right—or maybe you're the self-critical type who notices it on the left, too. Ditto in reverse if you're on the right. The truth is we all do it from time to time, unfortunately.

No matter which side of an issue the self-righteous shaming is coming from, it is invariably counterproductive. Think about it. When was the last time you changed your behavior because someone shamed you?

It is vital to understand the difference between *feeling shame* and *being shamed*. When we are held accountable for something we have done or said that harms others, we often *feel* shame, even though the person who pointed out the problem is not shaming us but rather is giving us valuable feedback. When we feel ashamed, we tend to deny we did anything wrong or to go on the attack—sometimes both. Instead, we must learn to work through our feelings of shame and get to a place where we recognize what we have done wrong.

As an upstander, you don't want to indulge in self-righteous shaming, *and* you don't want to allow another person's feelings of guilt or shame to silence you either. Several "flavors" of self-righteous shaming can be particularly dangerous to your efforts to be an effective upstander:

1. moral grandstanding,
2. the Incredible Hulk,
3. the knight in shining armor, and
4. White savior complex.

Below are more detailed explanations of what I mean by each of these terms.

1. Moral Grandstanding

Few things will kill good communication on a team faster than moral grandstanding: when some people talk about sensitive topics in a way that shames others and puts themselves on a pedestal of virtue. Moral grandstanding usually results in deeper misunderstanding, and it almost always exacerbates the problem it purports to want to fix.

Online communications—in particular, social networks—speed up the process by which we exaggerate both our own virtue and the perfidy of others. In the real world, people tend to show their annoyance at self-righteousness, so there's a natural slowdown mechanism. For example, if you jump on your soapbox in a meeting, subtle eyerolls will warn you to get off. But there are no subtle eyerolls online. Moral grandstanding gets rewarded with likes and shares online, creating more of it and a more extremist, toxic environment. Our online tools have not benefited from the evolutionary learning of our IRL responses. This snowball effect also explains why it's even *more* important for leaders to confront both moral grandstanding and the behaviors it's most often objecting to—bias, prejudice, and bullying—when managing teams working remotely than when everyone is working together in person. The answer is obviously not to ignore bias, prejudice, and bullying because leaders are tired of the drama that the moral grandstanding creates . . . The answer is to teach people more effective responses to bias, prejudice, and bullying.

Moral grandstanding tends to be used more by people on the extremes of *both* sides of any issue. And it's a vicious cycle. In an environment with a lot of self-righteous finger-pointing, people tend to move to the extremes.

UPSTANDERS &
| BIAS   PREJUDICE   BULLYING | ⚡ DISCRIMINATION   HARASSMENT   PHYSICAL VIOLATIONS

Research shows that most of us tend to believe in our own superiority along any number of dimensions, especially our moral judgment. This moral certainty, ironically, makes us unaware of our own moral failings. That's why shaming other people rarely causes them to look carefully at their own behavior. Rather, it causes them to retreat deeper into their sense of moral superiority. It's *very* hard to listen to criticism from someone who is shaming you. This fixed mindset leads to the kind of denial that renders otherwise tractable problems insoluble.

The Reverend Jamie Washington offers excellent advice for avoiding self-righteous shaming. He explains the difference between *calling out* and *calling in*. Calling in invites people to consider one another's experiences and thoughts rather than getting locked in a vicious cycle of "convicting, converting, and convincing."

Inviting in may not give you the jolt of instant gratification that shaming others or hurling an insult does. Admittedly, having a difficult conversation won't give you the quick-hit rush that condemning another person wholesale often provides. It's hard work. But, unlike shaming, this work creates a more collaborative, less coercive environment. You get more out of it than you put into it.

This is especially important in an era of remote work and communication tools that allow us to broadcast harsh judgments from behind the safety of a screen.

2. The Incredible Hulk

Sometimes it's tempting to try to out-bully the bully. Don't give in to that temptation. I have been guilty of this, and the results were not good.

My team and I were pushing hard on a project late one Friday night when Amy, a woman who'd recently joined the company right out of college, came into my office in tears. Charles, a guy on another team, had taken one look at some analysis she'd done and said, "There you go doing sales math again. I am an engineer; don't worry your pretty little head about the math."

When she told me this, I was *pissed.*

"That little shithead pip-squeak!" I exclaimed. "Watch this."

I picked up the phone, and when Charles answered, I started shouting. I was behaving like an asshole and enjoying myself way more than I should have. (Helpful hint for avoiding self-righteous shaming: if it feels too good to say it or to hit Send, stop!)

Years later, as my sister and I were watching *The Avengers* with our kids, a scene reminded me of this incident. Loki, the bad guy, says to the Hulk, "I am a god, you dull creature."

The Hulk looks at him for a moment, then picks Loki up by the feet and smashes his head on the ground. *Bam bam.* Pause. *Bam bam bam.* Pause. *Bam bam* to the left, to the right, to the center a few times, back to the left. Loki is left humiliated and unable to get up.

"Puny god," Hulk says, stomping off in disgust.

Something about that scene so perfectly encapsulated the way bullying makes me want to respond—just grab the person by the ankles and smash them all around. The way I treated Charles was a Hulk moment for me. But did it make the situation better for Amy? No! I had engaged in bullying myself. Ultimately, I regretted my behavior.

About five years later, my husband wound up working on a project with Charles. When Andy mentioned I was his wife, Charles's eyes grew wide. "You are married to *Kim Scott*?"

3. The Knight in Shining Armor

The desire to help others is good. But when it becomes about you, not fairness, your help may not be so welcome. You may be reflecting and reinforcing the stereotype, in fact.

UPSTANDERS &
BIAS PREJUDICE BULLYING ⚡ DISCRIMINATION HARASSMENT PHYSICAL VIOLATIONS

If you cast the person being harmed in the role of "damsel in distress," for example, you reinforce the problem that you're supposed to be interrupting. I have been cast in that role several times by well-meaning colleagues, and let me assure you: I didn't like it, and it wasn't helpful to me one bit.

It's worth noting that the damsel in distress need not be a woman and the knight in shining armor need not be a man.

4. White Savior Complex

A related but different complex happens when White people arrogantly decide they are going to "save" Black people and are in a position to do so because they are "better" in some way. There's a big difference between on the one hand realizing that as a White person it may be easier for me to point out the bias, prejudice, or bullying of another White person, and on the other hand deciding that I am going to go "save" a person who's been harmed by my White colleague's attitudes or behaviors because I am superior in some way to both my White colleague and to the person harmed by their behavior.

One predominantly White private school I knew bragged that their high school students had designed houses for people in a developing country. These kids' parents wouldn't trust their children to design a woodshed on their own property. Where did they get the notion that they could design houses that people would actually live in? This is just White supremacy in a different cloak.

This approach often demonstrates that the White colleagues are in fact unaware of their own racism. Teju Cole has written about "the White Savior Industrial Complex." He explains it "is not about justice. It is about having a big emotional experience that validates privilege."

Sometimes it can be hard to know where the line is between being a helpful White upstander and succumbing to White savior complex. If you're wondering where that line is, here's some advice: to avoid reinforcing the very injustice you're trying to address, be clear about the purpose and meaning of what you're about to do. This is not about you demonstrating virtue. Nor does it mean that the person you're trying to help can't stand up for themselves. You are standing up to a broken system and trying to do your part to create a work environment that allows all people to work together well.

WHEN UPSTANDERS INTERVENE PRODUCTIVELY, EVERYBODY WINS

Fairness Wins

Remember, as an upstander, you are standing up to injustice, you are not standing up for someone who is "weaker" than you. You are asserting that you'd rather work in a more respectful, collaborative working environment. You are helping to create a fairer and more reasonable working environment.

People Harmed Win

When you confront bias, prejudice, and bullying on your team, the people who are harmed by these attitudes and behaviors benefit. You dispel gaslighting, making it easier for them to defend themselves and perform at their best.

Upstanders Win

When your colleagues can all do their best work, it helps you do your best work, too. As we saw with the baby shower story, everyone's work suffered because Adriana's boss insisted on assigning her the "office housework" even though she was on a tight deadline.

UPSTANDERS &
| BIAS   PREJUDICE   BULLYING | ⚡   DISCRIMINATION   HARASSMENT   PHYSICAL VIOLATIONS

Another problem with not intervening is that your inaction can leave you feeling guilty by association or by inaction. A young man I know reported feeling "ashamed to be a White man" after another White man on his team said some cringe-worthy biased things to a Latina woman. He realized his feeling of shame came not from his own gender and race, or from the other man's behavior—but from his own inaction. He went and spoke with the woman, apologized for not intervening sooner, and asked her if she would like him to go talk to their colleague. She said she would. He did, and their colleague, chagrined, apologized. It won't always work out so well—but often enough, it will.

People Who Cause Harm Cut It Out

In the story above, the person who had said the biased things was grateful to his colleague for making him aware of what he'd done wrong. He wanted to make it right. Telling him was doing him a favor.

It's trickier in the case of prejudice, but often people who do have a prejudice do not want to violate the law or an HR policy. They'll fall into line if they know where the line is.

A person who is prone to bullying is likely to push past the line. But if they experience consequences for their bullying early, they're less likely to escalate and suffer worse consequences later. Also, people are often not aware that they are perceived as having bullied others and will change their behavior when they understand the impact they are having. I worked with a man who had been called an asshole his whole life. When I took the time to explain to him what exactly he was doing that upset others, he was able to change.

Leaders Win

Leaders cannot prevent bias, prejudice, and bullying from destroying respect and collaboration on their teams without the help of upstanders. These attitudes and behaviors make themselves manifest so often and in so many ways, it's really impossible for leaders to catch it every single time. Leaders need engaged upstanders on their teams.

Results Are Better

It may seem that disrupting bias, prejudice, and bullying is a distraction. But it's actually bias, prejudice, and bullying that are the distraction—so often the elephant in the room, preventing people from getting things done. Disrupting them is the solution, not a distraction. Radically Respectful teams that optimize for collaboration and honor the individuality of each team member simply get more done than teams rendered dysfunctional by coercion and conformity.

UPSTANDERS &
BIAS   PREJUDICE   BULLYING   ⚡ DISCRIMINATION   HARASSMENT   PHYSICAL VIOLATIONS

RADICAL RESPECT FRAMEWORK FOR UPSTANDERS

BIAS
NOT MEANING IT

**HOLD UP A
MIRROR**

PREJUDICE
MEANING IT

**HOLD UP A
SHIELD**

BULLYING
BEING MEAN

**5D'S: DIRECT, DISTRACT,
DELEGATE, DELAY,
DOCUMENT**

UPSTANDERS HAVE AN OBLIGATION TO INTERVENE

4

What to Say When You Don't Know What to Say

How to Choose a Response When You're the Person Harmed

Your silence will not protect you.

—Audre Lorde

The poet Claudia Rankine expresses the disorientation and discomfort of being harmed by someone else's bias, prejudice, or bullying:

What did he just say? Did she really just say that? Did I hear what I think I heard? Did that just come out of my mouth, his mouth, your mouth? The moment stinks . . . Then the voice in your head silently tells you to take your foot off your throat because just getting along shouldn't be an ambition.

CHOOSE A RESPONSE

THE RESPONSIBILITY OF PEOPLE HARMED

When you are the upstander, you have an obligation to intervene. But when you've been harmed, you have every right to pick your battles. My goal is to help you make an *intentional choice* about how or if to respond so that you retain your sense of freedom and agency.

Viktor Frankl wrote, "Everything can be taken from a man but one thing: the last of the human freedoms—to choose one's attitude in any given set of circumstances, to choose one's own way." You may not have the full range of responses you wish you had. But you still get to make a choice in how or if you respond, what you think.

Sometimes you may decide to save your breath. If you do, make a *proactive* choice. There's a world of difference between choosing to be silent and being silenced. Other times you may decide it's worth it to respond. In these moments, it's often hard to know what to say. This chapter will give you some ideas about that and, more importantly, help you cut yourself some slack for not having the perfect response at the tip of your tongue.

For much of my career, I was more acutely aware of the downsides than the upsides of responding. Then I became aware of how often I built solidarity when I responded, and the cost of not responding to my own sense of agency. That is why Audre Lorde's warning that "your silence will not protect you" resonated so strongly for me.

Of course, choosing your response is not the same thing as *always* confronting people or allowing other people's problematic attitudes and behaviors to consume or distract you from your own goals. Toni Morrison warned: "The very serious function of racism . . . is distraction. *It keeps you from doing your work.*" When you decide not to respond, do so because you have something more important to work on or something more fun to do, not because someone else thinks it's not that big a deal.

If you're the person harmed, it's not your job to educate the person who just harmed you. But you may decide to do the work anyway because you care about them or want to stop them from doing the same thing to someone else.

Do the work *you* choose to do, not the work that others are imposing on you with their problematic attitudes and behaviors. Sometimes ignoring a remark may help you get your own work done; other times ignoring it will eat at you and you'll decide you're better off responding.

What follows is a story to help build a shared understanding of how difficult these moments can be, and then some ideas that might make it easier to make your decision about whether to respond. If you decide not to respond, I hope these stories will help you feel good about making that choice. If you decide to speak up, I hope these stories will give you some ideas of what to say when you don't know what to say.

The Haircut

A colleague of mine who is gay gave a big presentation to a client. Upon meeting her, the client complained that her short hair was "unprofessional."

It is strange that one person would think they get to tell another what haircut to get or what clothes to wear, but it happens all the time.

PEOPLE HARMED &
BIAS PREJUDICE BULLYING   ⚡ DISCRIMINATION HARASSMENT PHYSICAL VIOLATIONS

It's worth parsing what was going on here. Since all the men in the room had short hair, there was nothing inherently unprofessional about short hair. If she'd been wearing a more traditionally feminine business attire with makeup and heels rather than a pantsuit, it's unlikely the short hair alone would have bothered the client. But she was not conforming to their expectations of the way a woman "should" look.

This incident illustrates why intersectionality makes experiencing bias, prejudice, and bullying even more difficult. Even if she could be certain that it was unconscious bias, which bias was presenting? Gender bias, a bias toward assuming everyone is straight, or both? Or did it reflect real prejudice? If so, was the prejudice against women in business or against gay people, or both? Or was the client trying to bully my colleague? If so, why? Because she was a woman? Because he assumed she was gay? Or both?

And given all this uncertainty, what might she have said to him? Let's go deeper on how you can use an "I," "it," or "you" statement in these moments, should you choose to respond.

BIAS

If you are on the receiving end of bias, you may choose to help the person notice the mistake. You may also choose not to, and that is your prerogative.

If you choose to disrupt the bias, remember, you're inviting the person in to understand your perspective, not trying to assert your moral authority or shame them. Of course, while you want to be as kind as possible, it's not your job nor is it even possible to prevent the other person from feeling defensive.

Easier said than done. Remember: even if you don't know what to say, start with the word *I*.

The easiest "I" statement is the simple factual correction. For example, in the safety pin story from chapter 1, I could've said, "I'm about to go onstage and give a talk; I think one of the staffers in the yellow T-shirts can help you find a safety pin." An "I" statement doesn't need to be perfect, doesn't have to be clever or witty. It can even be clumsy. The point is to say *something* if you decide it's worth your while to respond. The hardest thing to overcome is inertia. So say "I" even if you don't know what's going to come out of your mouth next.

An "I" statement can hold up a mirror for a colleague without being antagonistic or judgmental. For example, "I don't think you meant that the way it sounded . . ." Or, in the case of the haircut, my colleague could've said with a laugh, "I don't think *your* short hair is unprofessional."

An "I" statement is a generous response to someone else's unconscious bias. The goal is to point out a mistake to help that person avoid repeating that mistake—not to shame them. Shaming is an ineffective strategy. When a person feels attacked or labeled, it's much harder for the person to be open to your feedback, to become aware of what they did wrong, and therefore unlikely they'll make it right. Shaming a person attacks personality attributes, which they can't change, rather than their behavior, which they can change. It's a form of ad hominem attack—not helpful. When was the last time you saw someone reply to "You are worthless" or "You are an asshole" by saying, "Oh, now I understand what I did wrong. I won't do it again." Not gonna happen.

PEOPLE HARMED &
BIAS | PREJUDICE   BULLYING ⚡ DISCRIMINATION   HARASSMENT   PHYSICAL VIOLATIONS

Another benefit of an "I" statement is that it's a good way to figure out where the other person is coming from. If people respond politely or apologetically, it will confirm your diagnosis of bias. If they double down or go on the attack, then you'll know you're dealing with prejudice or bullying.

What if you're not sure it's bias? It's okay. You don't have to be 100 percent sure to speak up. If it was bias, you've given the person an opportunity to learn; if it wasn't, you've given the person an opportunity to explain what was meant.

The ROI on Speaking Up

Calculate the return on investment (ROI) of speaking up so that you're making a proactive choice rather than being silenced. Ask yourself what the pros of speaking up are, and be conscious of them, recognizing that you'll likely feel the cons in your gut.

Here are seven benefits of challenging bias to consider.

First, by speaking up, you are affirming yourself. For me, every time someone says something that bothers me and I ignore it, a tiny feeling of helplessness creeps in. Every time I respond, my sense of agency is strengthened. I know I am not alone—this is true for many others as well.

Second, affirming that the bias is an error, not the truth, can prevent you from internalizing the bias. In a TED Talk, the Reverend Paula Stone Williams, a transgender woman, describes what she learned about the biased assumptions men make about women: "The more you're treated as if you don't know what you're talking about, the more you begin to question whether or not you do, in fact, know what you're talking about." Bias is corrosive.

Third, when you help someone become aware of and change a bias, it will improve things not only for you but for others. When you disrupt gender bias, you help every other woman you work with, and those who will come along after you—ditto racial bias, sexual orientation bias, gender identity bias, class bias, regional bias, political bias, and every other kind of bias.

Fourth, by disrupting bias, you make it likelier that others will point out biases. When we ignore bias, we allow it to be repeated and reinforced. When we correct it in the moment, we create a virtuous cycle that helps us grow together.

Fifth, your relationship with your colleague may improve thanks to your intervention. They may appreciate that you took the risk to help them, and it's easier to get along with someone who isn't saying or doing some biased thing that pisses you off over and over.

Sixth, you are doing the person who is saying or doing the biased thing a favor. Nobody wants to go around being biased, making mistakes, often cringeworthy, that they aren't even aware of.

Finally, your team's results will improve. Bias disrupts collaboration, and a team that doesn't collaborate well doesn't achieve good results. Bias demands conformity; people can't do their best work when their individuality is not honored by their teammates.

PREJUDICE

What do you say when people consciously *believe* that the stereotypes they are spouting off about are true—when you are confronting active prejudice rather than unconscious bias?

For me, it's hard to respond to bias, but it's much harder to respond when someone asserts some sort of unfair stereotype that claims I am incapable or inferior. I am *way* more pissed off when someone asserts their belief that it's been scientifically proven that women are biologically programmed to be this or that than I am when someone makes a remark that reveals some unconscious bias. Anger can make it harder to respond—especially for people who are not "allowed" to show anger as a result of bias. It's bias piled on top of prejudice.

Also, I'm usually less optimistic that a confrontation will result in change when I'm confronting prejudice. People won't apologize for their prejudiced beliefs just because I point them out; they *know* what they think. So why bother discussing it?

The reason to confront prejudice is to draw a clear line between that person's right to believe whatever they want and your right not to have that belief imposed upon you.

Using an "it" statement is an effective way to demarcate this boundary. As mentioned in chapter 1, one type of "it" statement appeals to human decency: "It is disrespectful/cruel/ridiculous to . . ." Another references the policies or a code of conduct at your company; for example, "It is a violation of our company policy to . . ." The third invokes the law; for example, "It is illegal to . . ."

An "it" statement follows the same principle as "good fences make good neighbors." The goal is to protect yourself from another person's intrusion. This may not get the two of you on the same page, it probably won't change their beliefs, but it can prevent an unnecessary conflict.

What follows are two different stories that show how "it" statements can play out.

Don't Let Colleagues Impose
Their Prejudices on You

I once was chatting amiably with a colleague before a meeting when, out of the blue, he said it: "My wife stays home because it's better for the children."

At first, I thought this was bias. It was inconceivable to me that he consciously believed that I was a bad parent because I chose to have a career. So I made a little joke to give him a chance to clarify: "Oh. I decided to show up at work today because I thought it was better to neglect my children."

He didn't let it go. "But, Kim, studies show it really is better for the children if the mother doesn't work."

That's when I reached for my "it" statement: "It is an HR violation to tell me I am harming my kids by showing up at work. Plus, it's just mean. I love my kids as much as you love yours."

As I intended, the simple words *HR violation* shut him up. But I still had to work with him. His idea that I was harming my children could play out in all kinds of subtle ways that would hurt me. I worried that he wouldn't want to work with me on projects that required travel because he'd feel uncomfortable about my being away from home. (It was strange that he'd worry about my time away from my kids but not his time away from his kids.) So I decided to engage with him.

"Look, I'm not going to make a thing of this with HR." He relaxed visibly, and I continued. "I could give you studies that show the opposite of what yours show.

But I'm guessing you don't want to read my studies any more than I want to read yours. Besides, there's not just one right way to live, one right way to raise your children. What is best on average may have nothing at all to do with what is best for your family or for my family."

He laughed, acknowledging neither of us wanted to spend more time talking about this: we were ready to get back to work.

"Can we agree on these three things?" I proposed, going back to some other "it" statements. "It is my decision, with my husband, how we raise our kids. And it is your decision, with your wife, how you raise yours. And is it fair to say that you and I respect one another enough not to judge each other's decisions harshly?"

"Of course." He smiled and stuck out his hand. I shook it. I didn't change his belief, and he didn't change mine, but he never again accused me of neglecting my kids. Engaging took a little time and some emotional energy, but not engaging would've made it hard for me to work with him in the long run. Speaking up cost me less than remaining silent would have. That is why we do any kind of work. We get more out of it than we put into it.

"F**K That Noise" Is Not an "It" Statement, but It May Be the Opening Salvo You Need

In business school, I took a class called Economic Strategies of Nations. One evening, my friend Alex and I were studying together, reading an article by the sociologist Charles Murray our professor had assigned. I couldn't believe this was assigned reading in 1995, as it felt so 1950s to me: "Young males are essentially barbarians for whom marriage—meaning . . . the act of taking responsibility for a wife and children—is an indispensable civilizing force."

"F**k that noise!" I said. This was not unconscious bias; this was a conscious prejudice. And it was assigned reading! I read it again out loud, threw the article on the table, and exploded, "I'm supposed to make myself economically and physically vulnerable to a barbarian so that I can civilize him? He can figure out how to civilize his own damn self. And, Alex, why aren't you more offended than I am? You are no barbarian!"

Perhaps the professor had deliberately assigned a provocative reading, knowing that we would encounter such prejudiced beliefs in our careers and needed to be ready to confront them. Or perhaps he believed that crap. Either way, I dreaded class the next day.

When I got to class, nobody voiced an objection to the prejudice of what we'd read. I sat there mutely. I wasn't sure I could make my feelings known about Murray's argument without dropping an f-bomb. Of course, men dropped f-bombs all the time at business school. There it

BIAS [PREJUDICE] BULLYING ⚡ DISCRIMINATION HARASSMENT PHYSICAL VIOLATIONS

PEOPLE HARMED &

was: bias repressing my emotion, making it harder for me to confront prejudice.

Alex kept shooting me meaningful looks, silently urging me to say what I'd said the night before. The longer the minutes ticked by and nobody else called BS, the more alone I felt. Had nobody else found the article offensive? If not, why not?

Finally, Alex, in an upstander moment, raised his hand. "I was talking to Kim about the article last night, and she made some really good points."

"Yes, Kim?" the professor asked.

"Well . . ." I pulled out the text about civilizing barbarians and read it out loud. "Here's what I have to say about that: *F**k that noise.*" Before I could say more, the whole class, including the professor, burst out laughing. It turned out I *could* get angry and I *could* curse and it was okay—more than okay. It was an important revelation.

Twenty-five years later, I am still grateful to Alex.

At the core of so much prejudice against women is the pernicious belief Murray articulated in that essay: that men can't be held accountable for their own executive function and, implicitly, that it's women's responsibility to keep them in line. It's not just Charles Murray. It's an old and persistent myth that women *should* remain subordinate to men and be responsible for managing their behavior at the same time.

Also, it astounded me that the men in the class didn't object to the notion that they should cede their executive function to women. They were all planning to become executives, after all! Yet they often seemed to feel they "couldn't" control themselves. This wasn't just an abstract intellectual prejudice. Some of my classmates tried to impose this idea on me in the classroom.

For example, the guy who sat above and behind me in the class's stadium seating complained to me that when I stretched or even just sat up straight, my breasts distracted him. He suggested that I sit hunched over to hide my chest or wear baggier clothing. His friend backed him up, doing an exaggerated imitation of me, arching his back and sticking his chest out. "How can he possibly concentrate with you sitting there like that?" I was infuriated—but also suddenly self-conscious. Since I'd been raised to repress my anger, self-consciousness won out.

I slouched a little the next couple of days. I found that as I tried to make myself disappear, I talked less in class. And that was a problem, as 50 percent of our grade was based on class participation. Then I wondered, why was I letting this guy's inability to manage his own eyes and thoughts cause me to slouch in class, to feel ashamed of my body in that roomful of men?

I decided to confront him with an "it" statement: "It's not my job to control where your eyes or your mind go. It's not reasonable to ask me to slouch or wear different clothes because you can't manage yourself."

He conceded the point. From then on, if I saw him glancing at my chest, I'd raise my eyebrows, and he'd look away, embarrassed. Pretty soon, he managed to stop staring at my chest.

Years later, I coached a woman who was having a hard time being taken seriously in meetings at a male-dominated company. As I watched, I noticed her slouch, and I knew exactly what she was doing and why. I played her psychologist Amy Cuddy's famous TED Talk[1] where she talks about "postural feedback," the idea that sitting up and standing up straight can make you feel more confident. I had her practice Cuddy's Wonder Woman pose, which I'd come to understand was what I was doing at business school before class started. The woman I was coaching still slouched during the meetings.

Finally, I just said it bluntly. "Look, I may be wrong, but I think I know why you slouch like that. You are trying to hide your chest. I did that in my business school class, and it was bad for my performance. You will look and feel more confident if you sit up straight with your shoulders back."

I knew I was giving her good advice, but even I was astounded to notice how well it worked. At the next meeting, the difference in her performance was remarkable. Her boss, a woman, called to thank me and asked me what in the world I had recommended to get such a dramatic improvement in such a short time. I told her, and we had a good laugh: we'd both been there.

It would have been easy simply to dismiss the guy at business school who gave me a hard time for sitting up straight. But I was glad I took the time to identify the core prejudice and respond. I don't know if I persuaded him to think differently, but the conversation proved helpful to *me*—and, later, to the women I coached. And he and I are still friends to this day. If I'd given in to the silence and rage cycle, we would not be.

BULLYING

When someone is bullying you, the person's *goal* is to upset or knock you off your game. Using an "I" statement like "I feel X when you Y" simply informs them they succeeded. Ignoring bullying doesn't work either, because even if you don't react, they often get some sort of charge out of their behavior. The only way to stop bullying is to create negative consequences. When you're the victim of bullying, though, you may feel powerless to create the kind of consequences that stop it.

As mentioned in chapter 1, one way to push back is to confront the person with a "you" statement or question, as in "What's going on for you here?" or "You need to stop talking to me that way." A "you" statement can be surprisingly effective in changing the dynamic. That's because the bully is trying to put you in a submissive role, to demand that you answer the questions to shine a scrutinizing spotlight on you. When you reply with a "you" statement, you are now taking a more active role, asking them to answer the questions, shining a scrutinizing spotlight on them.

An "I" statement invites the person to consider your perspective; an "it" statement establishes a clear boundary beyond which the other person should not go. With a "you" statement, you are talking about the bully, not yourself. People can let your statement lie or defend themselves against it, but they are playing defense rather than offense in either case.

Remember, your "you" statement can be an act of kindness for the person who is acting like a bully. You're not trying to punish the person. You're holding them accountable because there is at least some chance they can do better.

In his book *The No Asshole Rule*, Bob Sutton distinguishes between the "temporary" asshole and the "certified" asshole. I don't know anyone who hasn't bullied others or acted like a jerk when they were having a bad day and could get away with it.

I've worked with several people who had been labeled certified bullies or assholes by their colleagues. When I worked more closely with them, however, I found there were underlying issues that once resolved allowed them to work more productively with others. For example, sometimes people who for whatever reason have trouble understanding the impact they're having on others are accused of being "bullies" or other epithets. The issue is not that they don't care but they don't understand, and when it's explained clearly to them, their behavior and therefore their reputation totally changes. Hold people accountable for their behavior, but try not to label the person, just the behavior.

In an ideal world (which this is not), there would be consequences for bullying, whether involving a temporary asshole or a certified asshole. It's only your job to create these consequences if you are a leader.

Unaffiliated or Unattached?

Early in my career, I was invited to join a very formal institution dedicated to increasing knowledge about foreign policy. Members convened regularly in the group's stately Manhattan headquarters for a luncheon and an address by an academic expert or a government official. One such meeting concerned US policy toward Kosovo, where I had recently lived. After the speaker finished his talk, he offered to answer questions from the audience.

Even though I knew more about the situation than most of the other people in the room, I was reluctant to ask a question myself. The protocol required stating your name and affiliation (where you worked). The room was full of high-powered people, most of them older men, and I was working on a novel and unemployed.

A well-known investor and philanthropist rose to ask a question. When he stated his name and affiliation, everyone chuckled because they already knew who he was. The idea of standing up and saying, "I'm Kim and I'm unemployed" or even "I'm Kim and I'm writing a novel" felt too humiliating. The next question came from a well-known, recently retired investment banker. He stood up, stated his name, and said he was "unaffiliated." Oh! So that was the word the club members used when they didn't have a job. I put my hand back up. When the speaker called on me, I rose to my feet and said my name and that I was "unaffiliated." A man in the back of the room shouted out, "Unaffiliated or unattached?" The room burst into laughter. I wish I could say that I took this in my stride. But the threat of hot, humiliated tears stung my eyes. I took a deep breath, pretended not to notice the remark, and asked my question.

If an upstander had stood up, turned to Mr. Unaffiliated-or-Unattached, and said, "Why are you being so rude?" or "You can't talk to other members so disrespectfully," *he* would have felt embarrassed instead of me. If even one person had come up to me afterward and said this behavior was bullying and unkind, that *also*

BIAS   PREJUDICE   **PEOPLE HARMED &**
                   [**BULLYING**]   ⚡   DISCRIMINATION   HARASSMENT   PHYSICAL VIOLATIONS

would have made a world of difference to me. But nobody did.

Because nobody there, including me, challenged the remark, and in fact many rewarded his remark with their laughter, it hurt me, not him. I never felt comfortable there again and I wound up resigning, even though that meant giving up access to an extraordinary network. In retrospect, I wish I had responded in some way. Speaking up would have restored my sense of dignity—and it would more than likely have helped my reputation and hurt his.

If I were advising my younger self, I'd tell her to open her mouth, say the word *you* to buy a moment and get the ball rolling, then trust whatever came out next. Here are some things I might've said:

- "You . . . What is going on for you here?"
- "You . . . Why would you ask such an inappropriate question?"
- "You . . . Are you uncomfortable having women join this organization?"
- "You . . . Do you make it a habit to bully women members?"
- "You . . . Are you trying to haze me? This isn't a fraternity."

People often want a script, but it's much better if you first make your own calculation about whether it's worth speaking up. If you decide it is, choose language that works for you; my words won't necessarily feel right in your mouth.

Take a moment now to choose a few "you" statements or "you" questions that you can imagine actually saying when you feel bullied. Make it generic so it will apply to many different situations. For example, my go-to "you" statements are either "You need to stop now" or "What is going on for you here?" What are yours? Once you have them in mind, practice saying them. Practice in the mirror, practice with other people. Break them in, like a new pair of jeans, so they will feel more comfortable when you need to use them.

Bullying vs. Conflict

Of course, if you're having a disagreement or a healthy conflict, you don't need a "you" statement. You want to get on the same side of the table, not push the person away.

What is the difference between bullying and conflict? Here's a simple way to think about it, adapted from the work of PACER, a nonprofit that leads a bullying prevention center.

CONFLICT	BULLYING
Disagreement in which both sides express their view.	One person aims to hurt, harm, or humiliate another.
No status difference between those involved.	Person bullying has more in-group status.
Person causing harm generally stops and changes their behavior when they realize it is hurting someone.	Person causing harm continues their behavior when they realize it is hurting someone.

Don't Let Bullying Rob You of Vulnerability

Vulnerability is necessary to form relationships, so don't let bullies rob you of this asset. You don't want to expose your vulnerability to a bully, whom you cannot trust. But that doesn't mean you can't show your vulnerability to anyone. And it's important to show it, because, as Brené Brown writes, "We need to trust to be vulnerable. And we need to be vulnerable to trust." The more people we can trust, the more successful working relationships we can have that unleash our best work.

One way to build those relationships with others is to share openly with your colleagues what happened and how it made you feel. Telling your story, showing vulnerability, rather than hiding from the world the harm that bullying caused, can be a much more effective response to bullying behavior than ignoring it. Whatever you do, don't allow the bullying to turn you into a bully or to push you to behave in a way that you aren't proud of.

Comedian and author Lindy West describes her response to bullying: "Do a good job. Be vulnerable. Make things. Choose to be kind."

NO MATTER WHICH PROBLEM IT IS . . . KEEP THESE THINGS IN MIND

Whether you're being harmed by bias, prejudice, or bullying, or are unsure what the hell is going on but know that something doesn't feel right, there are a few things to keep in mind.

- Resist the default to silence
- Break the silence and rage cycle
- Cultivate upstanders

RESIST THE DEFAULT TO SILENCE

If you decide not to respond, make your silence a proactive for-bearance, not a passive avoidance. The risks of responding may indeed outweigh the rewards. When that's the case and you de-cide not to respond, it doesn't mean you aren't confident or cou-rageous; it means you're a rational actor. You may be worn out and choose to save your energy. You may have already disrupted bias five times that day, and you're ready to do something else. Maybe you know there's not just a risk of retribution, there's a certainty of it. When you are the person who has been harmed by bias, prejudice, or bullying, you get to choose whether or not to respond.

But make it your choice, not someone else's. There's often ex-ternal pressure to be silent. Recognize that pressure and resist it.

Here are some common excuses I've used for remaining si-lent when it would have been better for me to speak up. I bet you've said some of these things to yourself, too.

1. *"I want to be nice."*
2. *"I have to protect the fragile male ego."*
3. *"I can't question feedback."*
4. *"They are a good person / didn't mean any harm."*
5. *"It's no big deal."*
6. *"I don't want to hurt my relationship."*
7. *"It will only make things worse."*
8. *"It's not worth putting my reputation at risk."*
9. *"I don't even know what that was."*
10. *"I am afraid of retribution."*

PEOPLE HARMED &
BIAS PREJUDICE BULLYING   ⚡ DISCRIMINATION HARASSMENT PHYSICAL VIOLATIONS

1. "I Want to Be Nice."

One of the reasons I wrote *Radical Candor* was to confront
the deeply ingrained tendency to remain silent when it would be
kinder to speak up. That is an instinct born of "If you don't have
anything nice to say, don't say anything at all."

But of course it's not actually kind to withhold critical
feedback simply to spare someone's short-term feelings at the
expense of their long-term growth. When we deliver critical
feedback kindly and clearly, we help the people improve. Failure
to speak up prevents the other person from addressing a fixable
problem—and sometimes that problem gets them fired. Not so
nice, after all.

Let's take a simple example: The other person has spinach in
their teeth. Most people would agree that it's kinder to point it
out than to ignore it. The same principle applies to more fraught
situations. But if someone makes an offensive remark, our instinct is often to let it slide rather than to let the person know.
And yet if you care about your colleague who said or did the
problematic thing, you don't want them to keep repeating the
mistake. And if you care about the other people on your team
who were also on the receiving end of the bias, prejudice, or
bullying, you know it's better for everyone to say something.
There's nothing "nice" about ignoring it.

This is hard enough when the problem is bias. Prejudice can
be even more uncomfortable to confront. But it's even more
important. If what a person is saying or doing violates a rule or
a law that could get them fired or in legal trouble, you are doing
them a favor when you give them a heads-up and say, "It is a
policy violation to . . ." or "It is illegal to . . ."

Same with bullying. Bullying that runs unopposed escalates
until the bully does real harm, and eventually, such behavior
gets the bully into real trouble, but not before it has caused huge
problems for everyone else. And of course sometimes people
aren't aware their behavior has crossed a line to bullying. The

world would truly be a kinder, more productive place if every-one confronted bullying early and often.

2. "I Have to Protect the Fragile Male Ego."

In *Radical Candor*, I describe Ruinous Empathy as the tendency to be so concerned about someone's short-term feelings that you fail to tell them something they'd be better off knowing in the long run.

When gender is added to the equation, there's another dy-namic as well: the tendency to feel the pain of men and dismiss the pain of women. Moral philosopher Kate Manne calls this *himpathy*. So perhaps the "I don't want to hurt his feelings" or "you have to protect the fragile male ego" arguments are best characterized as Ruinous Himpathy.

Ruinous Himpathy is memorable, but it risks making light of something that is serious. A friend of mine told me a story about a neighbor who summoned her to his car window. He gestured inside. He was masturbating. She had no idea what he was holding or what he was doing—she was eight years old. Her mother called the police, and it turned out the neighbor had been doing this to little girls all over the neighborhood. When he was arrested, her mother tsk-tsked, "Such a shame. He had such a promising career." Even as a child, my friend thought this response was strange. As an adult, she could ask, "This guy jisms at me, traumatizing me, and my own mother is sad about him and his *career*?"

Ruinous Himpathy is bad for the targets of the "him" in question, bad for the other men around him who often suffer from guilt by association with his bad behavior, and even bad for the "him" in question. That's why I've tried to eliminate the phrase "He's a good guy" from my vocabulary. We all do good things and bad things. People who are committed to being good

PEOPLE HARMED &
BIAS PREJUDICE BULLYING ⚡ DISCRIMINATION HARASSMENT PHYSICAL VIOLATIONS

people want to know about the bad things they do so they can make amends and avoid doing them again.

3. "I Can't Question Feedback."

As described above, bias, prejudice, and bullying often masquerade as feedback. It is especially damaging because when it happens too often, it can shut you down to any feedback, and we all need feedback to grow in our careers.

So if someone is giving you that kind of non-feedback, take a moment to show that you are open to criticism. Find that 5 or 10 percent of what they said and agree with that, just to make your listening tangible, to show you're not defensive. And then push back with your "I," "it," or "you" statement. The only way to stay open to helpful feedback is to be able to push back on the BS part of the feedback.

For example, if someone says, "I'm just going to tell you the truth," and then says something biased, you can take a page from the Daniel Craig character in *Glass Onion* and say, "It's a dangerous thing to mistake speaking without thought for speaking the truth."

The bias that most bedeviled me, especially early in my career when I felt most vulnerable, was being called "not likable" or "abrasive." In my first job out of college, the CEO of the company called me a "pushy broad." This was name-calling, not feedback. I wish I could have told myself and him that and asked, "What name would you have called Bob if he did just exactly what I did?"

Being told I was "not likable" made it tempting to pretend to be less competent than I was. But when I did, I didn't do as well at my job, and, surprise, surprise, people didn't like me any better. More importantly, I liked myself best when I was doing my best. And it turns out when I liked myself, other people liked me better, too.

I have found that when I confront the bias and hold my

ground, I do better work, build better relationships, and wind up with a better reputation. Paradoxically, it was learning not to care about my "likability" that made me feel more "likable."

Don't get pushed around by bias, prejudice, or bullying masquerading as feedback; push back on them!

4. "They Are a Good Person / Didn't Mean Any Harm."

Good people do bad things all the time. The only way for us to become the good people we want to be is to become aware when we fall short. And good people want to know when they are falling short so that they can do better next time. Acknowledging that you believe someone to be good should allow you to address the bad behavior. You aren't critiquing the person, you are critiquing the behavior.

5. "It's No Big Deal."

If it's no big deal, then it's also no big deal to correct it. And if it's no big deal, why do these incidents often jolt one awake at 3:00 a.m.?

Furthermore, if bias, prejudice, and bullying were rare, they *wouldn't* be that big a deal. But they are not rare. They happen all the time. Sometimes they are called *microaggressions*. But there is nothing micro about something that happens so often it feels like a repetitive stress injury.

6. "I Don't Want to Hurt My Relationship."

Allowing someone to continue to hurt or annoy you will not improve your relationship with that person. I *know* this. And yet I have made the mistake of thinking my silence will improve the relationship. I bet I'm not alone.

When I express my annoyance early, I can usually be radically candid—I can show I care even as I challenge the behavior

PEOPLE HARMED &
BIAS PREJUDICE BULLYING   ⚡ DISCRIMINATION HARASSMENT PHYSICAL VIOLATIONS

directly. When I repress my annoyance, it usually builds and then blows up. I wind up being obnoxiously aggressive. And then I'm mad at the other person for their behavior *and* at myself for my response.

7. "It Will Only Make Things Worse."

A common technique of bullies is to punish anyone who calls them on their behavior. So the fear of retribution is reasonable.

At the same time, we often have a negativity bias when it comes to confronting bullying. It's easy to overestimate the risks and underestimate the rewards of speaking up. As a result, we often fear challenging bullying more than we need to. So if you're worried about retribution, stop and ask yourself how likely it really is. When you stop to think, you may find you're less vulnerable than your instincts are telling you. Also, stop and think about the costs of not speaking up. They may be higher than you instinctively think.

8. "It's Not Worth Putting My Reputation at Risk."

I get questions like this from young women all the time: "The literature shows that when women are funny, they don't get taken seriously. Is humor dangerous for me in the office? Will being funny hurt my reputation?" "This study shows that when women negotiate hard, they are punished. Will being a good negotiator hurt my reputation? Should I quit negotiating so hard?" "When I am as aggressive as I must be to get the job done, I get a reputation for being 'abrasive' or 'not likable' and dinged in my performance review. I can't succeed in this catch-22. Should I just quit?"

All these questions make me want to scream, "*Nooooo!* Don't allow bias to make you less than you are. If you're funny, be hilarious; if you're a good negotiator, go for it; if you need to be aggressive to get your job done, be aggressive—especially when your peers who are men are free to be as aggressive as necessary."

The worst thing you can do for your career *and* your reputation in the long term is to hide your talents or suppress your voice or not do your best work. But that is exactly what bias pressures people from historically marginalized groups to do.

9. "I Don't Even Know What That Was."

What if you're not sure whether what just happened was bias, prejudice, or bullying? My advice to you is this: *trust your instincts*. If you respond to a remark as if it's evidence of prejudice or bullying when it was in fact bias, that's okay. You've given them the opportunity to explain themselves and to learn how what they said or did is landing for you.

It's worth noting that sometimes we pretend to ourselves that we are confused about what's happening as a mechanism of self-preservation—we are repressing awareness of a threat because there's nothing we can do about it, and so we don't want to waste emotional energy on it. For example, there are times when we pretend that we think something is unconscious bias when actually we know it is prejudice or bullying, but we don't want to feel the strong negative emotions that confronting those things elicit in us. Other times we genuinely don't know.

10. "I Am Afraid of Retribution."

Being afraid of retribution is not irrational. People suffer retribution all the time when they confront bias, prejudice, and bullying. It's important to be aware of the risks of speaking up. And it's equally important to be aware of the risks of *not* speaking up. They tend to be less obvious but no less real. Power is a big problem in these dynamics. The second half of this book will address the ways you can speak truth to power without blowing up your career.

PEOPLE HARMED & ⎯⎯⎯⎯
| BIAS   PREJUDICE   BULLYING | ⚡ DISCRIMINATION   HARASSMENT   PHYSICAL VIOLATIONS

BREAK THE SILENCE AND RAGE CYCLE

I have found that when I default to silence in the face of bias, prejudice, or bullying aimed at me, I can fall into a vicious silence and rage cycle. Someone says or does something offensive, and I default to silence. When I don't respond, I feel powerless, I lose my agency, just a little. Since I haven't said anything, the other person is likely to repeat the offense, making me feel angrier with each repetition. But each time, I default to silence, and so as I get angrier, I also feel more and more powerless. The more powerless I feel, the silenter I am, the angrier I get, and pretty soon, I'm in a vicious cycle. In the words of Simon and Garfunkel, "Silence like a cancer grows."

In retrospect, I realize that often I would've been better served to speak up than to default to silence. That doesn't mean that my calculus is the same as yours. I have a lot of unfair advantages. I'm straight and White, which shouldn't but does make speaking up safer for me; I have degrees that give me all kinds of unearned credibility; and I have financial resources that buy me lots of options that should be available to everyone but are not. What may be true for me may not be true for you.

One thing is almost always true: being silenced is invalidating and enraging, and having your emotions squashed by others is invalidating and enraging. In an ideal world, it's better to speak up before you're enraged than after. But this world isn't ideal. So don't let your anger silence you. If the only response you can manage to being silenced is to rage, then rage.

Soraya Chemaly writes in *Rage Becomes Her*, "By effectively severing anger from 'good womanhood,' we choose to sever girls and women from the emotion that best protects us against danger and injustice." Rebecca Traister's book *Good and Mad* explores how our society tries to compel women to repress their anger, and how important anger has been to galvanizing women to push for change. Anger, long cast as unfeminine, has become an increasingly important tool for creating solidarity among women of all classes and races.

Of course, men's emotions are repressed at work, too. In his Instagram Curbside Ministries, entrepreneur and brand guru Jason Mayden, who is Black, gave some excellent advice about expressing emotion in the workplace: "Stop saying that us being emotional is somehow regarded as a negative thing in corporate America. . . . What's wrong with being emotional? It means I'm human, it means I care, it means I'm actually present, I'm available to understand with an EQ not just an IQ how to treat people."

Being constantly on guard against saying what you really think and showing how you really feel can disrupt sleep patterns and diminish one's ability to contribute at work. Research has only recently begun to measure this toll on the health of people from historically marginalized groups in the workplace.

When one group is allowed to express emotions at work but another isn't, it makes it difficult for the people who have to repress their humanity to do their best work. The double standard is that men's anger is "strong and reasonable" but women's anger is "hysterical"; or that I as a White woman can say what I think, but when my colleague Michelle did the same thing, she was "an angry Black woman."

Of course, it's also not great if everyone is allowed to use their emotions as an excuse to bully each other. For example, I thought the investment bank where my boyfriend felt free to scream profanities at his colleagues had a bullying culture. One problem was that people from systemically disadvantaged groups wouldn't have been allowed to behave that way while White men were. But the more fundamental cultural problem there from my perspective was that *nobody* should've been allowed to bully others.

PEOPLE HARMED & ———
| BIAS   PREJUDICE   BULLYING | ⚡ DISCRIMINATION   HARASSMENT   PHYSICAL VIOLATIONS

Who's Allowed to Drop an F-Bomb?

I once dated a White man who was an investment banker.
I watched in horror one evening as he started screaming
profanities at his colleagues on a work call. I was afraid
he might lose his job. When he hung up and I expressed
concern, he looked puzzled. "Oh, it's no big deal." And it
wasn't, I realized—not for him. But if I had expressed even
a tenth of the rage he had, I felt sure I would have been
fired instantly. And what would have happened to a Black
or Latino man who yelled and cursed at work the way my
White boyfriend had?

Years later, I had a chance to answer that question. I
was at a company where we were role-playing to teach
people how to give feedback. We had hired actors. One
of the actors was a man, the other a woman. The actors
decided to see what would happen if they dropped
an f-bomb in the role-play. This seemed a reasonable
experiment since this was a company where f-bombs were
not uncommon, especially from the CEO. The participants
didn't react to the f-bomb from the actor who was a man;
however, they "fired" the woman actor who dropped
an f-bomb in the role-play. When the actors wondered
whether these very different responses were a result of
gender, they were told "not to talk about gender."

CULTIVATE UPSTANDERS

Better to invest your time and attention on your friends than
your enemies. What are the things you can do to make sure
you have more upstanders and fewer people causing harm in

your career? Here are some things that have helped me do just that:

1. Positive target identification
2. Solicit feedback
3. Allow for clumsy curiosity
4. Use humor
5. Turnabout is not fair play

1. Positive Target Identification

A fighter pilot told me that when he learned to fly through dangerous mountains, he was taught to focus his attention and energy on the path through the mountains and not to waste too much of his emotional reserves staring at the mountains he was trying to avoid crashing into. Yes, he needed to be aware of them. But he needed to focus on the way through, not what might hurt him. He called this *positive target identification*. I think it's a good approach to navigating bias, prejudice, and bullying.

When you look for people who can be supportive, you'll often find them. You need to know who the detractors are, too, but don't waste too much energy on them. Spend your energy building solidarity with people who can help you, people who will be upstanders.

2. Solicit Feedback

Caroline Wanga, CEO of Essence Communications, explains that you can't be great at your job if you can't be who you are at your job, *and* you are well served to focus first on earning credibility at the basics of your job to accomplish everything you want to accomplish. Focus on being great at your job, staying true to yourself, and building real relationships; if you do that,

PEOPLE HARMED &
BIAS PREJUDICE BULLYING ⚡ DISCRIMINATION HARASSMENT PHYSICAL VIOLATIONS

a good reputation will follow. A good reputation is the result of being your best self, not something you can achieve by trying to be what you think others want you to be.

One thing that will help you get better at your job, build better relationships on the job, and be yourself at work is feedback—real feedback that helps you grow professionally, not bias, prejudice, or bullying masquerading as feedback. Ask for criticism. Don't tune it all out because in the past you've gotten too much bias masquerading as feedback.

3. Allow for Clumsy Curiosity

I once worked at a company where I was the only parent. One of the young engineers was curious about what it was like to juggle work and family, and he asked me how I managed it. I talked about blocking time to have breakfast and dinner with my family, and to do the bedtime routine.

"Oh!" he exclaimed. "It's kind of like baseball season."

At first, I was a little put off. My family was sacred to me. Baseball was not. I was tempted to write this guy off. But I asked him what he meant. "Well, I played baseball in college. Before the season started, I always wondered how in the world I was going to get all my schoolwork done. But I always found it was kind of like you just described—there were long chunks of baseball time, but I somehow still had time to get my work done."

I was immediately glad I'd asked and not just written him off. Once I understood what he meant, I realized he was exactly right. "Baseball season" became one of my favorite metaphors for parenthood. And he became one of my most important champions at that company. We are friends to this day.

I told this story to an HR leader, who said he tried to work with his team to "allow for clumsy curiosity." Often people's comments or questions stemmed from total unfamiliarity with another person's situation. They say things that are uninformed because they *are* uninformed—as we all are on a huge number of topics.

Educating people about yourself can be exhausting, especially when their ignorance prompts them to say strange or offensive things. But it may be less exhausting and more rewarding than assuming that clumsy curiosity is hostility. Of course, sometimes the person really is hostile.

What's the difference between allowing for clumsy curiosity and assuming good intent? Both approaches leave you feeling more optimistic about human nature. When you trust people, your good faith is often rewarded. From an economic standpoint, trust is key for free markets to work efficiently and with the lowest possible transaction costs. It's possible to remember that most people are well intentioned most of the time without being in denial about those who are not.

However, the exhortation to "assume good intent" is often weaponized. When another person insists that you "assume good intent" after they've harmed you, it's reasonable to ask them to focus on their impact, not their intentions.

If you are a person who has just gotten feedback that you've caused harm even though you had no intention of doing so, I'll talk about the other side of this coin in the next chapter.

4. Use Humor

Humor can be a great asset in building solidarity and cultivating upstanders. You don't have to be funny, nor do you have to be serious all the time.

In her forthcoming book *Funnier*, professor of comedy at Columbia College in Chicago Anne Libera offers evidence that the evolutionary purpose of humor is insight. This is what Libera calls "Ha-ha Ah-ha!"

Remember that the best humor tries to make things better, not worse. Lindy West says, "The world is full of terrible things . . . and it is okay to joke about them. But the best comics use their

PEOPLE HARMED &
BIAS PREJUDICE BULLYING ⚡ DISCRIMINATION HARASSMENT PHYSICAL VIOLATIONS

art to call bullshit on those terrible parts of life and make them better, not worse." This kind of humor can be an effective way to communicate with well-meaning but clueless people who are oblivious to the mistakes they are making.

For example, Amy Cuddy, whose work on the power pose I mentioned earlier, developed an excellent response to a frequent experience. She would be on a flight and the person sitting next to her would strike up a conversation, asking, "What do you do?" When she responded, "I'm a professor at Harvard Business School," the response would often be something along the lines of "Really?! You don't look like someone who would teach there. What class do you teach?" Amy would reply, deadpan, "Typing." Then she'd share a laugh with the person who asked the question. She was laughing with, not at, them, giving them an opportunity to notice their mistake and apologize.

5. Turnabout Is Not Fair Play

The best way to fight bias, prejudice, and bullying is to confront them but *not* mimic them. It's tempting to fight bias with bias, prejudice with prejudice, bullying with bullying. Someone asks a question like, "Why are women so neurotic?" It's tempting to respond, "Why are men such assholes?" In the moment, it can feel as if turnabout is fair play. Problem is, it's not effective. It just reflects and reinforces the very attitudes and behaviors we're trying to get rid of. "You're bad, I'm good, so I am entitled to treat you terribly." Thus, hypocrisy is born. That is not what we are shooting for.

As Michelle Obama said, "When they go low, we go high."

Note

1. There's been a lot of controversy surrounding this talk. After it went viral, some academics tried to replicate Cuddy's results, with only partial success. These efforts are an important part of the scientific process. Many studies from many academics have proved difficult to replicate. Usually, there is intelligent discourse around this. However, in this case, Cuddy herself (not just her work) was aggressively attacked— to the point that I perceived it had crossed a line from academic skepticism to bullying. Ultimately, Cuddy conducted another study that reinforced some of her initial findings and added to the overall discourse—but not before the controversy had done enormous harm to her career. To learn more, read the *Forbes* article in the notes: "Power Posing Is Back: Amy Cuddy Successfully Refutes Criticism."

RADICAL RESPECT FRAMEWORK FOR PEOPLE HARMED

BIAS
NOT MEANING IT

"I"
STATEMENT

PREJUDICE
MEANING IT

"IT"
STATEMENT

BULLYING
BEING MEAN

"YOU"
STATEMENT

PEOPLE HARMED: CHOOSE IF OR HOW TO RESPOND

5

Be Part of the Solution, Not Part of the Problem

> The source of everything respectable in man [*sic*] either as an intellectual or as a moral being, namely, that his [*sic*] errors are corrigible. He [*sic*] is capable of rectifying his mistakes, by discussion and experience. Not by experience alone. There must be discussion, to show how experience is to be interpreted. Wrong opinions and practices gradually yield to fact and argument; but facts and arguments, to produce any effect on the mind, must be brought before it.
>
> —John Stuart Mill

BE AWARE AND MAKE AMENDS

THE RESPONSIBILITY OF PEOPLE WHO CAUSE HARM

In her book *On Repentance and Repair*, Rabbi Danya Ruttenberg turns to Maimonides, a Sephardic Jewish philosopher, for advice on how to become part of the solution and quit being part of the problem when you realize you've harmed someone. Maimonides was born in 1138, but people hurting each other is nothing new, and his advice is as relevant today as it was then.

First, don't apologize before you understand what you've

PEOPLE CAUSING HARM &
BIAS PREJUDICE BULLYING ⚡ DISCRIMINATION HARASSMENT PHYSICAL VIOLATIONS

done wrong and done something about it. Acknowledge your mistake, as precisely and as publicly as possible. Accept the consequences for what you've done, and go beyond those consequences to make amends for what you have done. Only after you've done these things are you ready to apologize. And if you continue the offending behavior, your apology is worthless.

I summarized the responsibility of the person who caused harm as "Be aware and make amends," but there's more to it. One way to remember these steps for how to make things right after you realize you've harmed someone is an acronym of five As and a C: AAAAAC!

be aware (educate yourself, don't ask the people you're harming to educate you)
acknowledge your mistake as publicly as possible
accept consequences
make amends
apologize
change for good

It's your responsibility to be aware of the harm you've done. This can feel tricky, unfair even, when it comes to unconscious bias. How are you supposed to be aware of what you are not conscious of? It can feel like a catch-22. More on this is below in the section on bias.

Whenever I am tempted to use the "I wasn't aware" excuse for having hurt a colleague, I think of a horrifying conversation I once observed. It involved an entrepreneur who had brought his daughter to work at his new business. She was bullied and disrespected by both him and others at the company to the point that she contemplated suicide. When she told him, he responded that he "wasn't aware." As if that absolved him of any need to take action or change.

Even if the person you're working with is not your child, you have a responsibility to be aware of how your behavior is affecting them, and to adjust if you are harming the person. This doesn't mean don't hold the person accountable. Part of caring about people is holding them accountable for doing a good job.

Of course, some people *want* to cause harm. This chapter isn't going to fix that problem. It's written for you, and I assume that if you bought this book and have read this far, you want to be part of the solution, not part of the problem.

BIAS

HOW TO BECOME AWARE OF WHAT'S UNCONSCIOUS

> It is much easier, as well as far more enjoyable, to identify and label the mistakes of others than to recognize our own. Questioning what we believe and want is difficult at the best of times, and especially difficult when we most need to do it, but we can benefit from the informed opinions of others.
>
> —Daniel Kahneman

If you don't want to unintentionally harm or anger your colleagues, if you don't want to contribute to making your workplace an unfair or unreasonable environment, the first and perhaps most difficult part of your job is to become aware of your unconscious biases. As Nobel Prize–winning psychologist Daniel Kahneman points out, "Acquisition of skills requires . . .

PEOPLE CAUSING HARM &
BIAS | PREJUDICE BULLYING ⚡ DISCRIMINATION HARASSMENT PHYSICAL VIOLATIONS

rapid and unequivocal feedback about the correctness of thoughts and actions." Here are some tips:

1. Find your "bias busters"
2. Question false coherence
3. Be aware of how "small" things add up to a big thing
4. Manage your defensiveness
5. Be persistent

1. Find Your "Bias Busters"

I recommend explicitly asking people to be your "bias busters," people who will be on the lookout for the things you say or do that reflect your unconscious biases. Word of warning: People who are from systemically advantaged groups are often in the majority or supermajority; when each person in the majority expects a person in the minority to educate them, it becomes burdensome. Often, people who are systemically advantaged do not recognize, compensate, or even appreciate their colleagues for doing this work.

So if you're from a systemically advantaged group, don't ask your colleagues who are not to point out your biases, unless you have a close enough relationship to be certain that this is not a burden to them, or unless it's their job (for example, if they are on the DEI team at your company), or unless you are paying them as a consultant to do it.

If you're not in a position to pay, you can share your openness to feedback with everyone, over- and underrepresented colleagues alike. But if people take you up on it, make sure you find other ways to reward the candor. Often, changing your behavior is the best reward. A thank-you is rarely enough.

It's also essential to choose bias busters who are thoughtful, people whose judgment you trust and whom you can count on to act in good faith. Look for people who understand a wide range of perspectives. Don't choose one person; choose a few.

You want a diverse set of people helping you to identify your biases.

Finally, don't do this only once and assume you've attained self-knowledge: it's a continuous process.

2. Question False Coherence

Our brains love to sort the chaos of life into various boxes and buckets and patterns. That's what the brain does—automatically but not necessarily wisely. Daniel Kahneman teaches us to challenge the kind of false coherence our brains serve up. Kahneman's book *Thinking, Fast and Slow* describes how our brains process information along two tracks, which he defines as System 1, fast thinking, and System 2, slow thinking. "System 1 operates automatically and quickly, with little or no effort and no sense of voluntary control. System 2 allocates attention to the effortful mental activities that demand it, including complex computations. The operations of System 2 are often associated with the subjective experience of agency, choice, and concentration." System 1 manages what happens when the light turns green. You put your foot on the gas without thinking. Someone presents you with a crossword puzzle or a calculus problem: System 2 takes over. Now you are working. Kahneman explains, "The defining feature of System 2 . . . is that its operations are effortful, and one of its main characteristics is laziness." In other words, System 2 will defer to System 1, often when it shouldn't. Unless you make a conscious effort to stop and think, System 1 and System 2 will conspire to avoid work that seems hard.

When System 2 over-delegates to System 1—that is, when you rely on a stereotype instead of looking at the actual situation, or when you don't stop and think even though the situation demands real thought—we get destructive biases. Sometimes System 2 lazily accepts the biases that System 1 energetically serves up.

It's okay to defer to System 1 at the green light; not okay to defer to gender or racial bias when making a hiring decision. It takes discipline, effort, and self-awareness to question the assumptions we make and to understand that the categories we construct are often arbitrary. In other words, if we don't want to get duped by our own brains, we must become conscious of our biases. That means learning to question them, and allowing others to question them, energetically.

3. Be Aware of How "Small" Things Add Up to a Big Thing

Sometimes the response to your bias may feel disproportionate to you. It seems like "no big deal" to you, but the other person is upset. You may be tempted to say, "Chill out," or "Don't overreact," or "Don't be hysterical." My advice to you? *Don't.* Get curious, not furious. Be aware that your biased comment or action may be the straw that broke the camel's back. Even though it's not your fault that this person has experienced the same biased remark you just made five thousand times before you said it, you still need to attend to the harm done.

When you understand that what seems a small thing to you may feel like a repetitive stress injury or death by a thousand paper cuts to the other person, it will help you respond with more compassion.

This may be a simple acknowledgment about why what you said was problematic. And if you're in a position to do so, offer to educate others on your team about the biased thing you just said or did so that this person doesn't face the same old shit day after day.

4. Manage Your Defensiveness

When you mess up, as we all are bound to do, it's natural to feel defensive. There's no denying that it can be hard to accept being told the things you do or say are biased. You might feel as if the zipper to your soul has come undone, revealing a shameful flaw. Or maybe you're not so deeply ashamed, but you fear that the consequences will be severe. This defensiveness is natural. And it may indeed be risky in your environment to admit that what you said or did was biased. But remaining unaware of your biases is even riskier. Don't hide from your mistakes. But don't double down on them either and risk being like the guy in this cartoon by Sine Anahita.

You can't do right if you don't know what you're doing wrong. So be open to learning about what you may be doing wrong and to correcting it.

5. Be Persistent
Changing biased behavior can be hard if that behavior has been your default. It may be that you've come to agree that referring to women as "guys" or "dudes" is not inclusive or accurate, but if you've been doing it your entire life, you may slip up or freeze at first as you attempt to change your default. Be patient with yourself—and even more persistent.

And remember, you may feel worse before you feel better.

Recently, I got some feedback that I tend to use language that assumes everyone identifies as either a man or a woman, an assumption that is both incorrect and harmful to people who are nonbinary. Shortly thereafter, I went on a live podcast and found myself saying, "Whether you are a man or a woman." I suddenly became aware I was doing it again, so I added, "Or whether you are . . . ," and then I couldn't retrieve the word *nonbinary*. I felt like a damn fool. Luckily, the host knew what I meant, filled in the word I'd forgotten, and we continued our conversation. It was embarrassing to find myself at a loss for words so publicly, but that was better than not attempting to make a change.

We all have to forgive ourselves for the mistakes we'll surely make when changing bad habits of speech from childhood or using a colleague's pronoun changes or any other change that causes us to change a deeply ingrained but incorrect pattern of thought or speech. And we have to be *persistent* with ourselves. The key is not to give up.

It is easy to feel utterly paralyzed by the awareness of the sheer volume of your newly discovered biases. In these moments, it can be helpful to do three things:

- Run the numbers
- Think of a person you care about
- Think about how bias busting improves your work

RUN THE NUMBERS

Breeze Harper, one of my bias busters, suggested I would benefit from thinking more deeply about the following words: lame, color-blind, blind, see, moron, psychopath, male, female.

What was my response? "Oh my God, every word in the English language is going to offend someone. There are no words I can use!" That kind of hyperbole is a common deflection technique. Analysis is the solution to hyperbole. When I stopped to count, I realized that there are over 170,000 words in the English language. Breeze had suggested I rethink my sloppy use of *eight* words. This math helped me gain some perspective.

THINK OF A PERSON YOU CARE ABOUT

Abstract "shoulds" can feel exhausting. Thinking instead about specific people you care about who will benefit from your efforts can reenergize you.

Three of the words that Breeze suggested I stop using were sight metaphors. Zach Shore, a historian who helped me edit this book, is blind. My first motivator to quit using language harmful to people who are blind was a desire to honor Zach, whom I admire. He never mentioned my use of ableist language. And as the person harmed, he shouldn't have to. He chooses to focus his energy on making a dent in the stubbornly high 70 percent unemployment rate among people who are blind and getting more of these folks interacting with people who can see.

I'd been unaware how often I was using ableist language and was glad Breeze had educated me. I thought I was aware and addressing the problem. But when I finished this book, I did a search on the word *see*. Guess how many times I'd used this word thoughtlessly? Ninety-nine times! When another bias buster read this, she pointed out another sloppy metaphor that is all too common and that I wasn't aware of: blinders. We all have a lot to learn.

THINK ABOUT HOW BIAS BUSTING IMPROVES YOUR WORK

Once I started making changes, I realized the sentences flowed better when I substituted the more accurate word. In the end, making the change improved the quality of my work. It probably benefited me more than people who are blind. I point this out not because I think that self-interest is a more significant motivator than altruism but because there can be arrogance in altruism.

You may not be a writer, but you may find that you make better promotion decisions, for example, when you are aware of not using biased language. You may find you sell more of your products when you eliminate biases about your customers, when you hire a team whose demographics mirror those of your customers. Becoming more aware of our biases pushes us to think more clearly. It's work, but we get more out of it than we put into it. A refusal to keep learning is like a child who says, "I know my addition tables. I don't need to bother with multiplication."

PREJUDICE

HOW TO QUESTION QUESTIONABLE BELIEFS

Be sure you choose what you believe and know why you believe it, because if you don't choose your beliefs, you may be certain that some belief, and probably not a very credible one, will choose you.

—Robertson Davies

It is never too late to give up our prejudices. No way
of thinking or doing, however ancient, can be trusted
without proof.

—Henry David Thoreau

A Prejudiced Belief

Until I was about eighteen, I believed that women were
superior to men. I didn't discuss this belief with anyone; I
just assumed it was a fact of life that everyone understood.

My family belonged to the Christian Science Church,
a religion founded by a woman, Mary Baker Eddy. She
wrote, "The Mind or intelligence of production names the
female gender last in the ascending order of creation." My
understanding of her words was that last meant highest,
or best; that women were more godlike than men. This
interpretation was reinforced for me by the fact that my
grandmother and her sisters dominated the church where
my family worshipped. Both at home and at church,
these strong women were in control. I thought this was
just the way things were for everyone.

The message about women's superiority was also
reinforced at the all-girls school I attended. We did better
on standardized tests than the students at the all-boys
schools. We were reminded of this fact constantly: we
weren't equal to the boys, we were *superior* to them—
smarter, nicer, and likelier to be guided by our ideals.
Looking back now, I assume these were not so much firmly
held convictions on the part of our teachers but rather an

effort to counterbalance negative messages about women in the wider culture. At the time, I thought it was just the truth.

It was inevitable that life would challenge my particular prejudiced belief. Unfortunately, it's far, far less inevitable that life will challenge a young man's assumption that men are superior to women. The number of dead White women writers he'll read will be dwarfed by the number of dead White men writers he'll read, the overwhelming number of world historical figures he'll study will be men, and so on.

Something analogous happens with racially prejudiced beliefs. Your life experiences won't automatically challenge them. For example, if you are White, ask yourself how old you were when you had an authority figure in your life who wasn't White. For me, it wasn't until I was in college and took a class with Toni Morrison. I was lucky to get an incredible education on many dimensions from her. She taught us to go looking for racist beliefs that were hiding not so far below the surface in canonical American literature. She shared that education with everyone in her book *Playing in the Dark*. I recommend it.

If you do have such essentializing beliefs lurking in your mind, you may find it a relief to let go of them. As Simone de Beauvoir wrote, "What people have endlessly sought to prove is that woman is superior, inferior, or equal to man . . . To see clearly, one needs to get out of these ruts; these vague notions of superiority, inferiority, and equality that have distorted all discussions must be discarded in order to start anew."

Let's all just try to become our best, truest selves and break free of these prejudices that create false, limiting comparisons! How can you do it? Here are three things to keep top of mind:

- Don't dichotomize and degrade
- Don't make the fundamental attribution error
- Don't expect everything to conform to average

Don't Dichotomize and Degrade

People who hold prejudiced beliefs will often dichotomize and degrade. They will open a conversation by setting up a false, essentializing dichotomy and then degrading one side of the false dichotomy. Men are "this," women are "that," and "this" is better than "that." Boomers are "this," millennials are "that," and "this" is better than "that."

For example, Pythagoras wrote, "There is a good principle that created order, light, and man, and a bad principle that created chaos, darkness, and woman." Ridiculous. I'm not saying we have to reject the Pythagorean theorem. Pythagoras's ideas about triangles have stood the test of time. His ideas about women have not.

Challenge your beliefs rigorously.

Don't Make the Fundamental Attribution Error

The fundamental attribution error refers to an individual's tendency to use perceived personality attributes—"You're an idiot"—to explain someone else's behavior rather than considering the situational factors that may at least in part have been the cause of the other person's behavior (which is the grace we tend to give ourselves). It's a problem because: 1) it's generally inaccurate; 2) it renders an otherwise solvable problem hard to solve because it invokes a fixed mindset; and 3) it makes it less likely that we might consider how our own behavior may have influenced the situation and therefore less likely to start by soliciting feedback before dishing it out.

Don't Expect Everything to Conform to Average

Ask yourself, "Even if it is true on average, does it apply to the specific situation at hand?"

As Todd Rose describes in his book *The End of Average*, when the US Air Force designed a cockpit for the "average" pilot, they designed a cockpit for no one. This is why, if we want Radical Respect, we must always be defeating the tyranny of the average and instead respecting each person's individuality and adjusting to it.

If you find yourself questioning or mocking people who don't conform to some arbitrary average, stop and think. Why are you doing this? Is this a bias hardening into a prejudice? Are you misusing the data to insist that people conform to what is on average true but not always true?

HOW NOT TO BE MISTAKEN FOR A JERK

Here's my story of bullying a colleague. I tell it not to either shame or justify myself but because I know I can't do better if I refuse to notice what I'm doing wrong.

I Am Not an Asshole. But, Like All of Us, I Do Sometimes Behave Like One.

I was working on a podcast with Russ Laraway, a colleague of many years with whom I'd recently cofounded a company. One of the producers suggested we discuss Amy Cuddy, the Harvard social psychologist famous for a TED Talk on postural feedback effect. As mentioned earlier, Cuddy's research has shown how and why adopting a physical posture that projects confidence—standing up straight with your shoulders back—can make you *feel* more confident and therefore project confidence. It has helped me a great deal. Recently, she'd been subjected to what seemed to me some academic bullying, and I was eager to support her publicly.

As the podcast began, I brought up a much-quoted finding from her research. "It's remarkable," I said, "how a two-minute Wonder Woman pose, standing with your legs apart and your chest puffed out, can increase testosterone and decrease cortisol!"

I didn't know it at the time, but Cuddy herself had recently acknowledged that new evidence that good posture affects testosterone and cortisol levels was mixed. Her research about how good posture makes a person feel, however, was borne out. Russ had learned this after doing some research when the producer suggested we discuss it. He brought this up during the podcast and tried to give me a chance to correct myself. Instead of listening to what he was trying to tell me, I shut him down by bullying him.

"With all due respect," I began (helpful hint: any time you start a sentence with the phrase *with all due respect*, you're almost certainly not being respectful), "what you don't understand is that you were *born* doing the power pose." All the women in the room let loose with great whoops of laughter, and Russ clammed up.

Russ was the only man in the room, over six feet tall,

BIAS   PREJUDICE   [**PEOPLE CAUSING HARM &** **BULLYING**]   ⚡ DISCRIMINATION   HARASSMENT   PHYSICAL VIOLATIONS and a former marine. He seemed like fair game. In the vast majority of similar situations in my career, the shoe has been on the other foot—I was the only person of my gender in the room, being excluded and mocked in some way. But turnabout is *not* fair play. It's simply a repetition of injustice. My attitude was also highly problematic. *Because you are a man, you have no right to speak on this topic.* I was actively excluding Russ from the debate and excluding the information he had from my consideration by mocking him for his gender.

When I later realized what I'd done, I apologized. Russ confirmed that he'd felt that I'd shut him down harshly and that he'd felt powerless to fight back. But he forgave me.

Bullying was as inefficient as it was unjust. The podcast went out with me saying things that were flat-out wrong and then bullying Russ when he tried to correct me. It harmed the message we were trying to get out into the world. It harmed Russ, made me look like a jerk, wasted a lot of time, hurt the quality of our work, and put a strain on our relationship.

Here's what this experience taught me: When I'm about to behave badly, there are usually two warning signs. One, I'm in the majority. Two, I am mad. Russ was the only man in a room of five people. I wasn't mad at Russ, but I was angry with the world for the way it was treating Amy Cuddy.

A good way to prevent yourself from bullying people in the future is to examine times when you've bullied others in the past. Be as honest as you can with yourself about why you did it and its impact on the other person, on you, and on witnesses.

What were the circumstances? How did you feel just before you bullied the person?

NO MATTER WHICH PROBLEM IT IS, KEEP THESE THINGS IN MIND . . .

If you're getting feedback that you've been biased, that one of your beliefs is prejudiced, or that you've bullied someone, first take a deep breath. This is hard to hear. A few things are always helpful to keep in mind:

- Have a growth mindset
- Focus on your impact, not your intentions
- Communication is measured at the listener's ear, not at the speaker's mouth
- Avoid telling people they "should" act/be a certain way
- Know how to apologize
- Know how not to apologize

Have a Growth Mindset

Recognizing your own bias, prejudice, or bullying is painful, especially if you don't think of yourself as biased, prejudiced, or a bully. Success requires adopting what psychologist Carol Dweck calls a *growth mindset*. When we have a growth mindset, we view failure and criticism as an opportunity to learn and improve. The opposite of a growth mindset is a *fixed mindset*, which views failure and criticism as signs of a fixed/negative trait, signs of who we are, some indelible personality attribute we cannot change.

Let's imagine someone gets feedback that they've been biased. The response of the person with a growth mindset would be "I'd like to understand why so I don't repeat that mistake." The fixed-mindset person, on the other hand, would reject the feedback by asserting their fixed attributes: "I am not a biased person, so therefore what I said could not possibly be biased." And so the person continues doing the biased thing. When we assign bias, prejudice, or bullying to others or ourselves as labels of who we are as human beings rather than attitudes or behaviors that could be changed, it makes it much, much harder to fix these problems.

Developing a growth mindset in our approach to changing our own attitudes and behaviors is essential. For example, a person whose leadership I admire, call him Bart, started working with a new employee, Avery. Avery was transitioning from male to female and had recently started using she/her to refer to herself, but Bart often referred to Avery as he/him because of his incorrect assumptions about Avery's gender. The first time this happened, Avery corrected him, and Bart apologized. But he repeated the mistake. Now Avery was angry. Bart did respect Avery's individuality, but he knew that overcoming years of assumptions would take time. Bart asked for the whole team's support in changing his behavior. This meant that everyone would be willing to step up and interrupt Bart's mistakes when he made them so that the whole burden of correction wouldn't fall on Avery.

Bart's mistake was bias, not prejudice or bullying. At a conscious level, Bart really did believe that Avery was the only person who got to say who she was; he knew it wasn't his right to tell Avery who she was or what gender she was. At the same time, it was hard for Bart to change habitual, biased assumptions about gender. And so he asked his colleagues to correct him. But

Bart went further: he also worked with his management team to develop training to help everyone honor the individuality of each of their colleagues.

They developed a saying: "As our trans colleagues transition, we transition with them." Everyone demonstrated willingness to do their own work to be supportive of a colleague's stepping more firmly into their own true self.

This saying broadened from trans people on the team to everyone. As a woman on the team was learning to embrace a more confident stance, her colleagues worked to eliminate the biases they held (e.g., calling her "abrasive" when she spoke up) that were making it harder for her to change her behavior. The essence of leadership is to help people grow. When each individual flourishes, the leader's team achieves better results.

Bart's efforts to acknowledge his mistakes, apologize, and, crucially, change his behavior improved his relationship with Avery. This was important to their ability to enjoy working together and also important to the team's success. Avery proved to be a great asset to the department. And the work Bart did to support Avery's transition helped *everyone* on the team have the freedom to bring their best, most whole selves to work.

If you're not willing to do the work required to honor the individuality of all your colleagues, including those who may be very different from you, you're not going to be successful in the vast majority of professions.

I can't impose this kind of growth mindset on you or anyone else.

Nor can your boss. It's up to you.

Focus on Your Impact, Not Your Intention

Do not insist that others "assume good intent" after they tell you you've done something to harm them in some way.

PEOPLE CAUSING HARM &
BIAS PREJUDICE BULLYING   ⚡ DISCRIMINATION HARASSMENT PHYSICAL VIOLATIONS

Code-of-conduct consultant Annalee Flower Horne suggests thinking about it this way: If someone told you that you were stepping on their toe, would you continue to step on it while you delivered a lecture about how you didn't mean to step on it? Of course not! You'd get off their damn toe and then apologize.

Telling people to "assume good intent" often ignores the cumulative pain and anger that builds up in people when they experience bias many times a day, every day of their lives, and when they feel, or are, powerless to respond to it. This is a moment to step back and realize that while you are involved in this problem, it goes well beyond you—you are one tiny piece of this person's justified anger. Try to be one tiny part of making it better by changing your behavior.

Rather than focusing on your intention, take a moment to look for the actual harm your attitude or behavior may have done. If someone is upset, try to understand why rather than reject the person's emotions.

This sometimes turns out to be an exercise in enlightened self-interest. You may find that you have harmed yourself more than you've harmed the person. When you make a biased assumption that the man in a meeting is the decision-maker when in fact it's the woman sitting next to him, you may have annoyed her a little. But you've just killed your chances of landing the deal. So you're the person causing harm, and the person you've harmed the most is not she, it's you.

Communication Is Measured at the Listener's Ear, Not at the Speaker's Mouth

Once, I worked with a couple of people who objected to what they called the "word police" on the theory that they didn't mean any harm and people should just quit being so sensitive. My boss explained to them that he did not consider himself to be the word police but that he was responsible for making sure his team worked well together. He pointed out that we all have words that make us see red.

If we are going to communicate well with one another, we must care about the impact our words have on them. We need to be willing to learn to avoid each other's "red words." If you're trying to communicate with someone, why use a word that will make it almost impossible for the person to hear the next fifty words you say? It would be so much more efficient to choose another word.

Admittedly, habits of speech are hard to break. Even when your team knows one another's red words, people will still say the wrong thing from time to time. Asking for forgiveness in the service of changing a habit is reasonable; insisting that you get to use whatever word you want, no matter what, is not.

Recently, in a post on social media, I misused the word *crazy*. I recommended people solicit feedback by saying, "Tell me why I'm crazy," when it would've been better to ask, "Tell me why I'm wrong." A couple of people pointed out to me (with greatly appreciated kindness) how this harmed people with mental illness. I posted an apology and linked to an article explaining in more detail why what I'd said was inaccurate and harmful. A bunch of people replied to the post, thanking me for saving them from making the same mistake. But many others only wanted to "reassure" me that what I'd said in the first place was okay, that we as a society have gotten "oversensitive." Just as I was about to explain why this wasn't a case of oversensitivity, I was happy to have a colleague weigh in on this point:

> For the "we've become too sensitive" crowd . . . Please consider trying to evaluate this with a simple return-on-investment calculation. What does it cost me to change / not change, and what do we get if I change / not change?

PEOPLE CAUSING HARM &
| BIAS   PREJUDICE   BULLYING | ⚡ DISCRIMINATION   HARASSMENT   PHYSICAL VIOLATIONS

The investment: Adapting my language costs what? Some cognitive difficulty for like two weeks?

My search for an answer on this topic and many others tells me that it costs effectively nothing.

Then, I ask myself what I get in return. If I keep using insensitive aphorisms—especially as a White man—I will create ranging inclusion issues—big for some, small for some, nonexistent for others. If I change my language, though, I take a small step toward a more universally inclusive environment. I think that the "we've become too sensitive" take implicitly invalidates the perspective of those offended or hurt, and I'm just not sure we should be doing that.

Well said.

Avoid Telling People They "Should" Act/Be a Certain Way

I get to decide who I am, and you get to decide who you are. Yet all too often, we try to tell other people who they are, what gender they "should" be, what job they "should" want, what they "should" wear, how they "should" feel, whether their hair "should" be long or short, straight or curly, whether they "should" have kids, whether they "should" be in a relationship, and on and on. These are often forms of bullying, though they could also be bias or prejudice, or a toxic stew of all three.

Each of us gets to decide who we are and how we feel. Nobody else gets to tell us who we are, who we "should" be, or how we "should" feel. This is pretty basic.

Know How to Apologize

The AAAAAC! principles are featured in an apology to Lindy West, who was targeted by a troll after her father died. The troll opened a Twitter and Gmail account in Lindy's deceased father's name and started sending her cruel messages. Rather than ignoring the troll, West wrote about the experience on the website Jezebel and got this response:

> *Hey Lindy,*
> *I don't know why or even when I started trolling you. It wasn't because of your stance on rape jokes. I don't find them funny either.*
>
> *I think my anger towards you stems from your happiness with your own being. It offended me because it served to highlight my unhappiness with my own self.*
>
> *I have e-mailed you through 2 other gmail accounts just to send you idiotic insults.*
>
> *I apologize for that.*
>
> *I created the PawWestDonezo@gmail.com account & Twitter account. (I have deleted both.)*
>
> *I can't say sorry enough.*
>
> *It was the lowest thing I had ever done. When you included it in your latest Jezebel article it finally hit me. There is a living, breathing human being who is reading this shit. I am attacking someone who never harmed me in any way. And for no reason whatsoever.*
>
> *I'm done being a troll. Again I apologize.*
>
> *I made a donation in memory to your dad. I wish you the best.*

Before he made this apology, he acknowledged exactly and precisely what he did wrong. He did the soul-searching to try to understand why he'd done that, and he made himself vulnerable by putting it in writing. He accepted the consequences—deleted the Gmail and Twitter accounts. He went beyond these consequences and made a donation in memory of her father. And then he sent his apology.

He demonstrated that the change stuck when he was willing to go on the show *This American Life* with Lindy to tell the story of his behavior and explain why it was so wrong and why he was committed to helping others avoid making that kind of mistake.

Know How Not to Apologize

Here are a few common "apologies" that really are not apologies at all:

"I AM AN ASSHOLE."

Saying this focuses in a vague way on who you are as a person, implying that it can't possibly change, rather than focusing in a specific way on your behavior and how it might change. It shows no willingness to acknowledge how your behavior harmed someone or any possibility you are capable of not repeating the same thing in the future. And, it asks the person harmed to comfort you, to reassure you that you're not in fact an asshole.

"I WAS JUST KIDDING."

If your joke harmed someone, then it was a bad joke, and you're better off apologizing for it than trying to use humor to cover up what you did wrong. Good humor reveals hidden attitudes and behaviors in a way that creates change. Bad humor reinforces harmful attitudes and behaviors.

"THIS HAS BEEN REALLY HARD FOR ME."

Once again, it focuses on you. In this case, you are not apologizing, you are looking for sympathy, or himpathy. A VC who was accused of sexual misconduct began his apology with, "The past twenty-four hours have been the darkest of my life." An upstander, another man in tech, responded, "Are you kidding me? This is how you start? *No one gives a shit about you.* The only acceptable way to start this statement is with the words *I'm so sorry.*"

Another version of this happens when a person uses emotion to avoid accountability. If you are prone to tears, make sure you and others who are present remain focused on the person harmed. Don't allow the discomfort that others feel in the face of your tears to cause them to give you a pass when you're acknowledging what you did wrong. Don't let it become about you. Everyone is allowed to cry—and also responsible for making sure their emotion isn't a bid, intentionally or not, to avoid confronting a way in which you've harmed someone else. This is often called White Women's Tears. Men do it, too, though. And although I've never cried strategically or weaponized my emotions, I've still been in situations where my emotions were privileged over those of others in a room; so I'm glad for the reminder.

"I'M SORRY YOU FEEL THAT WAY."

This misses the point. It shows you still don't get that you caused any harm beyond hurting someone's feelings.

Sometimes this is a communication in bad faith, not an apology at all, as in "I'm sorry you feel I was harassing you." What the person in this case is really saying is "I wasn't harassing you, and if you feel I was, there's nothing I can do about it."

"I WAS HAVING A BAD DAY."

Nobody is interested in why you did what you did. People are interested in what you're going to do to make it right, and they want to make sure you don't repeat the mistake.

"LET ME EXPLAIN."
Now you are justifying, not apologizing.

"YOU HAVE TO FORGIVE ME!"
People often ask for or even demand forgiveness before they've taken a single step to make amends or to ensure they won't repeat the mistake. Don't say, "Will you please forgive me?" while literally blocking the person's path to an exit.

APOLOGIZE OVER AND OVER BUT KEEP REPEATING THE MISTAKE
An apology is not a substitute for fixing the problem. In fact, apologies repeated over and over without action become an irritation, like throwing salt in a wound.

RADICAL RESPECT FRAMEWORK FOR
PEOPLE WHO CAUSE HARM

BIAS
NOT MEANING IT

**FIND YOUR
BIAS BUSTER**

PREJUDICE
MEANING IT

**DON'T
DICHOTOMIZE
& DEGRADE**

BULLYING
BEING MEAN

**BEWARE OF
POWER & ANGER**

AAAAAC! BE AWARE, ACKNOWLEDGE YOUR MISTAKE PUBLICLY,
ACCEPT CONSEQUENCES, MAKE AMENDS,
APOLOGIZE & CHANGE FOR GOOD!

PART TWO

DON'T LET POWER
SCREW IT ALL UP

CAUTION

UNCHECKED
POWER

6

Design Principles for Radical Respect

I t's not enough for a leader to be a good person. A leader must design good management systems. When management systems are designed explicitly to optimize for collaboration, not co-ercion, and to honor each employee's individuality rather than demanding conformity, the result is Radical Respect and the fairness, innovation, and productivity that come with it.

To design these systems well, leaders need to be very con-scious of limiting power. When managers have too much power, bias and prejudice give way to discrimination; bullying gives way to verbal or psychological harassment. Unchecked power, whether positional or physical, paves the way for the full range of physical violations ranging from the unwanted hair pat to the creepy hug to the violent assault.

Dominance hierarchies do enormous damage. But that doesn't mean all hierarchy is bad. Hierarchies that facilitate col-laboration and prevent coercion can unleash each employee's capacity to do the best work of their lives and the team's ability to deliver excellent results. To design a collaboration hierarchy, you have to create enough checks and balances on power that people in positions of authority can be held accountable, are less likely to be corrupted, and don't rob people with less power of their capacity to do great work.

LEADERS &
BIAS PREJUDICE BULLYING ⚡ | DISCRIMINATION HARASSMENT PHYSICAL VIOLATIONS |

·I am extremely wary of any situation where one person has unchecked power *over* another person or group of people. I learned this the hard way. In 2000, I cofounded a software company and became its CEO. Part of my motivation was to create a fair working environment. I thought all that was necessary was for me to be in charge, rather than the assholes I'd worked for in the past. I went to great lengths to make sure I retained complete control over my company. I believed that since I'm a good person, if I was in charge, bad things wouldn't happen. But unfortunately, my good intentions weren't enough—the very same bad things happened at my company that I'd thought happened elsewhere because the leaders were "assholes."

Now who was the asshole? I was! I'm going to assert right here that I try really hard not to behave like a jerk. But I did fail to build the kind of management systems that would've allowed me to achieve my goal of creating a radically respectful work environment. My goal here is to help you learn the easy way—by reading—what I had to learn the hard way—by screwing up.

The rest of this book is going to look at systems rather than criticizing the character of individual leaders. It's much easier and more satisfying to look for the individual scoundrel than to analyze the systems that made it possible or perhaps even inevitable that bad things would happen. Looking for the "bad guy" can feel satisfying because it indulges the instinct for self-righteous shaming. But it's dangerous because it offers a false reassurance that the problem is all someone else's fault and there's nothing we can or should do about it.

Thinking about these systems doesn't *have* to be boring. In fact, building an institution that will outlive its leader, that will continue to innovate for generations, is one of the most exciting things a person can do. Too often, leaders reserve all their design cycles and the lion's share of resources for their products and short-term financial results. They over-delegate the design of their company's organizational structure and management systems—the very engine that produces the desired results—to HR. Then leaders under-resource HR and undervalue the systems they are building. When the systems don't work, they blame HR.

The key is to design systems to avoid disempowering employees. The system does not need to "give employees a voice." Each employee already has a voice. The key is not to silence it. The key is to design a system that makes sure each employee is free to use the skills they already have and to exercise their innate capacity for growth. Often that means putting checks on the power of people in authority.

The strength of your team depends on each individual, and the strength of each individual depends on the team. Unlike wolves, lobsters, or other animals, we don't have to organize into crude dominance hierarchies to get things done. We are human beings with spoken language, books, and supercomputers in our pockets. We *can* create working environments in which everyone can be their fullest self and so do their best work— thereby making the whole greater than the sum of its parts. And leaders who fail to do this will not be able to keep up with the dynamism innovation from the teams of those who do.

WHAT GOOD DESIGN LOOKS LIKE

TWO PRINCIPLES

When leaders apply two design principles to their management systems, they can mitigate the harm caused by unchecked power and unleash the potential of each individual on their team to do their best work and to collaborate with their colleagues. These principles are:

BIAS   PREJUDICE   BULLYING   ⚡ | LEADERS & ——— DISCRIMINATION HARASSMENT PHYSICAL VIOLATIONS |

1. Checks and balances
2. Measure what matters

1. Checks and Balances

A leader's job is to ensure that the whole is greater than the sum of its parts. But too often, managers attempt to gain power by minimizing and bullying the people who work for them. Most workplaces allow this by giving managers up and down the org chart unchecked authority to make decisions that have profound consequences for their employees. Traditionally, managers dole out or withhold resources; they decide who gets hired, fired, or promoted; they determine bonuses, who gets the plum assignments, who gets stuck with the grunt work, and so on. When managers make all these decisions unilaterally, it is too risky for employees to challenge bias, prejudice, or bullying, let alone to report harassment or discrimination; and so harassment and discrimination are likelier to happen. Poor decisions are made. Employees are robbed of their agency. Managers are not held accountable. Employees suffer, and so do results.

You can bake checks and balances into your organizational design, or you can design a system that creates mini-dictators. If you do the latter, the unchecked power you've given managers makes discrimination and harassment, as well as failure, much likelier. It's worth repeating: if you don't design your management systems for justice, you're going to get systemic injustice—and hurt your ability to achieve results.

Much has been written about "empowering" employees. But there's something arrogant about that framing. It implies that employees are lacking in capacity to do great work and that the powerful leader must bestow skills upon them, when really the problem is a management bureaucracy that has robbed people of their innate capacity for work and growth. The goal of leadership is not to treat people as though they are lacking but to recognize what they already have and to create systems that unleash their best efforts rather than robbing them of their agency.

In other words, the most important thing leaders can do is to stop *disempowering* employees by giving too much unilateral authority to managers. As I wrote above, it's not your job as a leader to "give people a voice." They already have a voice. Rather, it's your job to make sure their boss is not silencing them or punishing them for speaking up; it's your job as a leader to ensure managers are held accountable for *soliciting* criticism and rewarding the candor when they get it.

Research explains the reasons why limiting the power of individuals and replacing old command-and-control structures with a more collaborative approach is so important to achieving excellent performance:

- Cohesive, empowered teams will outperform a collection of individuals on a wide range of tasks.
- High-functioning teams tend to make better decisions than high-functioning individuals.
- Teams where everyone speaks up perform better than teams dominated by a tyrannical manager or a "superstar."
- Homogeneous teams tend to make poorer decisions than their diverse counterparts do.
- When teamwork replaces command and control, better decisions get made.

Management systems in which leaders are held accountable for doing their jobs well rather than given unilateral decision-making authority can help you build teams with those attributes.

BIAS PREJUDICE BULLYING ⚡ LEADERS & DISCRIMINATION HARASSMENT PHYSICAL VIOLATIONS

This means that no one person in an organization, including its CEO, should be able to hire, fire, promote, or pay another person without oversight. The sections below will go into more detail about how, exactly, such management systems can operate.

But if your organization is homogeneous, checks and balances will not do enough to help you notice when bias and prejudice are skewing your management processes. In addition to checks and balances, you also need to measure what matters—to proactively quantify the way bias and prejudice may be skewing your processes.

2. Measure What Matters

Do you want your organization to make biased or unbiased decisions? If you, like me, believe that unbiased decisions yield better results and a more reasonable work environment, you'll agree that you will raise the bar, not lower it, when you seek to strip bias out of your management systems.

Since bias is so often unconscious, you've got to get proactive about noticing and correcting the ways that bias is affecting decisions about whom to hire, reward, mentor, and fire. You've got to do so with the same energy you'd use to investigate a decrease in profitability, research a competitor, explore a new opportunity, launch a product, or enter a new market to grow your business. Think of bias and the resulting discrimination as a virus in your operating system. It will eventually kill your system if you don't proactively identify it and fix it.

There is a real upside to a "search and destroy" approach to bias and the discrimination it causes. You'll make better decisions about whom to hire, to promote, to manage out, and how to improve employee engagement.

There is also a big downside risk of *not* getting proactive.

Laws that mandate diversity disclosure are being passed with increasing frequency. As a result, many general counsels are recommending that leaders develop or strengthen existing policies; develop, benchmark, and monitor key performance indicators, such as employee engagement scores; employee retention and turnover; employee training budgets, time, and participation rates; diversity representation on the board and by employee category; and pay equality measured as a ratio of compensation by employee category.

After the Supreme Court's 2023 ruling on affirmative action at two universities, several Republican state attorneys cautioned companies about using race as a factor in hiring and employment practices. I definitely recommend you seek legal advice before taking any advice you read in any book. However, there's plenty of evidence that there are safe and legal ways to use data about race, gender, and other factors to improve management systems. And it's a truth in business that "you get what you measure." It would be anti-capitalist to argue that businesses are not allowed to measure any factor that improves results.

In other words, you'll be more successful at hiring and retaining the right people for the right jobs when you quantify your bias; and it may be illegal not to. For many years, to prove discrimination, one had to prove intentionality. If leaders were in denial, they were off the hook. Denial and ignorance, however, do not excuse discrimination any longer.

Measure the progress you're making toward creating a more diverse, inclusive organization at every stage of the employee life cycle—from interviewing to firing. Include these measures in all your management processes. Dig into the numbers, spend your energy looking for solutions—not excuses or rationalizations.

There is a world of difference between these kinds of measurements and quotas. These kinds of measurements are a way to check your work, to get proactive about examining the ways the unconscious bias harms good decision-making. You're saying, "Let's see if I've failed to hire/promote/pay/reward/ mentor people from this group. If I have, let me do the work to understand why, and whether I need to improve my management process." You're *not* saying, "Hire/promote a person from a systemically disadvantaged group, even if they are not qualified." That kind of cooking-the-books approach to making sure you hire the right people into the right roles will not work. That kind of unthinking approach to under/overrepresentation can also lead to discrimination against minorities. It is what led the Ivy League to set quotas limiting the number of Jewish students it admitted, which led to discrimination and a student body that wasn't as academically qualified as it could have been.

PROACTIVELY DESIGN MANAGEMENT SYSTEMS TO AVOID OBLIVIOUS EXCLUSION AND BRUTAL INEFFECTIVENESS

What happens when leaders don't consciously design their management systems to be fair? They get systemic injustice and subpar teams. Let's look at two different ways it can play out: Oblivious Exclusion and Brutal Ineffectiveness.

Oblivious Exclusion

Oblivious Exclusion is insidious because it's especially easy for the people causing harm and leaders to ignore it, to be in denial, or to be willfully ignorant. Things seem collegial, pleasant, and civilized—at least if you're on the inside. Everyone jokes around with each other; they talk about sports and TV and pretend to be interested when Bob brags about what a good chess player his seven-year-old daughter is. There's a generous parental leave policy. People generally get along, and there's a clubby atmosphere. One leader I worked with calls this *false harmony*. Another calls it *country club management*. Often all the leaders on such a team literally do belong to the same club, one that explicitly discriminated until recently.

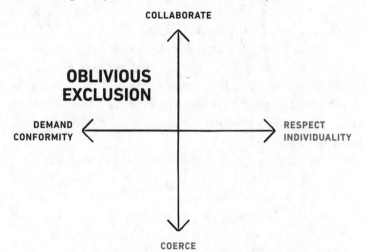

Sometimes leaders intentionally design a management system to exclude part of the population or to be homogeneous. Usually, though, leaders set up management systems with the intention of making it simpler to decide whom to hire, fire, and promote. Their goal is to create efficient meritocracies. But what they are actually doing is setting up what journalist Kara Swisher calls a "mirror-tocracy"—a workplace that rewards only those who look just like its leader.

People from systemically advantaged groups may well think of themselves as inclusive and collaborative. They do not *intend* to degrade or silence or discriminate against people who are from systemically disadvantaged groups. It's almost like what happens when a group of hikers passes a lone hiker on a narrow trail. The group doesn't intentionally set out to push that solo hiker to the side of the trail, but somehow, unless the group is communicating well and taking proactive measures to be considerate, chances are good that lone hiker ends up standing in a patch of poison oak as the group passes by, talking and laughing, waving in a friendly way, unaware they've just shoved someone aside and left them with a bad rash.

It's difficult for the people harmed to prove Oblivious Exclusion when it's happening. Brutal Ineffectiveness, that's something you feel. You know something is wrong because you are being harmed in pretty obvious ways. Oblivious Exclusion operates in the shadows. When you try to call it out, the answer is often just "Nothing to see here."

It's often hard to understand how senior leaders can be so oblivious to exclusion in the makeup of their teams. One team had nine White men, one White woman, and one Indian American man—and they bragged about their diversity. That's what I call Math of the Overrepresented. I've heard leaders whose teams look like this say revealingly biased things to shut down the conversation when they are questioned. "What do you want me to do, lower the bar? I'm just not going to do that!" Or they'll smile sadly and say it's because people from certain demographics "don't want the job." Often enough, they pull their photos off their website.

Here are two stories about what it's like.

Sally's Rise

I once advised the executive team at a tech company. Sally, the only senior woman on the product team at this company, asked me for some advice. She learned that one of her peers had gotten a stock grant worth many multiples of what hers was worth. That was pretty hard to swallow, but she was trying to stay focused on being positive, doing great work, and getting promoted.

Over time, though, she didn't get promoted, despite her many impressive contributions, and she was finding it increasingly difficult to stay motivated. She showed me her most recent performance review. Bob, her boss, had written that she was "abrasive" and "not technical" enough. My bias antennae perked up. By any objective measure, she was far less abrasive than several men who'd been promoted ahead of her recently. And it wasn't at all clear from their performance or educational background or work experience why the men who'd been promoted ahead of her were any more "technical" than she was.

Then Sally learned that Ned was going to be promoted ahead of her. Ned had accomplished less than Sally at the company. When Sally asked why she wasn't being promoted and Ned was, Bob again harped on the "abrasive" issue, since he couldn't point to any results to explain his decision. To Sally, her boss's rationale for promoting Ned over her seemed so obviously unfair that she was wondering if she'd missed something. When I told her, "No, it's not you; there's real gender bias here," she was visibly relieved. She could stop blaming herself.

In my next meeting with Bob, I mentioned an executive at the company who'd been promoted recently. I mentioned how aggressive this guy could be. "I know," Bob said. "He is a real asshole. But he has to be to get the job done."

I'd set a trap, and Bob stepped right into it.

"What about Sally?" I asked. "You told her she wasn't

getting promoted because she was too aggressive. Doesn't she have to be just as aggressive as Ned to get the job done? Aren't you putting her in a kind of catch-22?"

I continued, "You have two problems here. One is that you don't even notice your own biases—inconsistencies and double standards. That's causing you to skew your decision-making. Two is that if you keep talking that way, not only will you promote the wrong people, you are going to start losing the right ones."

He didn't address the problem, and Sally ended up quitting without even lining up another job. It was an agonizing decision. She wanted to stay for the sake of the women who worked for and around her. But it seemed futile. Women progressed to a certain level at this company, and then their careers stalled. Staying in a situation that would make her bitter or cynical wasn't going to help anyone—Sally or any other woman at the company. Leaving would at least signal to Sally's women colleagues that they didn't have to put up with a culture that treats women unfairly.

Sally's departure was frustrating for everyone. She didn't want to leave, the CEO tried to convince her to stay, and her team loved having her as their boss. But the leaders at the company were oblivious: they believed they were a meritocracy and didn't notice how the lack of promotions and leadership roles for women made it feel more like a men's club than a meritocracy. Discouraged by Sally's shabby treatment, several high-performing women at the company immediately started looking for new jobs.

A few months later, an even-faster-growing tech company offered Sally a VP-level job. A number of people, both men and women, who'd loved working with Sally followed her to this new company. She did well and quickly became the chief product officer there. So much for the "not technical enough" feedback. That company went on to be one of the most successful in Silicon Valley. Odds are high you have used their product this week, if not within the past few hours.

But for every success story such as Sally's, there are countless other women whose careers stalled after they were tagged as "abrasive," or "not technical enough," or some other form of bias masquerading as feedback. Countless women have been steered into less prestigious roles while less qualified men were fast-tracked into running the high-paying profit centers.

A "Real Mother Hen"

I once advised a CEO who initially didn't have any women on his team. To his credit, he figured this meant there was something wrong with his promotion process, not the women at the company. He hired me to sit in on his promotion committee meeting to help him figure out what was going on.

There were two leaders up for promotion, one a man, the other a woman. Both had exceptional results. Both had high-performing, exceptionally engaged teams.

As the committee started discussing the decision,

I noticed that they referred to the man as "a strong leader." Then someone said of the woman, "Oh, her team loves her. She's a real mother hen."

"Whoa, back up the train!" I said. "Who are you going to promote? The strong leader or the real mother hen?"

At first, the team pushed back. "Oh, come on, Kim, it's just a figure of speech." However, in the end, they had to agree, words matter. They referred to her as a real leader, not a real mother hen. She got the promotion.

See the next chapter for specific ideas on how to make sure biased language doesn't creep into your promotion processes.

Brutal Ineffectiveness

Brutal Ineffectiveness is what you get when, in addition to management systems that unconsciously reward conformity, the systems optimize for coercion rather than collaboration, producing more outright bullying and harassment.

The Weinstein Company was an example of Brutal Ineffectiveness. So is Elon Musk's Twitter/X, in a different way. The board of Uber made the determination that Travis Kalanick's behavior was both brutal and ineffective and removed him. The Jim Crow South, apartheid South Africa, and Putin's Russia are other examples of Brutal Ineffectiveness. Brutal Ineffectiveness is worst soonest for the people harmed, but in the end, it's bad for everyone. If we take the long view, everyone has a practical interest in changing these systems, even the people who benefit from them in the short term.

Sometimes Brutal Ineffectiveness springs from an evil leader, but it often springs from management systems that fail to hold people accountable for bad behavior or that even *reward* bad behavior. The assholes begin to win, and the culture begins to lose. Power dynamics, competition, poorly designed management systems, and office politics can create systemic injustice in ways that may be subtle and insidious at the outset but over time become corrosive, and often even criminal.

And, really, who cares about the leader's intentions? We should demand the same good results from leaders who create management systems as we do from CEOs when it comes to profitability. If the systems reflect and reinforce the injustice in our society, they need to be changed. If a leader can't figure out how to change the system, the leader must go.

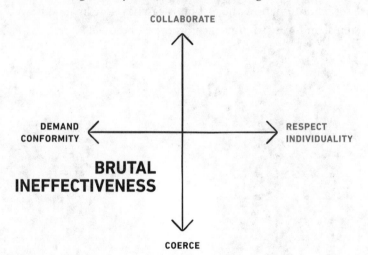

The examples of Brutal Ineffectiveness don't have to be as dramatic as the Weinstein Company or as bloody as Stalinism. Think about a time in your life when leaders demanded conformity and therefore hired homogeneous teams, passing over the most skilled people for promotion, touting their meritocracy while actually creating a mediocracy. And there were no consequences for bullying or harassment, so these behaviors

BIAS PREJUDICE BULLYING ⚡ | LEADERS & ───── |
| DISCRIMINATION HARASSMENT PHYSICAL VIOLATIONS |

were common, making it difficult for many to do their best work. A vicious cycle ensued.

It's hard to understand how or why we let things get so bad that we land in Brutal Ineffectiveness. Considering discrete problems like bias, prejudice, bullying, discrimination, harassment, and physical violations can't explain it. To understand, we need to consider the dynamics between these attitudes and behaviors, and the vicious cycles such dynamics can set in place. Chapter 8 will describe these dynamics. But first, let's look at how leaders can apply design principles to all management systems in a way that minimizes the odds that such bad dynamics are set in motion, how the rest of us can navigate around flawed systems, and how to prevent physical violations.

7

Apply Design Principles to Management Systems

What follows are specific ideas for how leaders can use checks and balances and measure what matters to make their management systems fairer and more successful at every stage of the employee life cycle:

1. Compensation
2. Performance Management
3. Coaching and Mentoring
4. Exiting
5. Eliminating NDAs and Forced Arbitration
6. Organizational Design
7. Hiring

Notice that hiring comes last in this list, even though it's at the beginning of the employee life cycle. That's because it makes sense to fix your other management systems *before* you focus on diversity in hiring. The reason is simple. If you hire people and then treat them like shit, they will quit.

Before describing the ways that leaders can create fair and reasonable management processes, let's return to a basic point. When building a team, leaders aim to identify the right people for the right job. Discrimination and harassment get in the way of that goal. It's not charity to create the kind of working environment that promotes and hires the right people and allows them to do their best work. It's enlightened self-interest. If your management systems have put unnecessary obstacles in the way of your employees' success, it's your job to remove them. That's just management. Just in both senses of the word.

1. COMPENSATION

In 2021, Latina women were paid fifty-four cents for every dollar paid to White men, and Black women sixty-four cents, Native American women just fifty-one cents, White women seventy-three cents, and Asian American, Native Hawaiian, and Pacific Islander women seventy-five cents. Over a forty-year career, Black women earn almost a million dollars less than White men doing the same job. Black men earn eighty-seven cents for every dollar paid to a White man doing the same job; Native American men earn ninety-one cents.

A 2019 report on wage inequality in tech from *Hired* magazine shows that "63% of the time, men were offered higher salaries than women for the same role at the same company. Companies were offering women between 4% and a whopping 45% less starting pay for the same job." And that only looks at salary. In some industries, a huge part of compensation is equity, where the data is more opaque.

Unless you believe that White men are superior to others and that's why they're paid more, it's impossible to believe that bias is *not* a factor. And if you do believe that, then prejudice is the factor.

Here are some things you can do to make sure your compensation system is equitable:

- Design a principled comp system
- Cut your pay data by demographic

DESIGN A PRINCIPLED COMP SYSTEM
DON'T RELY ON MANAGER FIAT

It's absolutely crucial not to give managers unilateral authority over salaries, bonuses, stock grants, or other forms of pay. Instead, develop a fair, transparent compensation system that everyone understands and stick to it. This is an important check on the power that individual managers have that will help prevent their biases or prejudices from translating into pay discrimination.

Someone in your organization—the compensation group in HR at a big company, the head of HR at a medium-size company, or you, if you're leading a small company and don't yet have an HR lead—should come up with salaries or salary ranges for particular jobs and functions. Do the research so you know what the market rate is and explain your rationale. There are many firms that offer this data.

Make some conscious decisions. For example, do you want to pay at market, above market, below market? People doing the same job should get job offers with the same salary and stock (if relevant) packages. Any exceptions should require an explanation and sign-offs from at least three different executives at the same level.

Doing this will do three things. One, it will mean that pay will be fairer, less subject to the bias of individual managers or the demands of employees who feel entitled to make them. Two, it will reduce your stress. You approach compensation in a consistent, structured way, rather than engaging in ad hoc haggling with each new employee. Three, employee engagement and productivity are improved; more people feel they are being paid fairly when pay is transparent. More and more companies are finding that the simplest way to address pay disparity is transparency. No negotiation. No secrets. Just like prices at the grocery store. Imagine if you had to haggle with the checkout clerk every time you wanted to buy bread. Why should hiring involve so much negotiation, which often winds up with someone feeling cheated? Put a page on your website that outlines different salaries and compensation for different roles. That solution will save you and all your candidates a lot of time and emotional energy.

In many jurisdictions, including California; Colorado; Connecticut; Maryland; Nevada; Jersey City, New Jersey; Ithaca, New York; and New York City, employers are required by law to make salary ranges transparent.

Even if you're not required by law to do this, I recommend it. You might lose some candidates to better competing offers. But the job market tends to be relatively efficient. If you set salaries at the right level, they will not be markedly different from those at other companies. If candidates let a small compensation difference determine which jobs they take, you haven't done a good enough job selling the opportunity. And if there is a big salary difference, try to understand why. Perhaps you need to adjust everyone's salary. Underpaying most of your employees and then paying the new person you just hired a lot more than everyone else kills morale and generates resentment.

CUT YOUR PAY DATA BY DEMOGRAPHIC

What is the pay gap, if any, between the compensation packages of people from systemically advantaged and disadvantaged groups? Examine the data. Payscale is one company that can help you do this pay gap analysis.

If one demographic in your organization is consistently paid less than the others, figure out why. I'm not saying there's never a valid reason; but be open to the possibility that bias may have crept into your pay systems. If that's the case, the sooner you figure it out, the sooner you can fix it.

You may be reluctant to pull data that could potentially be used against you in a discrimination lawsuit. Certainly you should seek the advice of your legal team as you consider advice in this book. But recall that new laws around diversity disclosure may *require* you to pull this data.

Cutting the data this way will allow you to do three things:

- Address negotiation bias
- Address market bias
- Address seniority bias

Address Negotiation Bias

A common reason why people from historically marginalized groups are paid less is that they are punished if they negotiate too hard. This doesn't mean they are bad negotiators; it means that they are rational actors. If a woman knows she is going to be penalized or called "abrasive," "selfish," or "not a team player" for negotiating hard, it is rational for her to pull her punches. Here we see two biases that create a catch-22. First is the bias against women who negotiate. Second is the bias that says women are bad negotiators, so it's their fault if they don't get paid more.

As a leader, you can do two things about this. You and your team can work hard to interrupt this negotiation bias, or you can simply not allow *anyone* to negotiate—set transparent salary bands as discussed above and do not deviate. Make sure that you offer bonuses and promotions as part of a routine process that looks at everyone at the same time.

Address Market Bias

Another reason why employees from systemically disadvantaged groups are so often paid less is that the market itself is biased. Even if you've done the hard work of eliminating pay inequity from your own system, you can still "catch" it from other companies.

If you ask a candidate what they were paid in their last job and match that, you may be reflecting and reinforcing the pay gap already in the market. You also may be breaking a law. It is illegal to ask a candidate what they are currently making in many jurisdictions.

In short, pay the rate you've decided is fair for the role, rather than paying the person as little as you can get away with.

But my company can't afford this! you may think. Ask yourself whether your company can afford to keep systematically paying some employees less when they are equally qualified. The problems you create may be harder to measure in the short run, but they are still very real. When you pay a person less than their peers, it's demotivating for them and harms their productivity. It creates resentments that make your teams less cohesive. It introduces the risks of class-action lawsuits. And it's just not fair.

If you are a leader, it is your responsibility to make sure this doesn't happen on your team. And the only way you'll know whether it's happening is to cut your compensation data by the relevant demographics. Measure what matters—proactively look for ways that bias may impact how you pay people.

Address Seniority Bias

Often the most glaringly unfair part of a compensation system is the gap between the highest- and the lowest-paid person. There are practical as well as fairness benefits to not allowing this gap to get too big. In his book *Loonshots* (purple flag!), Safi Bahcall explains that when the compensation step-up is too great at each promotion, people spend more time trying to get promoted and less time on their actual work. When the gap between the compensation of senior execs and junior employees is not so great, it will "reduce the return on politics," thereby encouraging people to focus more on innovation and less on pleasing their bosses.

One reason that the pay gap widens between the most senior executives and the rest of the company is that a CEO tends to be most aware of the gap between their compensation and that of their direct reports. They fix what they are most acutely aware of (how much more they are paid than their direct reports), rather than the problem that most needs fixing (that many employees are not paid a living wage). When leaders measure the gap, look hard at it, and look in the mirror, the analysis can correct the empathy bias they feel for the people who work most closely with them. Spending time with line employees is another way to close the empathy gap—and generally a good idea.

When a board of directors thinks about fairness, don't just compare the CEO's pay to the pay of other CEOs. Compare the CEO's pay to the pay of the lowest-paid employees. Of course it's okay for the CEO to get more. But how much more? When

BIAS PREJUDICE BULLYING ⚡ ┌ **LEADERS &** ──────────── │ DISCRIMINATION HARASSMENT PHYSICAL VIOLATIONS ┘

the CEO and top execs own private jets and the new employees are living in their cars or can't afford health insurance, there is a problem. Ben and Jerry said nobody at their ice cream company would be paid more than five times the lowest-paid employee. I'd be okay with ten times or even in some cases a hundred times. But in a number of places where I worked, it was more like a thousand times and occasionally ten thousand times. The highest-paid people were worth billions and the lowest-paid people couldn't afford to pay their rent. That's just not right.

Make sure even your lowest-paid employees get a living wage, especially when you are getting incredibly wealthy. I'm not talking communism; I'm talking basic human decency and common sense.

Pay Gap at the BBC

In 2017, a powerful lobby in the United Kingdom demanded that the BBC make the salaries of their highest-earning presenters public. The goal was to make sure the public knew how much money the BBC was spending to get top talent. The unintended consequence was clear, public evidence that the women were not paid as much as the men.

With so much pressure on the BBC to reduce their budget and pay top stars less money, they couldn't fix the problem by paying the women more. They could only fix it by reducing the men's salaries. Needless to say, the men resisted this solution. Conversations meant to be private were leaked. One broadcaster said to another, "I could volunteer that I've handed over already more than you f***ing earn, but I'm still left with more than anybody else and that seems to me to be entirely just." People who make a lot of money often do think they "deserve" it, whether they do or not.

A top BBC editor, Carrie Gracie, resigned. The BBC apologized to her and gave her back pay; she donated the full amount to the Fawcett Society, a charity focused on gender equality and women's rights. Since then, the BBC has issued a public gender pay gap report and has committed to fixing the problem. They have indeed reduced the pay gap every year. In 2019, it was 6.7 percent, significantly lower than the national average of 17.9 percent.

The BBC story reveals another way that bias plays out. It's hard not to contrast the man's bravado about how he deserves to be paid more with Carrie Gracie's decision to give her back pay to charity.

Wealthy women, even when they are dramatically underpaid vis-à-vis their counterparts who are men, face a level of intense scrutiny and resentment that wealthy men simply don't. Activating that resentment is an unintended consequence of revealing a pay gap between wealthy men and women—which is where the biggest pay gaps are. In tech, I know many women who are paid not 10 or 20 percent less than the men who are their peers but multiples less. Ten times less, twenty times less. It's worth repeating that the pay gap between the wealthy and the poor is a far, far greater injustice than a woman earning $1 million while the men who are her peers get $20 million.

Income inequality must be addressed across the board. But it shouldn't be addressed by paying women less than men. Journalist Kara Swisher put it well:

"You don't have to feel sorry for rich people, but if they're gonna be rich, they should be equally rich." It's important to recognize that this prejudice about women and money runs deep.

Justice is not a zero-sum game. Federal laws (e.g., the Equal Pay Act, the Equal Protection Clause, Title IX) apply to people across the wealth spectrum because equity is fundamental to a fair and just society. Economic injustice cannot be addressed by pressuring wealthy women to work for less and give their compensation to charity while assuming wealthy men deserve what they have earned and more.

2. PERFORMANCE MANAGEMENT

As people progress in their careers and get promoted, their compensation increases, often quite steeply, as noted above. Often people who are from disadvantaged groups get promoted more slowly. Comparing the salaries of people from systemically advantaged and disadvantaged groups who are at the same level doesn't even begin to capture the pay gap if the people who are being underpaid at their current level really should be at the next level.

Under-promoting is not fair. It's also not good for you, their leader, or for your shareholders. Your job as a manager is to put the right people in the right roles. When bias causes you to systematically underestimate some people and promote the people you are overestimating, you get suboptimal results.

Here are some things leaders can do to make sure that you are not unfairly under promoting people on your team:

- Design a principled performance management system
- Measure what matters in promotion data
- Mandate a linguistic analysis of performance reviews and promotion recommendations

DESIGN A PRINCIPLED
PERFORMANCE MANAGEMENT SYSTEM

Do Not Rely on Unilateral Managerial Decisions

In most of corporate America, and even more in small businesses, managers have had near-dictatorial powers in conducting performance reviews and doling out raises and promotions. If you get on the boss's bad side, or if your boss is biased, you're screwed, even if your results ought to earn you a top rating or a promotion. This state of affairs introduces inefficiency and injustice into management decisions. In the end, it results in worse outcomes for the organizations these managers lead.

The solution is to create systems that don't give unilateral decision-making about ratings and promotions to managers. When checks and balances limit the power of individual bosses to control these processes unilaterally, the results tend to be much fairer and more reasonable. You're likelier to wind up with the right people in the right roles.

Rather than allowing managers to write a unilateral performance review, try instituting a 360 process so that people's performance is assessed by their peers as well as others above and below them in the hierarchy. Create a ratings calibration process that makes sure managers are not easy or hard graders.

BIAS   PREJUDICE   BULLYING   ⚡   **LEADERS &**
DISCRIMINATION   HARASSMENT   PHYSICAL VIOLATIONS

Create promotion committees that review an employee's work and make promotion decisions. Managers give input to these promotion decisions, but they are not unilateral deciders.

Two words of caution:

One, sometimes when a person from a historically marginalized group joins a team, especially one that has up until then been pretty homogeneous, bias will often show up in the 360 process, especially if that person is a leader. It's important to proactively look for bias in these processes using augmented writing tools like Textio.

Two, over time, such systems can become bloated and time wasting. At one company where I worked, the performance review period began to be known as "perfcrastination" because no other work got done for a couple of weeks. So create your process, but manage it and keep it as simple and streamlined as possible.[1]

MEASURE WHAT MATTERS IN PROMOTION DATA

Cutting data about who was promoted to first-time manager by demographic is very telling: for every one hundred men promoted to management, only seventy-two women were promoted—eighty White women, sixty-eight Latina women, and only fifty-eight Black women. And it only gets worse with seniority: 86 percent of Fortune 500 CEOs are White men. Given that the population of the US is 29 percent White men, that's some significant overrepresentation. The promotion gap has a bigger impact than the pay gap, because the pay gap between the highest- and lowest-paid people in an organization is so great.

Are your employees from systemically disadvantaged groups

getting promoted at a slower rate than the people who are systemically advantaged? If so, why? Tracking these numbers and investigating discrepancies thoroughly and openly is as uncomfortable as it is crucial.

You want to be fair in both directions when you measure ratings and promotions. For example, at one company, promotion rates for women were measured using a color-coding system. Departments where the proportion of women getting top ratings was the same or higher as the proportion of men getting the same ratings were marked green. Departments where the percentage of top ratings were higher for men than women were marked red. The idea was that one wouldn't expect one gender to do better on performance ratings. If men were consistently rated higher than women, it was a flag that some investigation into why was needed.

It was great that this company had the desire to measure gender bias. But why did the system only highlight departments whose ratings were skewed in favor of men? Why was it considered okay for men to be consistently rated lower than women, when the reverse was viewed as a serious problem? *Any* gender disparity—toward men, women, or nonbinary employees—should be flagged red. And this analysis shouldn't be done only for gender but for any systemically disadvantaged group. The goal must be to ensure ratings and promotions are fair and unbiased across the board.

Sometimes people who object to such analyses claim that I'm advocating for a lowering of standards. This claim itself reveals a bias or even a prejudice. This implies that I will de facto lower my standards if I make sure bias isn't skewing promotion or rating decisions. The underlying assumption is that people from a historically advantaged demographic are automatically going to be better at the job. That seems extremely unlikely to me.

LEADERS &
BIAS PREJUDICE BULLYING ⚡ DISCRIMINATION HARASSMENT PHYSICAL VIOLATIONS

It's my instinct that if you've got a homogeneous team, you've overestimated the skills of some of the people on your team and overlooked the skills of some people not on your team. But one thing is sure: if you're not willing to look at the facts and to understand why they are what they are, we'll never get to a better answer.

MANDATE A LINGUISTIC ANALYSIS OF PERFORMANCE REVIEWS AND PROMOTION RECOMMENDATIONS

If managers are required to give employees written performance reviews or promotion recommendations, the language they use can reveal a lot about their biases.

If your team writes performance reviews, you can use an augmented writing tool to flag the kind of language that may indicate bias. There are other ways to correct bias that creeps into performance reviews, though. You could hire people familiar with how gender bias plays out in performance reviews and ask them to read performance reviews and flag possible bias.

When bias is found, it's crucial that the manager who wrote the review not be unduly punished but instead asked to reassess. The point here is not to punish but to learn to identify our biases and correct them. If the manager refuses to engage with the data, then you have a different problem and must deal with it as you would any other similar issue.

3. COACHING AND MENTORING

Formal systems such as compensation and ratings are important for an employee's career development. Often, informal mentoring is even more important. Having good mentors can be an enormous boost in a person's career. But employees from historically marginalized groups are less likely to get mentored.

Mentoring Matters

Evan Cohen, the Americas managing partner at the law firm Clifford Chance, had an experience that is broadly shared among leaders. He wondered why so few women were becoming partners at his firm and what he could do to change it. He got his answer during an exit interview with an especially promising woman who'd decided to quit the firm. Why, he asked her, was she leaving when she had such a clear path to partnership? She was taken aback by the question. She had no idea anyone saw a big future for her at the firm. The promising men in her class of associates were all mentored by various partners who told them they were on track. But nobody had sat her down and told her she was on track to make partner someday.

Cohen promised himself this would never happen again. He realized that when the mostly male partners chose mentees, they tended to select the associates who reminded them of themselves as young men. He took action and asked all the firm's partners to pick more diverse folks to mentor. He essentially held up a mirror and asked people to look into it: Are you mentoring only people who look like you? Without any quotas or formal mentoring programs, the number of partners who chose to mentor women increased, and the number of women

who've made partner has been on the rise ever since. Of
the Clifford Chance US lawyers promoted to partner in the
last three years, 45 percent were women, and the overall
percentage of women partners has more than doubled in
six years under Cohen's leadership.

Here are some things you can do to make sure that bias and
prejudice aren't creeping into decisions about who gets coached
and mentored, creating a situation where some employees are
systematically overlooked.

- Proactively look for bias in informal coaching and
  mentoring.
- Don't meet with men alone if you won't meet with
  women alone.
- Don't meet in venues that exclude.
- Compare psychological safety metrics of different demographic groups.

PROACTIVELY LOOK FOR BIAS IN
INFORMAL COACHING AND MENTORING

If you're a leader, be intentional about whom you're mentoring
and seek out people who are different. Write down the names of
the people you are mentoring. Stop and make sure you feel good
about the number of people from systemically disadvantaged
groups on that list. It's really not that complicated.

If you are a leader of leaders, pay attention to who is being mentored by your direct reports. If people are getting left out, do what Evan Cohen did. But remember, you've got to appeal to people's intrinsic motivations to mentor. Mentoring is not codified. The best kind of mentoring happens in ad hoc ways—in a shared car back to the office after a meeting, on a coffee break, over lunch when traveling. You need to inspire the people you manage to do better. Mandates won't work well.

DON'T MEET WITH MEN ALONE IF YOU WON'T MEET WITH WOMEN ALONE

A refusal to meet alone with over half the world's population is discriminatory, especially when the person doing the refusing is in a position of authority.

Meeting for Lunch Is Okay

Recently, I met a man, a colleague of many years, for lunch. When I returned home, a houseguest gave me a hard time. "Doesn't your husband worry when you have lunch with men?" she asked. My husband and I both found this question absurd. Refusing to meet alone with men would make it nearly impossible for me to do my job. I was the only woman on a board of directors, for example. My editor was a man. Refusing to meet alone with women

BIAS   PREJUDICE   BULLYING   ⚡   **LEADERS &** DISCRIMINATION   HARASSMENT   PHYSICAL VIOLATIONS would have been equally impossible for my husband, whose boss was a woman.

As it happened, my colleague and I had met not in a candlelit boîte but at a bustling restaurant in downtown Palo Alto where, between the two of us, we knew half the people eating around us. I had mentored him early in his career. In the intervening years, he had become an enormously successful entrepreneur and was now a mentor to me in turn. These kinds of relationships are an important part of one's professional growth. If I had refused to mentor him because he is a man, or if he'd declined to mentor me because I am a woman, both our lives and careers would have been impoverished emotionally and financially.

DON'T MEET IN VENUES THAT EXCLUDE

This headline may seem so obvious that it's ridiculous to write it down. But meetings in strip clubs, at plantations (a.k.a. forced labor camps), exclusive country clubs, or other venues that are bound to make some people uncomfortable still happen all the damn time, unfortunately. A Black colleague told me about a company off-site that was planned at a plantation. "Imagine how it would feel to Jewish employees if you had a company off-site at a concentration camp that honored the Nazis. That is how asking me to go to an off-site at a plantation feels." Unfortunately, this person's manager got defensive and said she was not honoring his Southern heritage. I, too, am a White Southerner. And I feel that part of honoring my heritage, honoring my ancestors, is to be aware of the sins of slavery, to acknowledge publicly the atrocities that were committed, to accept the consequences, to apologize, and to change for good. The worst possible way to honor Southern heritage is to glamorize slavery or pretend that it was anything other than what it was: a gross violation of human rights that did enormous harm. Atoning for sins of the past is the best way I know of to honor my heritage and my ancestors. Demanding that Black Americans attend work events at so-called plantations is to deny the reality of what was going on there—forced labor—and to perpetuate the harm.

Meeting at a Strip Club Is Not Okay

I once found out that an executive where I worked routinely took the men at the company out to strip clubs and told them information that the women on his team, whom he didn't invite on these excursions, were then not privy to.

The leader in question made a big deal about being open to feedback, so rather than fuming silently, I went to talk to him. All I had to do was say *strip club*, and he was appropriately chagrined. He apologized to all the women at the company. He also acknowledged that it wasn't only women who'd been excluded—it was also the men on the team who had no interest in lap dances. He apologized to them, too. Crucially, he talked to all the men who had ever gone to a strip club with him and let them know that this kind of thing had to end, immediately. And it did.

This leader did a really dumb thing, but when it was pointed out to him, he responded incredibly well. He felt embarrassed, ashamed; but he didn't let his shame manage him. He listened, accepted the feedback, apologized, and took responsibility to prevent future trips to the strip club. The leader in question had cofounded a hot Silicon Valley start-up. He could definitely have continued to take employees to the strip club. But he did not. He accepted the checks on his own power.

When a leader is open to criticism and willing to confront even big, boneheaded mistakes like this one, they can resolve a situation before it metastasizes into something much worse.

COMPARE PSYCHOLOGICAL SAFETY METRICS OF DIFFERENT DEMOGRAPHIC GROUPS

One of the best predictors of a team's success is psychological safety—whether everyone on the team feels that they can speak up without fear of retribution when they notice a problem or have a new idea. A good way to measure what matters on your team is to measure psychological safety. Harvard Business School professor Amy Edmondson has conceptualized psychological safety in the workplace and devised an effective way to measure it.

If you break the psychological safety measure down by the different employee demographics, you'll get a remarkably powerful indication of how people feel about the place they go to work every day. If the survey indicates that individuals or groups do not feel psychologically safe, work on specific things you can do to improve the situation. Maybe this is a sign you need to put bias disrupters in place, that you need to rewrite your code of conduct, or that there aren't enough consequences for bullying; or maybe it's a sign that people feel harassed or discriminated against. Don't assume. Ask. Act on what you learn. Give the changes some time to have an impact and then measure again to figure out what is working and what isn't.

4. EXITING

All too often, bias creeps into decisions about who to fire or lay off. When this happens, bias becomes discrimination.

Also, leaders often don't even know whether or why regretted attrition is higher for employees in different demographic groups. How can you better understand what went wrong and how to do better in the future as people whom you're trying to retain exit your organization?

- Look for bias in firing decisions
- Track why people quit

LOOK FOR BIAS IN FIRING DECISIONS

Analyze the data about who you are firing. Are you firing a disproportionate number of employees from systemically disadvantaged groups? If so, take the time to ask yourself honestly if bias or prejudice are skewing your decisions. If they are, figure out what you can do about it.

BIAS   PREJUDICE   BULLYING   ⚡   LEADERS &
DISCRIMINATION   HARASSMENT   PHYSICAL VIOLATIONS

TRACK WHY PEOPLE QUIT

When you have regretted attrition, you should do everything you can to get them to tell you why. Categorize the reasons why. When trends emerge, figure out what you can do to address them. Track these trends over time. Are you succeeding in addressing the key issues? Reassure the people who left that the truth will not burn bridges, and while you'd love to convince them to stay, that is not the purpose of the meeting. You are there to learn about mistakes that you or your organization made so that they aren't made again.

If you really want to know why that valued employee has quit, get as senior a leader as possible to do the interview. People usually leave managers, not companies. That manager might be the last person who'll hear the unvarnished truth. But the manager's boss? Then the employee might be eager to talk.

This is good management hygiene for all regretted attrition, but it's especially important when it's people from historically marginalized groups who are quitting. Investigate why the people you've worked hard to recruit and retain don't want to work for you any longer—whether it's mistakes you've made, mistakes others in your organization have made, or problems endemic to your workplace culture. Quantify it. What percentage of people from historically marginalized groups quit because they have experienced harassment or discrimination at your company? How many left because they've experienced bias, prejudice, or bullying? Ask this explicitly in the exit interview. How does this compare to people from historically advantaged groups who leave the company? The data doesn't necessarily point to a problem; but it does point to the need to investigate. If the investigation reveals a problem, figure out how to fix it!

5. ELIMINATING NDAS AND FORCED ARBITRATION

Nondisclosure agreements and forced arbitration are blatant attempts to dodge the checks and balances that our legal system puts on employers. The best way to avoid going to court is to do what you can to prevent discrimination and harassment from the outset; to offer multiple safe ways to report it when it does occur, despite your best efforts; to investigate reports fully and fairly; and to take appropriate action when the reports prove true.

NONDISCLOSURE AGREEMENTS (NDAS)

She Said by Jodi Kantor and Megan Twohey and *Catch and Kill* by Ronan Farrow detail how truly bad actors have been able to take advantage of NDAs to pursue victim after victim after victim. Use your NDAs to prevent disclosure of trade secrets, not wrongdoing. Nobody should have the right to buy silence from another person about wrongdoing.

Thanks to the efforts of Ifeoma Ozoma and other committed advocates, the Silenced No More Act was passed into law in California, so it's no longer legal to use nondisclosure agreements to

BIAS PREJUDICE BULLYING ⚡ ⌐LEADERS &⎯⎯⎯⎯⎯⎯⎯⎯⎯⎯
DISCRIMINATION HARASSMENT PHYSICAL VIOLATIONS

silence people in this state. Other states are likely to follow. But there are good reasons to stop these practices even before you're legally required to do so.

FORCED ARBITRATION

When employees make a complaint, especially about such things as discrimination, harassment, or sexual assault, many companies insist that they sign away their right to resolve the dispute in the justice system before they will discuss a settlement. Often employees have already signed away that right in the employment contract they signed when they joined the company, agreeing to take any legal claims to private arbitration.

There are a number of problems with forced arbitration, but let's focus on two: it's bad for employees and it's bad for the organizations where they work. Forced arbitration is bad for employees because the private arbitrators are chosen and paid by the organization, and their interest isn't so much in justice but in making sure the company keeps hiring them. Under such conditions, impartial justice is highly unlikely. While forced private arbitration may offer some short-term benefits to an organization—it can avoid the cost and publicity of a lawsuit—in the long run, it increases their operating risk.

Susan Fowler Rigetti, who documented many cases of discrimination and sexual harassment at Uber, explains it like this: "Forcing legal disputes about discrimination, harassment and retaliation to go through secret arbitration proceedings hides the behavior and allows it to become culturally entrenched."

Microsoft ended forced arbitration for sexual harassment cases in 2017. Uber followed suit, followed by Google, then Facebook, and many others. This is a welcome trend. The bad news is that approximately sixty million Americans still work under forced arbitration. You can end forced arbitration at your workplace and leave your corner of the world a little more just.

6. ORGANIZATIONAL DESIGN

What if the CEO is the one discriminating or harassing?

If the company has a board of directors, it is the board's responsibility to hold the CEO accountable—it's one of the reasons you have a board of directors in the first place.

For these situations, companies have a compliance function that should have a strong leader. The compliance function should report directly to the audit committee and can go around the CEO if needed. The internal audit function works the same way for the same reasons. If someone needs to report financial wrongdoing or discrimination or harassment, they need to be able to go around the CEO if the CEO is the problem.

This works better in public companies than it does in private ones. Dambisa Moyo, author of *How Boards Work*, explains that public corporations have far greater obligations—from all manner of stakeholders—for transparency and disclosures around forward-leaning social and cultural issues than privately held companies do. For example, issues of gender diversity, pay parity, climate change, and ESG (environmental, social, and governance) factors are all areas where public companies are subject to scrutiny and reporting whereas private institutions generally are not.

BIAS   PREJUDICE   BULLYING   ⚡   LEADERS &
DISCRIMINATION   HARASSMENT   PHYSICAL VIOLATIONS

The issue here is that the people who have the most power—the people on the board of directors—are generally best positioned to dodge accountability. This puts HR in a terrible position unless the organizational structure is deliberately designed to limit the power of the CEO. The board of directors must hold the CEO accountable and have HR's back.

At too many companies, CEOs appoint board members specifically *not* to challenge their authority, *not* to hold them accountable. CEOs also hire HR people who will serve them rather than be real partners who can hold them accountable. When this happens, HR investigations can go badly off the rails.

Of course, many small businesses—bars, restaurants, dry cleaners, bodegas, and so on—don't have a board of directors. The company I cofounded has no board of directors. How can small business owners hold themselves accountable? A few things can help. One is to appoint an ombudsperson whom people can go to with complaints. This ombudsperson needs to be someone who carries a lot of sway with the business owner—a mentor, for example—and who is willing to give a personal email address and phone number to all employees. Another idea is to form a complaints committee: two or three employees who are generally trusted by the rank and file because they will not be afraid to bring problems to your attention.

Good Intentions Are Not Enough for a CEO

Cofounding my first company gave me a chance to set up a fair and transparent compensation system. This was important to me. I had been dramatically underpaid in my first few jobs out of college. This even happened when I joined a start-up with a CEO who was a woman. A few months into that job, I found out I was being paid

30 percent less than my peer, a man. When I asked why, she replied, "You don't have a wife and child to support." I don't want to hold women to a higher standard than men. She paid me less than my peer who was a man for the same reason my bosses who were men did: because she could. Still, I didn't expect a woman to offer that particular rationale for discrimination.

So when I started my company, I told myself, *When I am in charge, women will be treated better.*

That didn't always happen, despite all my good intentions. Unfortunately, discrimination and harassment happen at companies with leaders who genuinely want to create fair working environments. I want to offer compassion for leaders who, like me, fail to live up to their ideal. But offering compassion doesn't mean not holding myself or others accountable. I could and should have done better.

Alex, one of my VPs, was doing terrible work. As we talked about how he needed to improve, I asked Alex what I could do or stop doing to help him turn things around.

"The problem here is that you are *the—most— aggressive—woman* I've ever met!" he exploded, punctuating each word by stabbing his index finger toward my chest.

Alex had been a senior leader at a tech company where executives threw chairs at people. Our industry was aggressive. He had to deal with aggressive people to do his job. So his problem couldn't be my aggression. His problem was that I was an aggressive *woman*. He was using my gender to bully me, to get me to back off.

It was my responsibility as a leader to respond in a way that would prevent him from bullying other women at the company in a gendered way. Instead, I ignored how he'd just spoken to me. If I'd been in the role of person harmed, that would have been my choice. But I was the CEO and so had an obligation to do more.

A few days later, after a company all-hands, Alex was sitting on a table that was over the garbage can. Madeline, a woman on the team, walked up to him with a couple of pizza crusts, clearly wanting to throw them away.

"Excuse me"—she gestured to the garbage can—"I need to—"

"Get in between my legs?" Alex asked, leering.

As a leader, it was my job to tell Alex on the spot that this was not an acceptable way to talk to Madeline, and to have a follow-up conversation outlining the consequences for him. Instead, again, as if I were the person harmed and not the leader, I chose to ignore him.

Here is the thing. Leaders, even leaders who care deeply about creating equitable workplaces, as I did, will fail sometimes to do the right things. Leaders are human. That is why they need to bake checks and balances into their organizational design and into their management systems. That will make it likelier that the right things eventually happen, even when the leaders fail to do the right thing, as they are bound to do. Madeline was early in her career, and I was the CEO. If Madeline wanted to report my lack of response to Alex's remark, she would have had to talk to—me. It had not occurred to me to create checks and balances or reporting systems as a check on my own power. Not surprisingly, she said nothing.

A few months later, she told me she felt I had contributed to a hostile working environment for women.

My first response was denial. After all, a huge part of my reason for starting the company was to create a good working environment for women.

To this day, I regret the way I responded. Madeline was telling me something important, and I was refusing to listen. Instead, I was replicating the sort of bad-boss behavior that I'd been determined to avoid. If I'd listened to Madeline instead of shutting her down, I might have had the opportunity to reflect on some other leadership failures on my part. Instead of learning something valuable, I paid her a small sum and asked her to sign an NDA. I am deeply ashamed to admit that, but it's the truth.

If I had embraced my role as a leader from the start, Alex would have known he couldn't harass women and get away with it. Perhaps this would have prevented his subsequent behavior; if not, he would have been fired. Having failed, if I'd listened to what she told me rather than paying her not to talk about it, I would have been an advocate for the women on my team rather than another leader who didn't care enough about harassment to prevent it. That would have taken some personal courage. If I had put in place an organizational design that gave Madeline a way to report what had happened and my failure to respond, then I could have been held accountable.

As always, I'll end this story by extending myself and other leaders a little grace. Leadership is hard, especially for leaders

BIAS   PREJUDICE   BULLYING   ⚡   LEADERS & DISCRIMINATION   HARASSMENT   PHYSICAL VIOLATIONS

from historically marginalized groups. And overall, I think I was a pretty good leader—precisely because I was able to learn from some pretty big leadership failures. It's worth repeating: we can't do right if we won't notice what we did wrong.

7. HIRING

Notice that hiring is coming last in this chapter. Too often, leaders focus on hiring before they've done all the things described above to make sure they can retain people they've hired. That's not just a waste of energy, it's painful and destructive for the people you hired and then treated unfairly. Don't do that.

After you've created a good working environment for your employees from historically marginalized groups, it makes sense to turn your attention to hiring. Here's a story of one leader who managed to get hiring right.

Christa Quarles at OpenTable

When she was CEO of OpenTable, Christa Quarles made improving diversity a priority. She knew it had to start from the top, so she and her team publicly emphasized the importance of hiring people from historically marginalized groups.

She started by focusing on hiring more women in engineering. She didn't set a specific target number but instead focused on the need to fix the process. The results were remarkable. By the next quarter, the share of newly hired women engineers at OpenTable had gone from 14 to 50 percent. They then averaged between 40 and 45 percent for the next four quarters.

When I asked her what the secret was, she said, "I was frankly surprised by the speed. But it's like any other business problem. You put effort toward something, you measure it, you get results." Use the same skills you employ to solve other issues that are priorities, and you'll improve the diversity of your hiring, too. Here are more details about how Quarles and her team improved their recruiting to hire more diverse teams:

- *They changed their approach to job descriptions.* Often homogeneity in a workplace culture starts with the way a position is described (e.g., using words like *killer* and *aggressive* that might read as though the company is seeking men, not women). OpenTable started using Textio Hire, a software program that helps recruiters write job postings free of unconscious or implicit bias.
- *They filtered personal identifying information out of résumés.* They used a product that helped them anonymize/redact gender-identifying info on résumés.
- *They cast a wider net.* Sourcers had to identify at least two women candidates for every job opening. This was important because research shows that when there's only one candidate with a particular demographic, the chance the person will be hired is statistically tiny because the person becomes the "diversity candidate" instead of simply being the "qualified candidate." The term *diversity candidate* often triggers an unconscious bias: many people who are overrepresented hear instead "less qualified candidate." This assumption is not fair to the candidate and will harm your ability to

hire the most qualified person.

- *They included women on hiring panels.* In an organization that was mostly men, this put a lot of burden on a small number of women to spend more time interviewing. Managers had to be aware of this and accommodate it. Quarles would also offer her services to cement key hires as a sign of the importance of closing highly qualified women.
- *They monitored the numbers.* The recruiting team measured and reported their performance on hiring women every quarter. Measuring the growth in women hires quarter over quarter was more revealing about progress being made than measuring the company's gender diversity overall.
- *They made sure everybody got the message.* Quarles and her leadership team spent a lot of time talking about improving diversity. The whole company needed to understand this was an important strategic effort. The leaders were focusing on improving diversity and inclusion in their hiring for two reasons. First, because it was important to have an employee base that mirrored their customer base—women make more reservations at restaurants than men do. Second, because diverse teams have quantifiably higher productivity, innovation, and outcomes relative to homogeneous teams.

RELY ON HIRING COMMITTEES,
NOT INDIVIDUAL HIRING MANAGERS

When leaders allow their own or their managers' biases and prejudiced beliefs to influence hiring decisions, good candidates get overlooked, and mediocre ones who look the part but can't do the job get hired. They wind up with a subpar team. Moreover, they are often breaking the law.

A great way to make sure a hiring manager's biases don't get in the way of making good decisions is to create a hiring committee. Don't give unilateral decision-making power to the hiring manager.

It's difficult for people to recognize bias in themselves but relatively easy for them to recognize it in others. This is part of the reason why hiring teams tend to make better decisions than individuals.

Furthermore, when there is a committee instead of just one person with unilateral hiring authority, sexual harassment is less likely to enter the equation. It's far less likely that a whole team of people would take advantage of their hiring power to harass a candidate than a single individual would.

Make sure your hiring committee is not homogeneous. Heterogeneous committees tend to make better decisions and have better close rates (the percentage of people who accept offers) than homogeneous committees. The hiring team at Qualtrics found this to be consistently true, according to cofounder Jared Smith. Other leaders I've talked to have reported the same thing.

If your team is homogeneous, how do you create diverse

hiring committees? Many companies try to solve this problem by asking underrepresented people to sit on more than their fair share of hiring committees. Problem solved, right? No. Now people who are underrepresented are spending a lot of hours helping other people fill jobs. People may get appreciated for "corporate citizenship" or told "everyone is *expected* to help with hiring," but in most companies, what gets people promoted is delivering results in their core function. So asking people to do extra hiring-committee work damages their prospects for advancement. This is unfair, especially when the people you're asking are in the minority in your organization and from historically marginalized groups.

This is not an impossible double bind, though. Unconscious bias training, combined with a norm of disrupting one another's biases and a disciplined approach to measuring what matters, can help even homogeneous hiring committees learn to recognize and question their biases. If you have the budget, you could hire a bias buster to join your hiring-committee meeting. Over time, as you hire a more diverse team, you get a reputation for being a great place to work, and recruiting becomes easier. You create a virtuous cycle.

Consider doing these four things:

- assess skills, not identity;
- be explicit about hiring criteria;
- look for culture add, not culture fit; and
- challenge biased comparisons in hiring committee.

Assess Skills, Not Identity

Orchestras offer a great example of the value of skills assessments that don't reveal the identity of the candidate. In 1970, the share of women on the highest-ranked orchestras in the United States was only 6 percent. This metric alone indicated that the orchestras were probably not hiring the best musicians. But the answer was obviously not to hand a woman, any woman, a bassoon or a french horn. The answer was to figure out how to eliminate bias from the selection process.

Auditions behind a curtain were an obvious answer. But they didn't go far enough. The candidates also had to be barefoot because the telltale tap of high-heeled shoes gave away the gender of candidates. After auditioning barefoot behind a curtain became common practice, the percentage of women musicians in orchestras grew to 21 percent in 1993 and just over 50 percent by 2016.

It's impossible to know whether it was unconscious bias or conscious prejudice that kept women out of the top symphony orchestras. It might also be that the women auditioning for these slots were operating under a bias of their own: they may have been experiencing stereotype threat. When people have the power to put their unconscious biases or conscious prejudices into practice, discrimination can become a self-fulfilling prophecy; dissipating those biases and beliefs can create a virtuous cycle.

Furthermore, auditions behind curtains have not done enough to address the issues that keep BIPOC musicians out of orchestras. It's too soon to declare victory here.

Be Explicit About Hiring Criteria

Here is some advice from Daniel Kahneman about how to avoid bias when interviewing: be explicit about the specific criteria you are looking for. Write them down—no more than six. Make sure all interviewers are interviewing for the same criteria. Ask each interviewer to rate the candidate for each criterion on a scale of one to five. Ask each interviewer to put the rating down for the criteria, together with evidence, before moving on to the next criterion—this avoids halo effects, a bias in which we assume that because people are good at one thing, they are good at everything.

BIAS PREJUDICE BULLYING ⚡ LEADERS &
DISCRIMINATION HARASSMENT PHYSICAL VIOLATIONS

Promise yourself you'll hire the candidate whose score is highest, not the one you like the best.

A word of caution: make sure your criteria themselves are not biased. In the example Kahneman used, one criterion was "masculine pride." Ugh . . .

Look for "Culture Add," Not "Culture Fit"

Often one of the attributes people are looking for in interviews is "culture fit." This is a big mistake that will give biases free rein. Melissa James, CEO of the Tech Connection, recommends that hiring committees look for "culture add," which she defines as "the likelihood that someone will not only reflect the company's values and professional ethics, but also bring an aspect of diverse opinions, experiences, and specialized skill which enhances not just the team, but the overall company culture."

The "cultural fit" screen in interviews—ostensibly designed to make sure the person will work well with others on the team—is too often a giant back door for bias, an unconscious code for "looking for someone who looks like us." It can reinforce the tyranny of the majority instead of interrupting it.

Challenge Biased Comparisons in Hiring Committees

In his book *The Undoing Project*, Michael Lewis tells the story of Houston Rockets general manager Daryl Morey's attempts to drive bias out of the process of evaluating draft picks. Like almost everyone else in the league, Morey had missed Jeremy Lin, the California-born son of Taiwanese immigrants, who was ignored in the NBA draft but went on to become a successful player. Morey had the guts to admit that he passed on Lin because Lin didn't look like a conventional NBA point guard. "He's incredibly athletic," Morey said. "But the reality is that every fucking person, including me, thought he was unathletic. And I can't think of any reason for it other than that he was Asian."

If you can own your biases and confess how they skew your hiring decisions like Morey did, others on your team will, too. Tell them where you screwed up and ask them to talk about times they have made similar mistakes. Once most people grasp how they might unconsciously be contributing to a problem, they will be motivated to fix it.

To prevent another Jeremy Lin mistake, Daryl Morey encouraged his scouts to focus on players' skills rather than their skin color. "If you want to compare this player to another player," he told them, "you can only do it if they are a different race." In other words, scouts could no longer compare a White player to another White player, a Black player to another Black player, an Asian American player to another Asian American player.

Not allowing simplistic comparisons is a good rule in business as well as sports. I wish I'd read *The Undoing Project* when I was advising the team who called a woman up for promotion "a real mother hen."

MEASURE WHAT MATTERS AT
EVERY STEP OF THE HIRING PROCESS

Even though any managers worth their salt know they shouldn't hire people who are "just like them," they do it anyway. To figure out where this is happening, take a look at your new hires every quarter. If the numbers don't reflect the population where you work or aren't at least moving in that direction, bias or prejudice may be creeping into your hiring process, even if you don't mean for them to, even if you can't imagine such a thing would happen on your watch. Measuring results is more fruitful

BIAS PREJUDICE BULLYING ⚡ ┌─ **LEADERS &** ──────────────────┐
                                          │ DISCRIMINATION HARASSMENT PHYSICAL VIOLATIONS │
                                          └──────────────────────────────┘

than measuring intentions. Go back and analyze every step in your hiring process:

- What is the breakdown of the résumés your sourcers looked at?
- What is the breakdown of résumés passed on for interviews?
- What is the breakdown of the percentage of people who are offered jobs?
- What is the breakdown of people who accept your offers?

What Is the Breakdown of the Résumés Your Sourcers Looked At?

Look for under- or overrepresentation across different demographics. Neither is a smoking gun. At the turn of the twentieth century, a disproportionate number of the world's top physicists were Jewish émigrés from Hungary. American universities benefited enormously from opening the doors to these scientists when Nazi anti-Semitism made it impossible to work in much of Europe. Setting quotas preventing the recruitment of these brilliant scientists would have been unjust—and stupid. However, underrepresentation is also a sign that your hiring process is systematically overlooking or underestimating some candidates. You can't afford to do that if you want to hire the right people for the right jobs. So ask yourself what you can do to make sure résumé sourcers are looking beyond traditionally tapped groups. Even if there is an explanation, you can still examine what you might be doing to discourage people from applying, and fix it.

For example, is bias baked into your job descriptions? You can use augmented writing tools to identify biased language. Also, make it clear which qualifications are necessary versus which are nice to have; if you list qualifications, women tend to apply to jobs where they meet 100 percent of criteria, but men tend to apply to jobs even if they don't meet all the qualifications listed.

Another thing to beware of: referrals. Many companies rely on employee referrals. This source of candidates rarely improves diversity. Our personal networks are often homogeneous. Measure the diversity of employee referrals, and if this source of candidates is making your company more homogeneous, then don't rely so heavily on referrals.

Look for Solutions, Not Excuses

When he was SVP of engineering at Google, Alan Eustace did a careful analysis of why there were so few women software engineers. Part of the problem was the lack of women graduating from computer science programs at the universities Google hired from. But Alan did not throw up his hands and say, "It's not my fault, it's a pipeline problem, there's nothing I can do."

Instead, Alan set out to learn more about the issue. He discovered that the computer science department at Harvey Mudd had studied the issue and realized that "weed-out" courses early in its programs favored people who'd been hacking code in junior high school—and for a variety of social reasons, more boys than girls code in junior high. The heads of the computer science department got rid of the weed-out courses; four years later, the college had significantly more women computer science grads. This wasn't about lowering the bar, it was about identifying a place where unequal starting gates existed

BIAS PREJUDICE BULLYING ⚡ LEADERS & DISCRIMINATION HARASSMENT PHYSICAL VIOLATIONS

and fixing it. Alan encouraged other universities to follow
Harvey Mudd's lead. Four years is a long time to wait
for new candidates to graduate, but it's not infinitely
long. Solving problems such as this requires patience and
persistence from leaders.

What Is the Breakdown of Résumés Passed On for Interviews?

If the percentage of people from a particular demographic who
are invited for an interview is lower than the percentage of that
demographic who applied, ask yourself why and what you can
do to improve it.

As mentioned above, one strategy is to strip identifying information out of résumés so bias doesn't creep into assessment
of résumés. You can use a tool designed to automate this, or hire
interns and ask them to redact with a Sharpie information that
identifies a person's gender, race, sexual preference, name, pronouns, and so on. That means getting rid of information about,
for example, membership in fraternities or sororities.

If you strip personally identifiable information out of résumés and more people from a particular demographic make it
through your screening process, you've not only identified bias
in your candidate sourcing system—you've also found a way to
interrupt it.

What Is the Breakdown of the Percentage of People Who Are Offered Jobs?

If there's yet another drop-off in the percentage of people who
are from a particular demographic, why? Do you make job
offers to 20 percent of the people who interview but only 5
percent of the people from that demographic who interview?

What can you do to improve that? Go back and look at what is happening in your interview process. If the interview panels don't have enough people from a demographic on them, see if you can address that without putting an undue burden on those employees. You could hire bias busters to sit in on your hiring meetings, for example.

What Is the Breakdown of People Who Accept Your Offers?

Do people who are from a particular demographic tend to reject your job offers? Ask yourself why and what you can do to improve that percentage. If your team is homogeneous, it's going to be more difficult for you. If that's the case, make sure you aren't getting in your own way. Look around. Does your company have a reputation for being a terrible place for people who are not systemically advantaged? Does your office look like a frat house or have other features that might make some people feel unwelcome?

It is your job to become aware of these things, even if you'd rather not know. Read the reviews of your company on sites such as Glassdoor and other such services to learn more about your company's reputation. Ask people to rate their candidate experience. But don't hide behind websites and surveys. When someone turns down your offer, take them out to coffee and try to find out why. Keep a tally of the different reasons candidates give you. If you notice trends, do something to address them.

If You Want Someone to Accept Your Offer, Make Sure They Feel Comfortable

For example, when Scott O'Neil, then CEO of the Philadelphia 76ers basketball team, was recruiting a senior woman to work on his team, he sensed during the interview that she wasn't entirely comfortable, but he had no idea why. Rather than ignoring the awkwardness, which was tempting, he asked her about it.

"It's your couch," she replied.

"My couch?" O'Neil asked, bewildered.

"Have you noticed how I've been sitting?"

O'Neil confessed he hadn't, and she pointed out that the couch was designed for seven-foot-tall basketball players. If she wanted to lean against the back of the couch, her legs would stick straight out, Thumbelina-style. O'Neil bought some cushions for his couch. A simple solution, but having the courage and curiosity to investigate the source of the woman's discomfort was far harder. Fortunately, O'Neil had the self-confidence and discipline to do so.

Bias Hurts Everyone

The movie *Moneyball*, which tells the story of how Oakland A's general manager Billy Beane changed the game of baseball by replacing bias with rational decision-making, perfectly illustrates the perils of "biasthink." In one scene, Beane is meeting with a bunch of scouts to evaluate minor-league prospects. Even though baseball has tons of statistics to objectively measure performance, Beane notices that his scouts base their judgments on irrelevant factors such as strong jawlines or how good-looking a player's girlfriend is. None of the scouts challenge one another's BS, because they don't notice it.

Beane himself had been hyped as a future superstar more on the basis of his looks and style than on his performance. Later in the movie, when he meets a statistician who is using data to improve decision-making, Beane asks him if he would've drafted him. The statistician says he wouldn't have. Beane, whose major-league career was hardly distinguished, agrees with that decision. In fact, he wishes he *hadn't* been drafted and had taken the full scholarship to Stanford he'd been offered. The bias, ostensibly in his favor, actually hurt him. He *looked* like a better player than he was. When bias results in a less qualified person getting a job over someone who's more qualified, it's bad for both people as well as the team. Bias hurts *everyone* when it skews decisions.

Moneyball illustrates three important points. One, bias creeps into everyone's decision-making, often unconsciously. Two, "expert" decision-makers habitually make bad calls based on these flawed observations, and all too often, nobody challenges the bias. Three, bias results in suboptimal decision-making that is usually bad for everyone, even the "beneficiaries" like Billy Beane.

Note

1. For more details on the kind of process I recommend, see the bonus chapter on performance review systems in the second edition of *Radical Candor*.

BIAS PREJUDICE BULLYING ⚡ LEADERS & ⎯⎯⎯⎯
DISCRIMINATION HARASSMENT PHYSICAL VIOLATIONS

Compensation

Performance
Management

Coaching and
Mentoring

Exiting

End NDAs and Forced
Arbitration

Organizational Design

Hiring

**BIAS
QUANTIFIER**
Proactively identify
where bias is skewing
decisions

**CHECKS AND
BALANCES**
No unilateral
decision making

**LEADERS ARE RESPONSIBLE FOR DESIGNING
FAIR MANAGEMENT SYSTEMS**

8

Create Virtuous Cycles, Prevent Vicious Cycles

> Everything that I have written is most minutely con-
> nected with what I have lived through, if not personally
> experienced . . . for every man [*sic*] shares the respon-
> sibility and the guilt of the society to which he belongs.
> To live is to war with trolls in heart and soul. To write is
> to sit in judgment on oneself.
>
> —Henrik Johan Ibsen

A t this point in the book, we've dismantled the engine of Brutal Ineffectiveness and laid out all the parts in the driveway.

BIAS PREJUDICE BULLYING ⚡ DISCRIMINATION HARASSMENT PHYSICAL VIOLATIONS

Now it's time to examine how the engine works when the
parts are operating together as a system. What are the dynamics
between the parts? How does bias lead to discrimination? To
harassment? To physical violations? And are there times when a
vicious cycle ensues? For example, a man believes women don't
handle stress well, so he discriminates against women, offering them lower-paying jobs. Having less power in the office,
a woman is more vulnerable to being sexually harassed. Not
surprisingly, she seems stressed, reinforcing his bias.

BIAS PREJUDICE BULLYING ⚡ DISCRIMINATION HARASSMENT PHYSICAL VIOLATIONS

What can we do to disrupt these dynamics and set in place a virtuous cycle that leads to systemic justice, instead of a vicious cycle that creates systemic injustice?

DYNAMICS

Let's look at what moves us away from collaboration and respect. Partly it's the discrete attitudes and behaviors already discussed. But it's also the dynamics *between* them.

The *Conformity Dynamic* drags us away from respecting individuality, usually offering a pretense of being rational, civilized, polite. But this dynamic excludes some people in a way that is not at all rational and can cause as much or even more harm in the long run as outright violence.

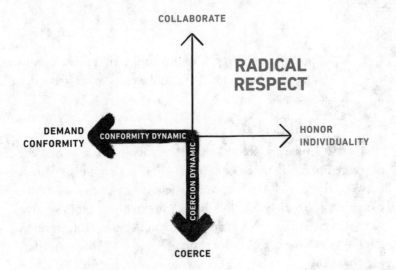

The *Coercion Dynamic* is what drags us away from collaboration. It makes no pretense at being polite—it is brutal. Bias, bullying, and harassment often implicitly or explicitly condone physical violations and therefore pave the way to violence. Bias, bullying, and harassment are not the moral or legal equivalent of a violent act. We don't want to overreact. But if they repeatedly and predictably lead to violence, we don't want to underreact either. We must be fully aware of the well-worn path from bias to violence if we are to treat bias seriously enough. That is why it's so important to be aware of these dynamics.

THE CONFORMITY DYNAMIC

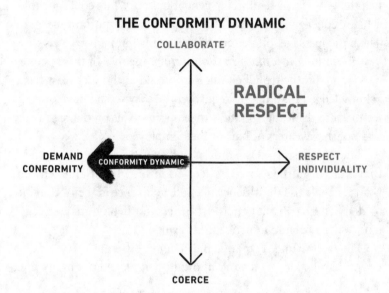

The Conformity Dynamic implicitly conveys an ancient message: *Be one of us, or make way for us.* And for many employees, of course, conforming to that "us" is not desirable or even possible. There are many things about myself I don't want to change—my gender, for example; and others I couldn't change even if I wanted to, like my age or my height. And when people are excluded from opportunity or subjected to unjust policies because they can't or won't conform with an arbitrary norm, it leaves them vulnerable to abuse, both emotional and physical.

The Conformity Dynamic often masquerades as "polite" or

BIAS   PREJUDICE   BULLYING   ⚡   DISCRIMINATION   HARASSMENT   PHYSICAL VIOLATIONS

"professional." This is BS. The fact that it's not overtly violent doesn't mean that it isn't destructive.

Shortly after I joined Google, a colleague told me not to wear a pink sweater to a meeting with the executives. The basic message, offered in the guise of helpful advice, was this: *Try not to look too much like a woman in this meeting.* He thought he was being helpful, but he was reinforcing gender bias. A White colleague told a Black colleague to cut off his locs before an important meeting. The basic message, offered in the guise of helpful advice, was this: *Try not to look too Black in this meeting.* If either of these people had wanted to be truly helpful, they would at the very least have acknowledged that in a more just world, they would have offered feedback to the leaders in these meetings to focus on the real work and not the sweaters or hair of their employees.

The Conformity Dynamic is reflected in the polite racism that Martin Luther King Jr. decried in his liberal allies in the North. People use the absence of explicit violence in their behavior to deny the harm that their attitudes and behaviors cause, to ignore the systemic injustice that results.

The Conformity Dynamic plays out in different ways for different people. Here is a story about how it played out in my life.

Hierarchy of the Absurd

When I was seven years old, my parents were playing tennis at their club as I amused myself by picking wild blackberries along the fence. Suddenly, two men approached the court. I was nervous because I knew the club's rules. Women were not allowed to be members; my mother and I were there as my father's guests. This translated to the following hierarchy for the tennis courts: If two women were playing, a man and a woman could take their court. Once the man and woman started playing, if two men walked up, the men could boot the man and the woman off the court. This, I feared, was about to happen to my parents. But then my mother, who was seven months pregnant, pointed at her belly and said to the two men, "I have a man-child inside of me. So there are two men on the court." The two men accepted this logic and went off to find another court.

I was astonished. My embryonic brother's penis had carried the day in a way that my brilliant, creative, strong adult mother could not have. I was outraged by the injustice of it. At school, we would never have been allowed to invent such ridiculous rules to exclude kids we didn't want to play with.

But this was the sexist hierarchy that governed our existence.

When I got my first summer job, at a bank in Memphis, an executive said to me, "Why, I didn't know they let us hire *pretty* girls!" I was eighteen, and I had no idea what an "I" statement was or how to respond. So I said nothing. I just felt deflated. This kind of erasure wore down all but the toughest women. And while I was getting underestimated as a result of my gender, I was getting overestimated as a result of my race. I was in denial about both dynamics for much of my life. It was conversations with women who weren't White that helped me notice what was really going on. This speaks to the importance of solidarity between people of different identities to challenge all the behaviors that contribute to a vicious cycle. United, we can create a virtuous cycle.

BIAS   PREJUDICE   BULLYING   ⚡   DISCRIMINATION   HARASSMENT   PHYSICAL VIOLATIONS

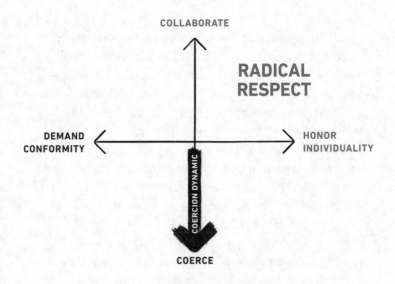

THE COERCION DYNAMIC

The Coercion Dynamic, which happens when people use their power to coerce others rather than creating a collaborative environment, is an equally ancient, well-worn path that leads from bias to bullying to harassment to violence. If you aren't aware of that path from bias to violence, you might give unconscious bias a "pass." But because bias can give way to violence, acknowledging that it matters is important, and we must take bias seriously.

My lived experience of the Coercion Dynamic has been of a privileged sort. I have rarely had to fear for my physical safety. But here is a story that illuminates why it's vital to recognize it, not to deny it.

The Office Party

I went to a holiday party a few months into a new job. The company's employees were predominantly (over 70 percent) men, so just walking in the door, I was a little intimidated. I was greeted by women, mostly naked, dancing in cages. That didn't help. As I did too often in my career, I tried to ignore what was happening around me. Women dancing in cages? Someone's terrible idea of a joke, I reasoned. I tried to ignore how uncomfortable I felt.

I looked around for a familiar face. A colleague, Simon, was headed my way. He handed me a beer. At first, I was glad to see him. Then Simon ruined everything by asking, "Do you know what a Southern girl's mating call is?"

I said I didn't want to know, but Simon told me anyway: "Y'all, I'm so *drunk*."

I didn't feel physically threatened by Simon, exactly, but this brief exchange tripped all my sensors. The context of the party mattered—predominantly men. At college, at business school, and throughout my career, I'd been in male-dominated environments. I'd had enough good experiences to know that ninety-nine out of a hundred men posed me no harm. And I'd had enough bad experiences to intuit that one out of a hundred would sexually assault me in some way if he got a chance. I just didn't know who that one man was. I didn't think it was Simon. But at the very least, Simon was signaling that he was not an upstander. He was reminding me—even if he didn't realize it—that it would not be wise for me to let my guard down that evening. If we lived in a world where

BIAS PREJUDICE BULLYING ⚡ DISCRIMINATION HARASSMENT   PHYSICAL VIOLATIONS

the Coercion Dynamic did not create a well-worn path from bias to sexual violence, his behavior would have been "only" bias. He was unconscious of the implications of what he was saying. He didn't mean it. A discrete event. But given the world we did live in, he was reflecting and reinforcing rape culture. Even if he wasn't aware of it, ignorance was no excuse.

DISCRETE INCIDENTS VS. DYNAMICS

It's important to understand the difference between a discrete incident and an incident that is a part of a *dynamic* that leads from bias to violence and contributes to systemic injustice. A discrete incident is bad but is far less threatening than the dynamic that carries with it the threat or past experience of violence. A man in tech can experience gender bias, but not sexism or misogyny. *Sexism* describes the dynamic between gender bias and discrimination, and *misogyny* describes the dynamic between gender bias and violence. A White person in the United States can certainly experience racial bias, but not racism. Racism describes the *dynamic* between racial bias and both discrimination and violence.

When I hazed my colleague Russ during the podcast recording, saying that he was "born doing the power pose," he experienced a discrete incident of bullying. He was in no way concerned that my behavior, while admittedly bad, posed any threat to his physical safety, nor did this incident trigger past experiences he'd had where a woman's bullying of him became violent—because he hadn't had any such experiences, nor had anyone he knew. My behavior was not part of a pattern in which women committed acts of violence against men. It did not play into the Coercion Dynamic, that well-worn slippery slope from bias to violence. It was bullying, but it wasn't misogyny (the dynamic that leads from bias to violence against women) or misandry (a theoretical but rarely seen dynamic that leads from bias to violence against men). For the same reason, when I as a White person say something that is racially biased, it's not just bias, it's racism. If I feel as a White person someone has said something racially biased to me, that may be true, but it wouldn't be accurate to say it was racist since there isn't a history of violence against White people in the US.

However, when Simon told me the rape joke, it was both bias and misogyny. I felt a menacing undercurrent. Simon himself wasn't overtly threatening me, but he was normalizing a sinister, criminal notion—that people think that having sex with someone too drunk to give consent is just a "party foul."

Whether he intended to or not, he was reminding me that I wasn't physically safe—especially if I had a drink. I'm not saying intentions don't matter. At the same time, impact also matters. I don't think it's too much to expect Simon to be aware of this dynamic or to hold him accountable for not playing into it. I knew Simon well enough to be pretty sure he did not think of himself as a person who would rape a woman or condone rape. However, if he wanted to show up to others as the kind of person he envisioned himself to be, he needed to understand the context in which he was making this joke and the impact it had.

If we are going to cultivate Radical Respect, we must be aware of the dynamics that can lead us from bias to discrimination to abuse or from bias to bullying to violence. Even if we ourselves have never committed an act of violence and don't think of ourselves as the kind of people who ever would, we need to be willing to notice the ways our words can reflect and

BIAS PREJUDICE BULLYING ⚡ DISCRIMINATION HARASSMENT PHYSICAL VIOLATIONS

reinforce patterns of violence. Yet this is hard, and many people are reluctant to notice these dynamics.

This reluctance played out painfully at a software company called Basecamp. Some employees at the company had created a list mocking the names of some of the customers; over time, the list had become quite racist. The management apologized and shut the list down. Some were concerned they hadn't responded in a way that would ensure something like this never happened again, though. In the ensuing discussion, an employee posted the Anti-Defamation League's pyramid of hate that showed how the dynamics between bias and violence work. This insight was so painful that it caused Basecamp's cofounders to attempt to ban political speech at the company. Thirty percent of employees quit in short order.

The reluctance of the founders to acknowledge the connection between a list that made fun of people's names and dramatic forms of violence like the Holocaust is at some level understandable. It *is* disturbing and jarring. And no violence was occurring at the company. However, the reaction begs some questions worth probing. One employee showed the ADL's pyramid of hate in the context of this incident, and a founder at the company was so reluctant to understand the connection between speech and violence that he forbade any discussion of politics at the company ever again. *What???*

My point obviously isn't that a list making fun of customer names and genocide were equally damaging. My point is that bias has historically led to violence and could do so again. So when the kind of violence that the biased "jokes" are making light of keeps repeating itself, the jokes are no longer funny and need to be taken quite seriously. The best way to prevent gender or racial violence is to take the seemingly "less serious" forms seriously.

Chanel Miller was a victim of gender and racial bias before she became a victim of rape. George Floyd was a victim of racial bias before he was murdered. In both cases, bias turned violent in a heartbeat. Part of the reason why these stories resonate so powerfully is not because they are unusual but because such violent encounters happen so frequently. Bias is not the same thing as violence. It doesn't lead inevitably to violence. But it can be an early-warning sign, and it can pave the way. We ignore the connection between bias and violence at our peril.

BOTH DYNAMICS CREATE VICIOUS CYCLES

Do discrimination and physical violations reinforce bias? Yes. Bias leads to abuse and violence. Abuse and violence reinforce bias. Two vicious cycles drag us to Brutal Ineffectiveness if we're not careful.

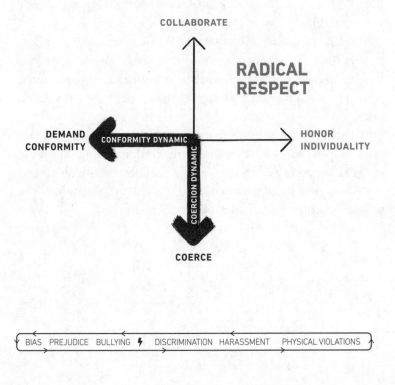

Here's a story that shows why. A decade after we'd quit working together, I got together with a colleague from that time, Steve. Over dinner, he and I enjoyed a good laugh about how stressful that period had been: the eighty-to-one-hundred-hour workweeks, the constant pressure. War stories.

"You always looked like your hair was on fire," he recalled, laughing. "I was kind of worried about you. Those kinds of hours are hard on everyone, especially women."

Evidently, he thought, *Oh, women can't take these long hours, that's why Kim seemed stressed.* In fact, it was not the long hours that had stressed me out. I had been stressed out because I'd experienced the full gamut of workplace injustice there: bias, prejudice, bullying, discrimination, harassment, and sexual violence. (The whole story is in chapter 11.) Those things hadn't happened to Steve. *That* was why Steve was less stressed than I'd been. Not because he was a man but because he wasn't dealing with all the shit I was dealing with.

This is how discrimination and harassment reinforce bias even in those who don't discriminate or harass. Being mistreated had an impact on my behavior, and my behavior reinforced Steve's bias, even though he didn't know what was really going on.

It's surprisingly difficult to interrupt this dynamic. Even years later, in a friendly conversation, I still couldn't summon up the energy to explain to him how unfair his bias about women and stress was. It seemed easier to leave it all alone. That's how the self-reinforcing cycle of workplace injustice rolls.

9

Speak Truth to Power Without Blowing Up Your Career

How to Protect Yourself from Discrimination and Harassment

I Was Safer Than I Felt

At one point in my career, I experienced some pretty blatant harassment and discrimination. When it reached a boiling point for me, I called up two of my mentors. The first one, a well-known Silicon Valley CEO, recommended I begin documenting what was happening in preparation for a legal escalation. My other mentor, also an experienced tech executive, gave me the opposite advice. "Just get another job. Quit quietly. Don't blow up your career."

I took the latter's advice. In retrospect, I regret it. I had a lot of options at the time, and thus the "blow up your career" risk was not actually so terrible.

As a person harmed, I had every right to choose my battles. However, over time, I came to notice that my silence hurt my self-respect and my sense of agency. For my own sake, I wish I had confronted what happened to me more forcefully. Worse, my silence left other people who were more vulnerable than I was without an upstander. For other people's sake, I also wish I had escalated the situation more effectively. And ultimately, as Audre Lorde predicted, it did not protect me. Again, I experienced discrimination and harassment.

I didn't consciously acknowledge my regret until a few years later, when I was on a panel about women in tech with Sarah Kunst. Kunst and six other women had recently called out venture capitalist Dave McClure for sexual harassment and assault, causing one of the early #MeToo reckonings in tech. Before our talk, I told her how my mentor had advised me not to blow up my career. I was planning to pass that advice on to other women.

"Do you know what the problem with saying that is?" Kunst responded. "The problem is that people will listen to you! If you tell people that they will blow up their career if they speak out, everyone will continue to stay silent, and nothing will change. Look at me. Is my career blown up?"

It would have been a hell of a lot safer for me as a White woman to speak out than it had been for Kunst, a Black woman. Plus, she'd had to work harder for success than I had. Yet she had been willing to take the personal risks required to challenge the sexual predation of a rich and powerful man. Not only had she left this world a little more just by doing so, not only had she survived, she had thrived. She went on to become managing director at a venture capital fund in addition to her then role as a contributing editor at *Marie Claire*. She is enormously successful by any measure.

I'm not saying that women have never had their careers blown up by confronting sexual harassment or predation.

Many have. And what I wish I'd done in retrospect may not be as safe for you to do as it would have been for me. I hope that, no matter what your circumstances, you can find support when thinking through your options. I hope the advice throughout the rest of this chapter will help you do just that. You are not alone.

This chapter is organized around the steps that I wish in retrospect I'd considered taking. The first three I think are always worth doing. Before you decide if or how you want to confront discrimination or harassment, take three preliminary steps:

1. Document
2. Build solidarity
3. Locate the exit nearest you

Once you have oriented yourself, you're in a better position to decide if you want to escalate. If you do, here are four escalation choices you may want to consider, depending on your situation:

4. Talk directly with the person who caused you harm (if worth the risk)
5. Report to HR (if worth the risk)
6. Take legal action (if worth the risk)
7. Tell your story publicly (if worth the risk)

BIAS   PREJUDICE   BULLYING   ⚡ PEOPLE HARMED & ─── (DISCRIMINATION   HARASSMENT   PHYSICAL VIOLATIONS)

1. DOCUMENT

If you are experiencing or observing discrimination or harassment, especially if it's from someone who is more powerful, you can document it every time it occurs—even if you're thinking you probably won't take any of steps 4–7 above. Take a few minutes to jot down what's happening. There are a couple of reasons to do this. One, it can help preempt gaslighting. Getting straight what is happening in your own head can be invaluable. Two, it will preserve options. If you later decide you want to take any of steps 4–7, your documentation will help.

Documentation doesn't have to be a heavy lift. Whenever possible, note the time and place, what was said or done and by whom, and who was present. Don't feel it has to be perfect—this is just a first step. You may never need to use this.

Documenting the Bizarre
Behavior of Boss "Tight Jeans"

Here's a basic example of what documentation might've looked like for me in one job I once had:

January 20—Boss told me I needed better clothes.
January 22—Bought new clothes. (receipts *here*)
January 24—Was presented with new clothing that my boss asked a colleague to purchase for me; included super-tight jeans, a revealing shirt, uncomfortable ballet slipper shoes, and a blazer; I would not wear the jeans, shirt, or shoes but didn't object too much since my boss told me the company would pay for

these items. (conversation with college roommate about the exchange that night)

January 27—Boss asked me to reimburse the company for these clothing items which I would not wear. (photo of check *here*)

February 14—Boss asked me to improve my relationship with Jack; speculated that I was suffering from competence-likability bias but then decided that I was "objectively not likable." (husband will recall discussing this at our Valentine's Day date)

March 18—Boss suggested that one thing that might help my relationship with Jack would be to seek fashion advice from him.

March 19—Jack told me that my biggest problem was that my jeans were not tight enough. Offered to take me shopping on the condition that I would agree to try on any article of clothing he suggested. I declined this "offer" and continued to wear jeans that were comfortable and shirts that did not show my bra when I wrote on the whiteboard and shoes that didn't hurt my feet. (discussed with my husband)

June 12—Jack told me he had been frustrated because our boss wouldn't assign him to the team I was on.

October 12—Boss suggested that a demotion might improve my relationship with Jack. (talked to my colleague, my husband, and my mentor about this; started looking for new jobs)

November 1—Took a new job and quit. Explained to my boss exactly why. He was really surprised. I don't think he got it.

PEOPLE HARMED &

BIAS PREJUDICE BULLYING ⚡ DISCRIMINATION HARASSMENT   PHYSICAL VIOLATIONS

When documenting, think about which of the facts can be corroborated by others or by some sort of paper trail. For example, in the case above: snapping a picture of the receipts for the new clothes and storing them in my personal Google Drive folder; keeping a picture of the canceled check I'd made out to the company to pay for the clothes in the same Google Drive folder. Also, after my boss bought me the clothes, I called my college roommate to discuss, so making a note of that was important. Regarding the February 14 meeting, my husband heard the story and would no doubt remember it, as it ruined our Valentine's Day dinner.

If someone is sending you offensive texts, emails, pictures, or videos, take screenshots of them and store them in a place you control. *Don't save all this information on a work computer.* Any documents you keep on a work computer, even personal journal entries, belong to your employer. You can email them to a personal email account, save them on your own computer or a thumb drive if you have one, upload them to a Google Drive or Dropbox account (or whatever other technology you use and control). Just be sure that you don't save any confidential or proprietary company information on a personal account, as this can be grounds for immediate termination.

If your work computer doesn't permit any of those things, pull out your phone and start taking pictures. Send them to someone you trust to establish what's called a *contemporaneous record*. For example, one of my mentors thought I should sue the company. He recommended that I send him an email each time these things happened, which I did. You can also establish a contemporaneous record by telling friends or trusted colleagues and then emailing confirmation of your conversation.

2. BUILD SOLIDARITY

Harassment and discrimination can leave you feeling isolated. Yet if you are experiencing these things, you are far from alone. Finding a way to feel connected to others is key. Often just one person at work can make all the difference. But how can you find that one person who is going to help you? Here are three things you can do to build solidarity:

- Ask for information
- Ask for help
- Find a "difficulty anchor"

ASK FOR INFORMATION

A big part of building solidarity and finding support is sharing information. I once shared my offer letter with a former colleague who was also considering joining the company. We would be peers, but I was pretty sure that I'd learn he was being paid more than I was if I asked. I wanted to know, but I hesitated to look at his letter because I was sure it would piss me off. If I hadn't, I might never have learned that I was, in fact, being offered a roughly comparable compensation package. That knowledge was enormously liberating. I was glad I asked and grateful to him for sharing.

If you have advantages that others don't, if you're getting paid more than others for reasons that are not fair, don't just sit around feeling guilty. Use your advantages to fix the injustice. For example, when White actress Jessica Chastain learned that her Black costar Octavia Spencer customarily made far less than

Jessica did, she famously suggested that they negotiate their next joint feature together—and they did.

If you complain to your boss, you may worry you risk having your salary lowered to your colleague's rather than your colleague's being raised to yours. Your boss may also get angry and defensive. It's important to proceed cautiously, while still finding a way to intervene.

If talking directly to your boss feels like tilting at windmills, find out if there are collective efforts you can join. If you can get together with a large number of people in your organization or even your industry and share information, your risk of being singled out and punished goes way down, and your chance of having a big impact thanks to collective action goes way up. When you support movements for pay equity, fundamental progress can be made. At the very least, you can share information with your colleague and acknowledge that it's not fair.

ASK FOR HELP

A mentor gave me some invaluable advice early in my career. Asking for help, he explained, is very different from asking for a handout. Asking for help is like asking someone to invest in you. And it's the gift that keeps giving. Once someone has helped you, the person has invested in your success and is likely to help again if you need it. You're not indebted to the person who helped you. You just need to pay it forward.

Here is a simple calculus you can do to figure out the best way to ask for help. Look for something *specific* the person can do to help you. Don't ask the person to have coffee or lunch with you—they are busy, and fifteen minutes can feel to them like a big ask. Look for things that are relatively easy for the other person to do but have a lot of value to you. A great ratio to keep in mind is low effort for the person / high value to you.

But don't limit yourself. Often people will go to a lot of effort to help you. People can be incredibly generous.

You can ask a mentor for advice on a specific decision you are making. Think through in advance how to present the decision in the most efficient way. Don't ask the person to do your thinking for you. "I could do A, or I could do B. Here are the pros and cons as I understand them. Is there another factor I should be considering?"

You can ask a senior colleague for help. Often people who have a little more seniority than you do can help you in a number of ways. They can:

- → Help you get assigned to a different team or to include you on a high-profile project that will help you on a path to promotion. Often you're doing them a favor when you put your hand up, so helping you helps them.
- → Support your promotion.
- → Make an introduction to a new job opportunity at a company where you think you'll face less discrimination.
- → Offer help in figuring out how to report HR violations in a way that won't harm your career.

FIND A "DIFFICULTY ANCHOR"

Mekka Okereke, an engineering leader at Google, shared some excellent advice on how to build solidarity with someone more senior to make sure you get proper credit for your work. The key is to ask for help from someone in your organization who is highly respected, known to have high standards, but is also objective. Someone who's known to be tough but fair. Explain what you're working on and ask the person to meet occasionally to

BIAS   PREJUDICE   BULLYING   ⚡ ┌ PEOPLE HARMED & ─────────────── ┐
                              │ DISCRIMINATION   HARASSMENT   PHYSICAL VIOLATIONS │
                              └──┘

give you guidance on your projects and the specific roles you're playing. This person will become your "difficulty anchor," who will be able to testify in detail about your contribution.

If your peers dismiss your work, assuming that the problem you were solving was easy (it must be easy if you could do it!), your "difficulty anchor" can objectively disagree and explain why it was a hard problem. This sort of evidence is much more effective coming from your anchor than from you. This is a big ask, but many people who are established in their careers enjoy this kind of mentoring. If you can build that kind of solidarity, it can help you get credit for your work. That's important because when bias means that people don't give you credit, you get passed over for promotions and the like—you get discriminated against.

Solidarity Moves the Needle

You don't have to be an SVP at Google or the president of your university to begin to address the problem of discrimination in your field.

When she was a sophomore at Colgate University in 2012, Lauren Yeary decided to take a computer science class. She loved the work, but there was one problem. The computer science intro classes had so few women, she was often a minority of one. For many women, that was reason enough not to study computer science.

Lauren wasn't going to let social awkwardness chase her away from work she enjoyed and a lucrative profession. Nor was she willing to accept the loneliness of being so outnumbered. She worked hard to recruit other women to major in computer science. She started a computer science club for women. By the time she graduated, the student enrollment in the computer science department at Colgate was well over 30 percent women.

Lauren moved the needle on an issue that has consumed millions of hours of impotent hand-wringing and excuses ("It's a pipeline problem, and it's not our fault, and we can't do anything about it") for the extreme gender imbalances at software companies. And her accomplishment does beg a question of university administrations. Why don't more universities make a conscious, proactive effort to make it more comfortable for women to enter male-dominated majors and for men to enter female-dominated majors?

3. LOCATE THE EXIT NEAREST YOU

Whether you want to stay or go probably depends on what your exit options are. So locate the exit nearest you. It's easy to feel stuck and never realize how many other job opportunities you might have. Sometimes we really are stuck in a bad situation. But often we are not as stuck as we feel.

If you look around and find several other jobs you could get, then suddenly the threat of being fired is not a big deal. You have a great BATNA (best alternative to a negotiated agreement). If you look around and realize this job is your only option or your best bet, then that will help you decide how much risk you can take. Either way, it's important to know your BATNA.

At times, you may realize that even though you can't easily

BIAS PREJUDICE BULLYING ⚡ **PEOPLE HARMED &**
DISCRIMINATION HARASSMENT PHYSICAL VIOLATIONS

find another job, you have to go. All the work you've done above—documenting what's happened, engaging the support of friends, reaching out for help—will, I hope, leave you feeling a sense of agency. And be skeptical of received wisdom about not quitting a job until you have another.

George, a person I care about deeply, once worked in a liquor store for a boss who was disrespectful to the point of harassment. Conventional wisdom was "Don't quit until you get another job." But it can also be hard to interview for a new job when you're angry and demoralized in your current one. George quit and started driving for Lyft and made ends meet while recovering from the harassing boss. That isn't possible for everyone, but don't assume you're stuck before giving it careful and creative thought.

Even if you can't immediately find another job, if the exit nearest you is not yet visible, you still have freedom: freedom to choose how you respond. I recommend two very different kinds of books to read if you find yourself in this situation. For inspiration and perspective, Viktor Frankl's *Man's Search for Meaning*. And for practical advice, Bob Sutton's *The Asshole Survival Guide*.

4. TALK DIRECTLY WITH THE PERSON WHO CAUSED YOU HARM (IF WORTH THE RISK)

Being direct is often less risky than it feels. You do take a risk, but you can get an outsize reward for doing so. When Ruchi Sanghvi, the first female engineer at Facebook, was negotiating her compensation with Mark Zuckerberg after finding out she was paid less than her male peers, she said, "Please bring me up to par on . . . compensation. I don't want to have this in the back of my mind while I'm working, nor do you. I only want to be thinking about building stuff!" Ruchi understood intuitively that she would not only be happier but also do better work if she knew she was being paid fairly in comparison with her peers. Receiving proper compensation gave her the freedom to do her best work.

I have mentored countless people frustrated by injustice in their workplace—by the lack of real efforts to recruit more diverse employees, by the visibly slower career growth for people from some demographic groups, by comments reflecting bias and prejudiced beliefs from senior leaders, and by other manifestations of harassment or discrimination. It's clear to me that these folks are ready to bolt.

"Why don't you talk to your boss?" I'll ask. "You've got one foot out the door already. You don't need to be afraid of getting fired. So why not try it?"

"Why bother?" they'll say.

"Would you rather keep this job or get another one?" I'll ask.

"I'd rather stay," they'll say.

"But you won't stay if this continues, right?" I'll ask.

"No," they'll say.

"And nothing will change if you don't say anything. So . . . ?"

For many people, it simply boils down to their reluctance to have an awkward conversation. Your boss is insufficiently invested in you and doesn't care enough to address that problem. Why set oneself up for further disappointment or even humiliation?

These sorts of direct confrontations are highly personal. You'll have to make your own list of pros and cons, costs and benefits. Here's one I made for myself.

PEOPLE HARMED &

BIAS   PREJUDICE   BULLYING   ⚡ DISCRIMINATION   HARASSMENT   PHYSICAL VIOLATIONS

COSTS/RISKS	BENEFITS
Confronting the problem makes it real	But it is real—and the only possibility of changing the reality is to confront it. Denial won't help solve the problem.
Time	Waking up at 3:00 a.m. pissed off because I've said nothing also takes time.
Emotional labor: Do I want to put myself through this?	I don't have to do this emotional labor. But the lack of resolution / being stuck working with someone I can't trust is also emotionally draining. If I confront them, I'll have a greater sense of agency and self-respect. That's a good ROI on my emotional labor.
Possible retribution	This person might fire me if I bring it up, or try to hurt my reputation. But I can get another job. And if I remain silent, it ensures this behavior will continue or even get worse for me and for others.
I might feel even angrier than I already do if there's no resolution or a bad response.	If I don't confront this, there's no possibility of resolving the situation or repairing the relationship that will otherwise be marred by lack of trust. That will also make me angry over time and also erode my sense of agency.
I might get emotional and feel ashamed.	It's okay to get emotional. If they can't deal with my emotions, it's their problem.
If I confront this situation too publicly, it will make it harder for me to get the next job.	That is true. How much is that next job worth?

Let's go back to the "tight jeans" situation I documented earlier. You might think that, given this cost-benefit analysis, I would have escalated. And I did confront my boss directly after I had quit, and then I went back after a couple of years to try again. I don't think I got through to him, unfortunately. I did not report him to HR or take legal action, though. I didn't tell the story publicly (until now).

Why not? The next job I took came with an enormous compensation package, and I decided the ROI just wasn't there for me. Did I want to take on enormous legal bills and the emotional cost of fighting this thing, or just walk away and take a new job that offered huge financial upside? In terms of dollars and cents, it was an easy decision. However, in terms of making the world a better, more just place, I'm not sure that I made the right call.

Navigating treacherous waters is difficult. These are complicated decisions, and I certainly don't have all the answers. I'm not sure I did the right thing, so I'm certainly not trying to tell you what you should do. The best I can offer is to share my thinking as honestly as I know how. I hope that my story helps you feel less alone and my frameworks give you a way to make sense of the things that are happening to you.

5. REPORT TO HR (IF WORTH THE RISK)

People are often cynical about reporting to HR. That is because there are too many instances when reporting an incident to HR actually winds up getting you, not the culprit, punished. This happens mostly when HR reports to the culprit. So, proceed with caution if you decide to take this step.

There are a number of important reasons to report any discrimination or harassment you experience to HR.

PEOPLE HARMED &
BIAS   PREJUDICE   BULLYING   ⚡ DISCRIMINATION   HARASSMENT   PHYSICAL VIOLATIONS

First of all, HR *can* be helpful. When HR resolves the issue, you are spared the time and hassle of having to find a new job or take another action. I have been lucky and have had strong relationships with most of the HR partners I've worked with. Throughout my career, they've given me excellent advice and helped me grow professionally. Given my fascination with creating business environments in which colleagues thrive and business prospers, I find HR the most intellectually interesting function at any company. That said, there are sometimes nightmare scenarios in which HR is in the pocket of the very person who's causing you harm. That's happened to me, too. But it is certainly not *always* the case.

Even in the event HR is *not* helpful—if HR seems more inclined to protect the person discriminating against or harassing you—it's still important to have reported the incident. For one thing, it is a form of evidence. If you wind up suing your company or going public with your story, creating a record of your complaint and how it was handled or not handled is an essential first step. If your issue is not resolved, that record will be crucial if you decide to take further action.

Reporting to HR Can Demonstrate When HR Is Solving Problems—and When It Is Not

A significant #MeToo reckoning in the tech sector occurred in 2017 when Susan Fowler Rigetti published a blog post detailing the sex discrimination and harassment she'd experienced at Uber, her former employer.

One of the things that made Rigetti's blog post about Uber so effective was how dispassionate and factual it was in describing the consistent refusal from HR and management to acknowledge violations she had reported.

When Rigetti was propositioned for sex by her new manager at Uber, she reported the incident to HR. She was told, "He is a high performer, this was his first incident, you are the problem." Over many months, Rigetti reported additional instances of sexual harassment and discrimination to Uber's HR department. She continued doing this even after it became clear to her that Uber's HR was part of the problem and not part of the solution. This was strategic. Continuing to report violations and to document lousy responses was part of what made her story so compelling and part of what helped her effect real change at Uber. Putting her complaints on the record was crucial to Rigetti's ability to document and communicate the depth of the problem of gender injustice at Uber. Her blog post would not have been nearly as powerful if she hadn't gone to HR each time.

It's important to acknowledge that a number of other employees who were not White, as Fowler is, also experienced sexual harassment and gender and racial discrimination at Uber. Ingrid Avendaño, Roxana del Toro Lopez, and Ana Medina reported to HR, sued the company, and told their stories publicly. Their lawsuit outlined how women and Black and Latine employees routinely didn't get pay raises, bonuses, stock, benefits, and opportunities for advancement because of the preference Uber was giving to men and White and Asian employees. Their stories did not go viral the way that Rigetti's did and did not get anything like the kind of media attention that Rigetti got.

BIAS   PREJUDICE   BULLYING   ⚡ PEOPLE HARMED &
DISCRIMINATION   HARASSMENT   PHYSICAL VIOLATIONS

Finally, reporting to HR may help others even if it doesn't help you. One of the things I felt worst about when I walked away from the job with the tight-jeans boss was that other women at the company experienced similarly bizarre, gendered behavior from him. Had I reported my issues before I left, it would have been harder for the company to soft-pedal future complaints. And it wouldn't have taken that much effort on my part—especially after I'd gotten another job and was leaving anyway.

Perhaps the lowest-risk way to report to HR is in your exit interview. This is a good moment to tell the people at the company exactly why you are leaving. Sure, you don't want to burn bridges. But this is a moment in which you can share some observations that you were hesitant to share while you were still at the company. This is an opportunity to state the facts of what happened, to describe the harassment or discrimination you experienced. It is also an opportunity to help the person you're talking to understand why the work environment was the cause of your departure. You can point out that you have no intention of suing but that you would like things to be better for those you are leaving behind. Doing so may enormously help the employees who are systemically disadvantaged at the company.

One risk of giving an honest exit interview is that you may be asked to sign a nondisclosure agreement. Do not allow yourself to be pressured to sign anything you don't want to sign. Be careful with exit documents and releases. I know several people who were so eager to leave they signed and then felt muzzled for years. Remember, you are always free to walk out any door. *You do not have to sign anything.*

6. TAKE LEGAL ACTION
(IF WORTH THE RISK)

Obviously, significant risks are associated with taking legal action, not least the time and emotional energy it can consume. I don't have any data behind this assertion, but it seems to me that getting an outsize payment is about as likely as winning the lottery.

But making a conscious decision about whether you want to sue, and seeking advice from multiple employment lawyers, does not have to be all-consuming. These conversations can help you zero in on how best to protect yourself, what you might want out of a lawsuit, and whether you're likely to get it.

Hiring a lawyer can feel daunting, and it's not uncommon to feel intimidated by lawyers. But a good lawyer can be the dogged ally you wish you'd had all along—full of practical advice, emotional support, and horizon-expanding wisdom. Oftentimes people dealing with workplace abuse issues find consulting with a knowledgeable, compassionate attorney gives them an invaluable plan of action. Numerous legal organizations are out there with resources to help you.[1]

Remember, you are about to hire someone to work for you. You are the boss, not the other way around. The lawyer will give you advice, but you don't have to take it. You get to decide whether you will act on the lawyer's counsel or ignore it.

Don't talk to just one lawyer, talk to several before deciding whom to hire. You don't have to pay for that first conversation any more than an employer has to pay people to interview for a job. Don't be afraid to ask hard, uncomfortable questions. Lawyers are used to that. Look for a lawyer who seems to respect your time and understand what's important to you.

Many lawyers work on contingency, meaning they only get

BIAS   PREJUDICE   BULLYING   ⚡ PEOPLE HARMED & ──────
DISCRIMINATION   HARASSMENT   PHYSICAL VIOLATIONS

paid if they win a lawsuit or if there is a settlement. If they think that they can win the case, or if the case will be so high profile that it's worth it to them to take it on, they will.[2] Because such lawyers get paid a percentage of a settlement, which often requires that you sign an NDA, they may push you to accept the settlement-and-NDA route. Be aware that if you sign an NDA, it will prevent you from helping others at the company by speaking out. And some NDAs will prevent you from getting the help you need—they can be so restrictive that you're forbidden from discussing what happened to you with anyone—even a therapist or a spouse. If you're not going to be comfortable doing that, make your position clear and make sure that your attorney respects it. Also, if you don't relish that kind of publicity, let the lawyer know.

Your endgame doesn't have to be winning a suit. Consider Lilly Ledbetter, whose pay discrimination suit went all the way to the Supreme Court. She lost there on a legal technicality, but the case was so grossly unjust that Congress later passed legislation, called the Lilly Ledbetter Fair Pay Act of 2009, to close the loophole. Ledbetter's willingness to fight this fight created a more just world for millions of women.

Cupcakes and Toxicity

When Françoise Brougher was fired as COO of Pinterest in the summer of 2020 due to gender discrimination, she decided to take legal action. Her lawyer thought she would win, but she knew that even a win would result in a negative financial ROI for her. The rewards for simply going quietly would have been significant, much bigger than anything she could win in a lawsuit. Françoise was at the height of a brilliant career. She was frequently approached by recruiters for other, bigger jobs and to serve on boards. She knew that if she chose to sue, many of these opportunities might evaporate.

She was not wrong. Some did. Shortly before her lawsuit, a recruiter had asked me for names of potential board members. I had recommended Françoise. After Françoise's piece came out, the recruiter dropped me a note: "I think it is great for her to speak up, but I do think it will make her candidacy tricky in the future." I replied, "Here is what I would advise companies. You want a board member who will hold the CEO accountable. Françoise will do that, clearly. This whole 'we don't want to hire people who speak out' BS has got to go." Given that the recruiter never called Françoise, it's safe to assume they didn't heed my advice.

When leaders quietly refuse to hire people who speak out against discrimination rather than *competing* to hire them because these are the very people who will help them and their teams do better, it perpetuates discrimination.

In the end, Françoise won $22.5 million in her lawsuit against Pinterest. That is a lot of money. But Françoise's stock options were worth *considerably* more than that. So she was not fully compensated for the discrimination. And the real penalty for Pinterest was not the $22.5 million but lost market capitalization, measured perhaps in the billions. Françoise is one of a handful of executives who knew enough about online advertising and online merchandising to monetize Pinterest. When she was fired, she was replaced by an executive without her expertise. Not surprisingly, the company has stumbled since. The CEO resigned. Françoise, Pinterest shareholders, and the

BIAS   PREJUDICE   BULLYING   ⚡ | PEOPLE HARMED &
DISCRIMINATION   HARASSMENT   PHYSICAL VIOLATIONS

Pinterest CEO would have been far better off if Pinterest had not discriminated against her.

Despite the fact that suing Pinterest has cost Françoise opportunities, she is glad that she decided to take this course of action. The toll of remaining silent would not have been worth paying. Being free to make that decision is a privilege that not everyone has. And not everyone will be rewarded for doing so.

Ifeoma Ozoma and Aerica Shimizu Banks are Black women who went public about the discrimination they experienced at Pinterest. They did not get anything like the settlement that Françoise got. This highlights the injustices that are at the intersection of race, gender, and seniority. Ifeoma and Aerica experienced both racial and gender discrimination, both at Pinterest and later in the legal system. Because of the way the legal system operates, Françoise was unable to reach out to Ifeoma and Aerica when they went public, although she wanted to and her case was no doubt bolstered by their decision to tell their story publicly. Because the most senior executives are paid so much more than even professionals with years of experience in tech, and because the legal system reflects and reinforces the racial bias in our society at large, Françoise's payout was much, much larger. She donated much of the money to nonprofits dedicated to making the tech sector better for employees from historically marginalized groups. But that didn't change the fact that Ifeoma and Aerica were not treated fairly by the system.

Ifeoma Ozoma channeled her anger at the way she was treated both by Pinterest and by the legal system into getting legislation passed. She worked tirelessly to get the Silenced No More act passed so that employers in California can no longer silence employees with NDAs. Her efforts to make the system more just for everyone are yet another example of the heroism of Black women in the face of systemic injustice. The best way we can celebrate that heroism is to fix both our management and our legal systems.

7. TELL YOUR STORY PUBLICLY (IF WORTH THE RISK)

Thanks to the #MeToo and #BLM movements, people who tell their stories today are likelier to be heard with compassion and solidarity than ever before in history. One of the things that makes me feel optimistic is the response that people have gotten when they've told their stories publicly, and the solidarity that these stories have built.

The #MeToo movement has offered many millions of people solidarity and support. It was born with a story, and it has unleashed millions more. It began when a thirteen-year-old girl told activist and community organizer Tarana Burke about being sexually assaulted. Burke, herself a victim of sexual violence, had been unable to respond to the girl's story in the moment. Burke later wished she had simply been able to say, "Me, too." She launched the phrase on MySpace in 2006 to help others find the strength both to *tell* their stories and also to *listen* to the stories of others. Thanks to Burke's brilliant call and the response on social media, countless victims of sexual harassment and sexual violence have done exactly that.

While #MeToo has been praised for providing support for people who tell their stories, it has also been criticized for discounting the contributions of women of color. If you are White, your

BIAS   PREJUDICE   BULLYING   ⚡   PEOPLE HARMED & ‾‾‾‾‾‾‾‾‾‾‾‾‾‾‾‾‾‾‾‾‾‾
                                   DISCRIMINATION   HARASSMENT   PHYSICAL VIOLATIONS

story is likelier to be picked up than if you are not, as we saw with Susan Fowler Rigetti at Uber and Françoise Brougher at Pinterest. Research demonstrates that these are trends, not anecdotes.

A special note for White women—including myself. No, it's not your fault that your story is likely to get shared more often because of your race. But it is your responsibility as an upstander to be aware of the fact. When you tell your story, make sure you are at the same time offering solidarity to other people who are also experiencing discrimination and harassment but who don't have the same access that you might.

Notes

1. American Civil Liberties Union, accessed August 13, 2023, https://www.aclu.org/know-your-rights/; MALDEF (Mexican American Legal Defense and Educational Fund), accessed August 13, 2023, https://www.maldef.org/; NAACP Legal Defense and Educational Fund, accessed August 13, 2023, https://www.naacpldf.org/; National Center for Lesbian Rights, accessed August 13, 2023, http://www.nclrights.org/forms/national-lgbt-legal-aid-forum/; National Immigration Law Center, accessed August 13, 2023, https://www.nilc.org/; National Women's Law Center: Legal Help for Sex Discrimination and Harassment, accessed August 13, 2023, https://nwlc.org/times-up-legal-defense-fund/.
2. Most of the top law firms take on unpaid, or pro bono, work. Many retired lawyers take on pro bono cases. Search terms such as "legal aid near me" or "pro bono lawyers" on Google for leads.

FIGHTING DISCRIMINATION, HARASSMENT, AND PHYSICAL VIOLATIONS

What Upstanders and People Harmed Can Do

DISCRIMINATION

Bias / Prejudice + Power
to exclude

HARASSMENT

Bullying + Power
to intimidate others

ALWAYS

Document

Build solidarity

Locate exits

IF WORTH THE RISKS

Talk directly

Report to HR

Take legal action

Tell your story

FIGHT THE POWER
WITHOUT BLOWING UP YOUR CAREER....

10

Reinforce a Culture of Consent

It would be nice, at least from the manager's perspective, to have absolute rules regarding physical contact in the workplace. No touching. But would that really work?

Ban handshakes? Ban hugs? Nope. That won't work.

While it's effectively impossible to ban every physical interaction or to legislate matters of the heart, you can put guardrails in place to make sure people understand that they cannot impose their desires on others, any more than they can impose their beliefs on others. Here is a basic articulation of a culture of consent:

> *If you want to touch someone, even just to shake their hand, it's your responsibility to know if they are okay being touched. If the other person doesn't want to be touched, don't touch. If you aren't sure, don't touch. If you're too drunk to know, don't touch. If you can't control yourself when you get drunk, don't drink, especially at work.*

But how can we apply this rule to all the myriad ways that both unwanted and consensual touch can manifest in the workplace? To answer that question, it's important to differentiate between four very different categories of touch and to consider a major contributing factor to each: alcohol.

As I wrote this chapter, a journalist called me to ask about an executive I knew. The journalist was comparing the executive's romantic relationship with a much younger, much more junior employee to a very different story about an entrepreneur who was a sexual predator. While I believed the executive had abused his power and really hurt this woman's career, I also believed it wasn't fair to compare it to rape. The comparison simultaneously exaggerated the severity of what he'd done wrong and let him off the hook. Just because he didn't rape her didn't mean he didn't do anything wrong.

This chapter will cover different ways that touch can go wrong at work, how to try to prevent the problems that can result, and what to do if they happen despite your best efforts. Leaders can't create a culture of consent all by themselves, so each section will cover what you can do no matter what role you're in.

1. Unwanted touch
2. Consensual touch between peers
3. Abuse of power relationship
4. Violence
5. Alcohol and drugs in the workplace

1. UNWANTED TOUCH

Let's start with unwanted touch, even simple interactions like a handshake or a hug. Plenty of people simply don't want to be touched in any way at work. And if we go back to a culture of consent, that's their prerogative. It doesn't matter what most people consider "appropriate." What matters is how the person being touched feels about being touched. The point is not to

BIAS   PREJUDICE   BULLYING   ⚡   DISCRIMINATION   HARASSMENT   ⌐EVERYONE &⌐
                                                                     PHYSICAL VIOLATIONS

ban all handshakes or hugs because they make some people uncomfortable. The point is to honor how each individual feels, rather than demanding they conform to how other people feel about being touched.

Indeed, some of the companies I work with have found that returning to in-person work after COVID lockdown gave them an opportunity to use the handshake to reinforce a culture of consent. As people came back together in person, some were comfortable greeting each other with a handshake; others were not. Learning to ask, "Handshakes okay?" before sticking your hand out toward someone and expecting it to be clasped was a good way to make sure people learned to check in with each other.

Often racism and sexism creep into the way that people feel comfortable touching each other. Many Black professionals have stories about colleagues who felt free to touch their hair in a way that is totally unwelcome. Pregnant women often tell stories about how colleagues feel free to rub their bellies.

The following pages will explore how all of us, no matter what our role, can reinforce a culture of consent so that such examples of unwanted touch don't happen in the workplace.

FOR LEADERS

As mentioned above, establishing a culture of consent to avoid "little" violations can help prevent way bigger/worse violations down the road. The lessons people learn from relatively minor violations can prevent more serious ones. Here are some things you can do to get it right.

- Overcommunicate your culture of consent
- Make it safe and easy to report violations
- Give people a chance to learn, but not too many chances

Overcommunicate Your Culture of Consent

For a whole host of reasons, it's tempting not to talk about consent at work. One, it can feel embarrassing. Two, it doesn't seem as if it ought to be necessary. Isn't it obvious? No, it's not obvious. Yes, it is embarrassing. Pushing through the discomfort is one of the many things leaders get paid to do. Here are some guidelines you can share with your team—it's worth repeating this from page 254:

> *If you want to touch someone, even just to shake their hand, it's your responsibility to know how the other person feels about being touched. If the other person doesn't want to be touched, don't touch. If you aren't sure, don't touch. If you're too drunk to know, don't touch. If you can't control yourself when you get drunk, don't drink, especially at work.*

If you like that, take it, it's yours. If you don't like it, write one you do like. But don't imagine you've done your job because you sent an email around. You've got to communicate it over and over again. Read it out at an all-hands meeting. Post it in high-visibility areas. Then, to make sure that people aren't ignoring it, put it in some new places from time to time. Put it on your intranet and feature it sometimes. Tape it over the mirrors in the bathroom.

When you read in the news about terrible things happening because someone didn't understand what a culture of consent meant, take the opportunity to share these examples with your team and remind them of your culture of consent document.

No matter how clear your written policy around a culture of consent is, you'll get a lot of objections like these:

BIAS   PREJUDICE   BULLYING   ⚡   DISCRIMINATION   HARASSMENT | EVERYONE & PHYSICAL VIOLATIONS |

Q: Don't you think that a world without hugs would be a
   cold, cold world?
   A: I didn't say no hugging. I just said don't hug people who
   don't want to be hugged.

Q: But how could I possibly know if the person wants to be
   hugged?
   A: Try asking, "Is it okay if I give you a hug?" You may like
   hugs, but the other person may not. Pay attention to the
   other person's body language. It's usually not too hard
   to figure out. If people's arms are crossed, if they look
   uncomfortable, back off.

Q: This is just too complicated. Why isn't there just a no-
   hugging rule at work and zero tolerance for any violation?
   A: Human behavior has rarely been successfully governed
   by simple absolute policies like a "no touch" rule.
   Sometimes a hug at work is really welcome.

Answering questions like these is a good way to make a
culture of consent real—and part of your job if you want to
establish a culture of consent.

Make It Safe and Easy to Report Violations

No matter how well articulated your culture of consent is, it's
not going to prevent violations from happening. That means
as a leader you must do everything in your power to make it
as safe and easy as possible for people to report inappropriate
touching. And if they prove true, create consequences. Remember, unwanted touch, whether it be a hug or sexual violence,
can feel to the person hugged like a form of bullying. Bullying +
power creates the conditions for these things to happen.

Give People a Chance to Learn, but Not Too Many Chances

If there are multiple complaints of unwanted—or lingering or too-tight—hugs, and if the person doesn't seem to be changing behavior despite clear feedback, it is probably time to think about firing that person.

You and your managers are going to have to investigate and make some hard calls. That's what managers do. They create systems that make it safe for people to report problems. Then they listen to that truth and to conflicting "truths." They use their judgment to interpret them. They confront people who need to be confronted. They tell people what's expected of them and help explain to them how to get there. If they can't do what's expected, then it's a manager's job to fire them.

To ensure fairness, establish a transparent process that everyone in your organization understands and trusts. Make sure there are checks and balances so that one manager is not making a unilateral decision. Just as promotion and hiring decisions are better made by a small team than one individual, so it is with these calls.

Even well-intentioned people will make mistakes. Talk to offenders compassionately but firmly. Communicate that you understand that mistakes are inevitable and also that you will hold people accountable for their mistakes. Holding people accountable doesn't mean harsh punishment. But it does mean that there must be a shared understanding of the mistake and a clear commitment to not repeating it. If people make a mistake and are called on it, require them to demonstrate active listening so that you know they got it. Ask them to apologize without defensiveness. Help them notice that the person who shared the discomfort with the touch was offering feedback—and that they should recognize that as a gift. Let them know that you'll be paying attention. And if the behavior persists, if they continue to be the object of complaints, or if they retaliate, let them know that their behavior is affecting their own performance and that of their colleagues. It's going to show up in their performance review, and if it causes enough harm, it's cause for termination.

A Kick in the Pants

One of my employees who was joshing around with his colleague made a Hacky Sack–like maneuver and tapped his foot on a woman colleague's rear end with a sideswipe of his leg. He intended it as a friendly gesture. She found it obnoxious. Nobody, including the woman kicked, thought it was a federal case. But she wanted him to knock it off, and it was my job as the boss to make sure he did.

I'll admit that at first I wanted to let it slide. It was my job to grow a billion-dollar business, not to adjudicate butt kicks! But I knew if I didn't sit down with each of them individually, a small thing could blow up into a huge problem.

First and foremost, she had to feel safe. I spoke with her to understand what had happened from her perspective.

Next, I talked to him. At first, he was a little defensive and focused on his good intentions. But after a few minutes of conversation, to my relief, he showed he could AAAAAC! He acknowledged what he'd done wrong. He said he understood that one consequence was that it would be harder to work with her if he didn't make this right. He said one thing he wanted to do to make amends was to tell the story about what he'd done, without using her name, so that others on his team wouldn't make similar mistakes. And finally, he apologized to her.

Happily, everything got resolved relatively easily. They worked well together for years after that. The two of them deserve most of the credit for the easy resolution. But if I, their boss, had ignored what had happened, things could have turned out worse. The whole thing took a little of my time that I would've rather spent analyzing our growth numbers, but by nipping this early, I saved myself and the company time, money, and hassle in the long run.

FOR UPSTANDERS

If you see something, say something. Go back to the five Ds described in chapter 3 for Upstanders: direct, distract, delegate, delay, document. At the very least, delay, and check in with the person harmed afterward. Here is a story that shows why an upstander's willingness to say something would have made a big difference.

The Hand Slobberer

I was working at a large company. My team and I were teaching a leadership class to five hundred salespeople. On stage when that organization's VP, Frank, introduced my two colleagues (both men) to the crowd, he shook their hands. When he got to me, I stuck my hand out for

BIAS PREJUDICE BULLYING ⚡ DISCRIMINATION HARASSMENT | **EVERYONE &** **PHYSICAL VIOLATIONS** |

a shake, but Frank made an absurdly low bow, took my hand in both of his, and kissed it, holding the pose for a painfully long time and leaving the back of my hand damp with his saliva. I experienced two equally unpleasant things that both made me feel awful. I felt singled out and demeaned in a gendered way in front of my colleagues. And I was being touched in a way that left me disgusted. All I wanted to do was to wipe my hand on my pants, but for some strange reason, that felt rude. I kept a pinched smile on my face even though I felt like vomiting.

That was gross. But even worse was what happened next. Nothing. Five hundred people witnessed Frank slobber on my hand and nobody said *anything*. If just one person had come up to me afterward and said, "Ugh," or, "Well, that was awkward!" it would have made a world of difference.

FOR PEOPLE HARMED

If you are getting touched in a way that feels creepy or inappropriate, or even if it just bugs you, you have the right to tell the person to knock it off.

You are the *only* arbiter of what sort of touch is okay for you. "I am not a hugger" is a perfectly acceptable response. So is "I would rather fist-bump/bow/whatever than shake hands." If the person is dismissive and defensive and doesn't stop, they are bullying or harassing you. Try a "you" statement. "You need to back off."

If you ask a person to back off and they respond to your "you" statement by doubling down, what do you do? In theory, you escalate to your boss or HR. Why is it that the simplest and fairest outcome—that if you report an unwanted touch, your boss or someone from HR just takes the person aside and tells them to knock it off or face consequences—feels like such a long shot?

There's plenty you can do, though. Return to the seven steps in the previous chapter: document, build solidarity, locate the exit nearest you, talk directly with the person who caused you harm, report to HR, take legal action, and/or tell your story publicly.

FOR PEOPLE WHO CAUSE HARM

If someone doesn't want to be touched, don't touch. Read the social cues. If you can't read the social cues, default to no touching.

If you're not a mind reader—and who is?—asking out loud is a reasonable thing to do: "Hug, handshake, fist bump, elbow bump, toe tap, or a smile?" Err on the side of caution—a smile from six feet away. I know that can feel strange. But it's also awkward for the person you're touching to say, "I'm not a hugger!" or "I'm not a handshaker!" or even just, "No." If you are initiating this contact, it's your responsibility to deal with the awkwardness. Figuring out how to do this, through words and gestures, in a way that doesn't put too much pressure on the other person will require some effort on your part. But it's also the fair and reasonable thing to do, and doing it will keep you out of hot water.

BIAS   PREJUDICE   BULLYING   ϟ   DISCRIMINATION   HARASSMENT | EVERYONE & | PHYSICAL VIOLATIONS

The Handshake

Once when I stuck my hand out to a business contact, offering a "nice to meet you" handshake, I noticed he looked extremely uncomfortable. I pulled my hand back and said, "Do you have a cold? I always appreciate it when people don't shake hands when they are sick."

"Actually, " he said, "my religion forbids me from touching a woman who is not my wife."

"Oh, I am sorry I put you in an uncomfortable situation," I said.

"No, thank you for giving me a chance to explain. I never know what to say," he replied.

We talked about how this handshake thing happened to him every single day, usually more than once. Together, we came up with a line he could use quickly: "I'm very glad to see you, but I don't shake hands because of a religious belief."

Taking an extra beat to notice his discomfort and to inquire took under a minute. But after that, we both worked better together. I did a tiny bit of work, and I got a lot more out of it than I put into it.[1]

If you're worried about getting into trouble around touch in the office, here are some things to consider:

- Don't overgeneralize
- Don't demand absolute rules

Don't Overgeneralize

Avoid applying generalizations to specific individuals—otherwise known as *stereotyping* or *essentializing*. This muddles your ability to understand things clearly, to respect individuality. You may have heard that Italians are more comfortable touching one another than Americans, but of course that doesn't mean you should assume you could/should kiss every Italian you meet on the cheeks three times.

Don't Demand Absolute Rules

Is it better to just say, *No hugs*? Many of us long for simple, clear-cut rules: *Here is the line: step over it once, this will happen; step over it twice, that will happen.* But many people, myself certainly included, would recoil from the idea of living in such a cut-and-dried world. There'd be so many exceptions that the rules would quickly become meaningless. What if someone at work gets a phone call and learns that a family member has died? Can you hug the person at that moment? Or if a person is going through a medical crisis and breaks down in tears of pain at work, surely a hug might be in order? Or if someone is just having a crappy day? What if both you and that other person are huggers?

I propose this approach to answer those questions. If you are a hugger, think about times when a hug was welcome and when it wasn't. Ask yourself, how did you know? One person's smile might indicate your hug is welcome. Another's smile might reflect discomfort. If you're not sure what a person's smile means, you can always express sympathy and ask, "I'm so sorry. Would you like a hug or a cup of tea?" Asking the person if they want a cup of tea (or water) gives them a polite way to tell you they'd rather be alone and not have a hug.

If you feel too awkward to even ask the question, that's probably a sign that verbal sympathy would be better. If you're paying attention to the other person and not expecting the person to conform to your preconceived notions of how others "should"

BIAS PREJUDICE BULLYING ⚡ DISCRIMINATION HARASSMENT |EVERYONE &— PHYSICAL VIOLATIONS|

act, you'll most likely make the right choices. If you are open to feedback when you get it wrong, you'll learn quickly. If you ignore the feedback and instead insist that everyone should assume you have good intentions so nothing you do could possibly be wrong, you're bound to misstep.

2. CONSENSUAL TOUCH BETWEEN PEERS

Touch can go wrong in a lot of different ways. And sometimes it can go right. Employee romance is not *always* a bad thing. Before we got married, my husband and I dated while working at the same company. Work is where many of us meet our life partners. And it can also be where we start and end a Bad Romance. How can we manage this so that things don't go sideways?

FOR LEADERS

People spend most of their waking hours at their jobs. As noted, it's unreasonable and ineffective to adopt a zero-tolerance approach to relationships at work. Especially if you have a young team with a lot of single people, people will get romantically involved sometimes. But for reasons already discussed, such relationships do need to be managed.

Here are some simple suggestions: First and foremost, reiterate your culture of consent.

Also, establish an explicit "No sex or physical intimacy in the workplace" policy. You might assume that not having sex in the office is common sense and does not require a policy. Who does that anyway? Quite a few people, as it turns out. I have observed "sex in the office" problems several times throughout my career. So I recommend making this rule explicit and known.

Don't undermine that policy or your culture of consent by tacitly (wink, wink, nudge, nudge) encouraging hookups. This seems obvious, right? Yet over and over again, I've seen leaders encouraging their employees to hook up. I myself did this inadvertently. Trying to adopt a casual atmosphere, I turned a conference room into a "team cozy" with couches and bean bag chairs instead of a conference table and chairs. One morning, I came into a staff meeting to find a bra and a pair of boxer shorts in the folds of a couch. I got rid of the couches and bean bag chairs. I also told the whole team why I'd done it.

Later, I worked at another company that had a conference room that felt designed for hookups: low lights, lots of fabric with a tentlike feel, no windows, and a nook with a couple of bottles of whiskey in it. I was like a broken record, agitating for the leadership to change that décor. They didn't do it until *after* sexual misconduct occurred there.

FOR UPSTANDERS

Nobody wants to be in the middle of someone else's romantic entanglement, especially at work. But pretending problems aren't happening never helps to solve them. If you notice one person treating another cruelly or disrespectfully, check in with the person harmed to find out how you can best support that person. If the behavior is disruptive to the team, report it to your manager or HR.

If you hear folks making offensive comments about one of the two people in the romance, say something. Sometimes a problem arises not between the two people who had a fling but in the rest of the team. Sometimes people form a sort of "competition pod" around one of the two people, usually the woman in a heterosexual pairing, treating her as though she is "fair game," competing for "whose turn" it is next. It becomes uncomfortable for her to come into the office.

Needless to say, this is unacceptable. Just because she dated one man on the team does not mean she is interested in any of the other men. And their bad behavior is in no way justified by the fact that she dated one person at work.

Sometimes this kind of competition pod happens to a woman working on a team that is predominantly heterosexual men even when she is not dating anyone. People start spreading false rumors about her. Or they'll make comments like, "Eventually, you'll have to choose one of us." It's certainly possible that something similar could happen to a man on a team that was predominantly heterosexual women or on a team where most people were not straight. But cultural norms make this kind of behavior most likely in the first case.

If you notice this sort of thing happening, intervene, using the five Ds. You can speak with the person directly or delegate—report their conduct to your manager or HR. Document. Distract. You can delay—check in with the person harmed after the fact.

FOR THE HEARTBREAKER AND THE HEARTBROKEN

My first advice about casual hookups with peers is simple: don't do it. If you fall in love, that's something different. It's probably worth risking your job for true love. But a fling with someone you're going to have to keep seeing day after day at work risks so many potential problems that it's best avoided.

Of course, things happen. If you hook up with a colleague and then one or both of you regret it, first let me offer some compassion. It's a difficult and painful situation—for the two people involved, for the people around them, and for their manager(s). But it's going to happen. So let's talk about how to deal with it in a way that is fair to everyone and minimally disruptive.

Here are some guidelines:

Don't Pressure

If the other person no longer wants to be romantically involved and you keep pressuring that person to resume, you are violating the rule of consent. If you find it impossible to be around that person without violating boundaries they have established, it is your responsibility to find another job.

Manage Your Own Emotions

If you can't contain your emotions and are disrupting the team, you are the one who should get a different job. The disruptive one has to go.

Don't Make It a Habit

If you regularly hook up with people in the office, you should take the steps necessary to break this destructive pattern.

3. ABUSE-OF-POWER RELATIONSHIPS

Things can go badly wrong, financially and emotionally, when one person in a romantic relationship is the manager of the other, or considerably more senior in the organization. That is why they have traditionally been discouraged or forbidden, and why such rules have come to be enforced more often after #MeToo. However, they still happen. And when they do, all too often, the more powerful of the two people demands that the less powerful person bear all the consequences of the relationship. Or they use their power to become emotionally abusive. Or both.

BIAS   PREJUDICE   BULLYING   ⚡   DISCRIMINATION   HARASSMENT   ⌐ EVERYONE & ⎯⎯⎯
                                                                  PHYSICAL VIOLATIONS

FOR LEADERS

When you read the job description for your role, it probably didn't mention that you should prevent abusive romantic relationships from harming your team's productivity. However, if you as a leader don't give some thought to preventing that from happening, it probably will.

Here are some preventative steps you can take and some suggestions for what to do when prevention fails.

Lead by example. Don't get romantically involved with the people at your company.

Put in place a "No sex, physical intimacy, or dating in your chain of command" rule. In other words, bosses who have sex or sexual intimacy with or date their employees—or the employees of their employees—must be terminated. When people violate this rule, which they inevitably will, the more senior person is the one who must leave a job, not the more junior person. To be fair and also to prevent undesirable behavior from powerful people, the rule must protect the less powerful. If executives do not create any penalties for senior leaders who date more junior employees but instead push all the penalties onto the more junior people, at least some of these powerful people will keep having sexual encounters with the less powerful.

The most senior leaders at a company—the direct reports of the CEO and *their* direct reports—should not date or have romantic or physical involvements with *anyone* at the company. The theory behind this policy is that at a certain level of seniority a person has so much authority that sexual advances or relationships risk feeling coercive and/or abusive. That's bad for the person coerced, and it also creates unnecessary financial risk for the company and a dysfunctional dynamic on a team.

Enforce the rule. This may mean letting go of some leaders who are getting results. For example, the board of directors of McDonald's fired the CEO when it emerged that he'd been sexting with an employee, despite the fact that under his watch the company's share price had doubled.

Leaders must disclose past relationships. After it was alleged that the McDonald's CEO did not disclose relationships he was having with three other employees, in addition to the one that got him fired, McDonald's sued him to get back the severance it had paid him.

Don't create environments in which abusive relationships are encouraged. One venture capital firm in Silicon Valley used to host two parties every holiday season: one for the wives and one for the mistresses. (There were no women partners or gay partners.) Don't be surprised when your culture goes toxic in a damaging public way if you do things like that.

Educate yourself.[2] If you are not sure what constitutes an emotionally abusive relationship, here's a simple definition: one person has power over another and uses that power to control or coerce the other to do things the person doesn't want to do.

FOR PEOPLE CAUSING HARM (TOO OFTEN, SIMULTANEOUSLY THE LEADER)

As hard as it is to recognize it when you are being abused, it may be even harder to recognize it when you're abusing your power in a relationship, especially if you love the person, and/or are physically attracted to them. It may not be your *intention* to abuse your power—it may be the logic of the situation, logic that you may be unaware of because your power or your wealth or your privilege insulates you from facts that seem obvious to people in different circumstances. But it is your responsibility to be aware of the impact you have on others, *especially* if you care about those people, and/or have a sexual relationship with them.

For example, Nina, a friend of mine, asked Stanley, an executive at her company, to endorse her for a promotion. He admired her work and agreed readily. A couple of days later, Stanley asked Nina out on a date. She wasn't in his chain of command, so technically, he wasn't violating any HR rules. But given that he was writing in support of her promotion, he did have some power over her. And she simply wasn't interested. After she politely declined, she called me, worried that he would withdraw his support for her promotion.

I knew Stanley reasonably well. I doubt it ever occurred to him that he had put Nina in an awkward position. But it *should* have. If he was smart enough to become an executive at a major tech company, he was smart enough to figure out this dynamic. Cluelessness was no excuse. If he'd taken just a moment to think about it—and all overtures of this nature in the workplace deserve that moment—he would have realized this was not the time to ask her out.

Here are a few guidelines to help you avoid becoming the abuser.

Don't get romantically involved with people who work for you or with people who are significantly junior to you in an organization. Don't flirt with them, don't allow them to flirt with you, don't ask them out on dates, don't touch them in a sexual or flirty way, at all, ever.

If you begin to have romantic feelings for someone who works for you, ask yourself this question: Would you be willing to give up your job to pursue this relationship? If so, by all means, quit your job and ask the person out. If not, exercise the executive function that got you into this role in the first place to manage your own behavior. Do not announce your feelings and then expect the other person to clean up the situation you just created.

If you wind up romantically involved with someone who

works for you or is junior to you, it's time for *you* to find a new job. Don't expect or allow this person to sacrifice a career for yours. The all-too-common but flawed expectation of such situations is that the junior person is the one who changes departments or gives up their job. After all, you have the "bigger" job. But the other person's career is just as important to them as yours is to you. And the person can likely *less* afford a career derailment, being the more junior with fewer resources.

FOR PEOPLE HARMED

Just because you're a strong, independent person doesn't mean you couldn't find yourself in an abusive relationship. And the corollary is also true: just because you are in an abusive relationship doesn't mean you're not a strong, independent person. If you are in a relationship with someone who is more powerful than you are and is using their power to be emotionally abusive, you can find healing in work and in solidarity with others.

Work can be a huge part of recovering from the trauma of abuse. Not only can a job ensure you are not financially dependent on the person abusing you emotionally, it can restore a sense of agency. If the person who is abusing you is your boss, locate the exit nearest you—find another job, even if they ought to be the one to quit.

Solace can also come from solidarity with other strong, independent people who have had the experience of an abusive relationship. There are lots of us out there. You will read in the next chapter about one of my big mistakes: dating my boss. It was the friends I made who helped me begin to heal; it was taking a new job that really set me on the path to mending my broken heart.

4. VIOLENCE

As #MeToo has revealed, sexual assault happens in the workplace with horrifying frequency. One out of six women and one out of thirty-three men is the victim of rape or attempted rape. Twelve percent of sexual assaults occur while the victim is working.[3] Of course, other forms of assault happen in the workplace. While the following pages will focus on sexual violence in the workplace, much of what is written applies to any violence.

FOR UPSTANDERS

Interrupt

If you witness a sexual encounter in which you question the presence of true consent, call the police and/or interrupt it if your own physical safety is not at risk.

In *Know My Name*, Chanel Miller describes how two young Swedish men rode by on bicycles while she lay unconscious behind a dumpster with her attacker, Brock Turner, on top of her. When the cyclists realized what was going on, they intervened, yelling at him to stop. After Turner fled, they first checked on Miller, then chased after him. "They represented the seers," Miller writes, "the doers, who chose to act and change the story . . . What we needed to raise in others was this instinct. The ability to recognize, in an instant, right from wrong. The clarity of mind to face it rather than ignore it." She describes how the Swedes pinned Turner to the ground and said, "What the fuck are you doing?" and how that inspired her to press charges: "The Swedes had introduced this new voice inside me. I had to teach myself to talk like them. To one day face my attacker and say, 'What the fuck are you doing?'"

Listen with Compassion

At the very least, if you witness or hear about a sexual encounter where there is no consent, don't deny it, minimize it, or lie about it. Don't reflect and reinforce the gaslighting that makes reporting this kind of behavior so difficult.

Listen. Don't Ask, "Why Didn't You Tell Me Sooner?"

Here's an example of the additional harm that failed upstanders can do. Once at a party hosted by an executive of a company where I worked, someone came up behind me and groped me. When I whirled around, there were four people close by. I was certain it was the company's CEO, who had a reputation for such behavior. Years later, when I told a friend who'd also worked at that company what had happened, the first thing she said was, "Why didn't you tell me sooner?"

Leaders, upstanders, friends, take note. When someone tells you something like this, *never* ask why the person didn't tell you sooner. That question has been asked and answered a thousand times over. In the vast majority of cases, victims don't say something sooner because they are afraid that if they speak out about what happened to them, they will be punished. Listen to what happened with compassion, even when it's hard to hear, and an open mind.

Then she made another common mistake. She started cross-examining me. "You can't say for sure it was him."

"No, I can't. But here's who else was there." I listed the

BIAS   PREJUDICE   BULLYING   ⚡   DISCRIMINATION   HARASSMENT   EVERYONE & _____
                                                                PHYSICAL VIOLATIONS

names. We both knew them well. "Do you really think it was any of them?"

She made a noncommittal noise.

"Come on. I really, seriously doubt any of those men would do a thing like that. And you and I both know Phil *would*."

"It wouldn't hold up in a court of law."

"I'm not in court. I'm just talking to you."

"Besides, how do you know it wasn't just an accident?"

"Have you ever been grabbed like that? It's an unmistakable gesture. That kind of grab doesn't happen accidentally."

"You can never prove it."

"No, I guess not."

Why was she asking me to prove it? I viewed her as a friend and was talking to her in that capacity. She no longer worked at the company where this had happened, and neither did I. I couldn't help but think she was quietly telling me to keep my mouth shut, as if the real danger here was that rumors about *me* might start flying around, not that Phil would keep attacking women at the company.

"Be careful," she warned. "There's a backlash coming."

"Why a backlash? He got away with it! There was nothing I could do. What is he lashing back at?"

Clearly, my friend was not an upstander. In some ways, this was more upsetting than what the CEO had done. I knew the CEO's reputation and *expected* him to behave that way. But my friend? That felt like a *betrayal*.

FOR PEOPLE HARMED

If you are a victim of sexual violence, I am with you in words, and I know that my words are inadequate. If I could scale infinitely, I'd be there in person with you as well. Here are some things that I hope can help:

- Choose your response
- How to find support and solidarity
- Be explicit if it helps
- Tell your story if it helps

Choose Your Response

When you are the person who has been harmed, you get to choose your response, and you may choose not to respond. This is always true, but it is especially important to remember this in cases of assault, including sexual assault. Nobody can tell you what you "should" do. What follows are ideas for what you can do, not what you "should" do.

Find Support and Solidarity

I wish I could say turning to the people who love you most for support will always work. And more often than not, it will. But sometimes the responses from the people closest to you can be hurtful or even retraumatizing. Sometimes the people who love you most cannot bear your pain, and so they don't respond well. Other times, they just don't get it.

Even if that happens, there are other places to turn for support. The National Sexual Assault Hotline is available twenty-four hours a day at 1-800-656-4673, and you can also chat online with professionals at RAINN, the Rape, Abuse & Incest National Network (online.rainn.org). The NO MORE Global Directory (nomoredirectory.org) is a directory of domestic and sexual violence helplines and services, which can be searched by country, state, and region, as well as by community served. Tarana Burke's organization, the #MeToo movement, also has some helpful resources and tool kits.

You can go to a hospital to get a forensic exam.[4] You can reach out to your local rape crisis center to discuss the examination before you go. Rape crisis centers often have advocates who can go with survivors to the hospital. Having an advocate can be important if the medical staff or the police are misleading or treat the survivor poorly. It still happens too often that officials doubt the victim, respond in a way that feels cold or unfeeling, or even tell the victim lies or misinformation. So some people prefer to have an advocate accompany them.

After such a traumatic experience, your first instinct may be to take a shower; try to keep in mind that you may be washing away important evidence. But even if you do shower, you can still go to the hospital: there still may be important evidence to gather, and you may have injuries that require medical attention. It's also a good idea to write down what happened to you and to email what you wrote to yourself or to a trusted friend. Taking these steps doesn't mean you have to report the crime. But if you later decide to do so, the more evidence you have, the better.

Be Explicit If It Helps

If we can't use the right words, we can't give the right descriptions, and that allows perpetrators to get away with their crimes. If someone is touching you in a way that is not OK, try to liberate yourself to use whatever words you need to describe exactly what they are doing. I once failed to report a man who assaulted me in the elevator to HR because I couldn't bring myself to use the words I needed to explain exactly what he'd done. Don't make that mistake.

Whose Hand Is This?

I was once groped on the subway. Part of the reason I didn't yell was that I didn't dare shout the words that would accurately describe what he was doing to me. The words "You are digitally penetrating me" do not fall trippingly off the tongue; nor did I feel comfortable yelling, "Get your fingers out of my body!" Or even "Why is your hand up my skirt?" Somehow, I felt that describing accurately what was happening was shameful for me but not for him.

The most satisfying response to being groped I've ever heard comes from author Deborah Copaken. She was on a bus and someone grabbed her butt. The bus was crowded and she couldn't tell who it was, so she reached down, grabbed the man's hand, pulled it away from her body, and shouted, "Whose hand is this?"

Take a page out of Deb's book. She was not ashamed!

Liberating yourself to use the words that come to your mind, rather than feeling you must censor yourself, works preventively as well as reactively. If someone asks you to do something that makes you feel uncomfortable, you can tell them exactly and explicitly why you're uncomfortable. I learned this by accident when I was on a train from Moscow to St. Petersburg. I had bought four tickets so that I could have a sleeping compartment to myself and

---

would not have to sleep with three strangers. A man barged in anyway. When he went to the bathroom, I threw his stuff out into the hall and locked the door. He came back pounding on the door and yelling at me. My Russian wasn't good enough to be subtle, so I said, "You are a large man. I am a small woman. It is not safe for small women to sleep with large strange men." He apologized and found another seat.

It is important to be explicit about what makes you uncomfortable. You are not accusing the other person of anything when you say what worries you. Rather, you are explaining why you're uncomfortable.

Tell Your Story If It Helps

Many people find telling their story, either in writing or orally or in an artistic medium, to be enormously helpful in recovering from the trauma of sexual assault. You never know what might happen with your story. But even if your story doesn't go viral, if it helps you heal, it has moved mountains. I wrote a three-hundred-page memoir to help me digest and get out of an abusive relationship. It never saw the light of day, and it never will. I wrote it for myself. And writing it helped me get it out. That was enough! I like to write, so that worked for me. If you hate to write, find another way to get it out. Sing it. Dance it. Act it. Make a video. Tell it to a friend on a hike or over a meal. Try therapy. Join a support group.

"Fear comes from focusing on the costs of speaking up," actor and activist Ashley Judd observed, and "courage comes from focusing on the costs of staying silent."

That doesn't mean you are a coward if you decide it's not in your best interest to tell your story. Ashley Judd has resources you might not have. But you don't have to be a famous actor to ask yourself: Does the cost of silence outweigh the cost of speaking up?

FOR PEOPLE WHO CAUSE HARM

Henry Kissinger famously said, "Power is the ultimate aphrodisiac." In my experience, what this means is *not* that powerful people are sexier than less powerful people. It means they *think* they are sexier. They are wrong.

Studies have shown that power makes people likelier to think about sex, to be sexually attracted to those around them, and to demonstrate disinhibited sexual behavior and dominance more broadly. But it does *not* mean those feelings are reciprocated by the less powerful people around them. This is a big problem because having power makes people likelier to touch others, whether or not the others want to be touched.

So if you are in a position of authority, remind yourself that every promotion puts you into a higher-risk group for getting in trouble around touch. *Every promotion means you think you are sexier than the people around you think you are.* Let that sink in. And back off.

Whatever you tell your people about being mindful of others goes double for you. Keep in mind that an unwanted hug from a leader will likely kick up a much bigger problem than one between two people with no power over each other. Also, keep in mind that unwanted touch is likelier to happen when there is a power imbalance.

BIAS   PREJUDICE   BULLYING   ⚡   DISCRIMINATION   HARASSMENT | EVERYONE & ⎯⎯⎯⎯⎯ PHYSICAL VIOLATIONS |

FOR LEADERS

When a person who trusts or depends on an institution is sexually violated, it is a leader's job to demonstrate institutional courage. When they refuse to take accountability, leaders demonstrate institutional betrayal and cause further harm for the victim, for the organization, and for themselves.

As described in chapter 2, institutional courage demands a leader show a commitment to seek the truth and to take action on behalf of people who are harmed by others affiliated with the institution. Courageous leaders are forthright, thorough, and fair in handling reports of sexual violence—even when it's unpleasant, difficult, and costly.

Institutional courage is a radical departure from its all-too-common opposite: institutional betrayal. Institutional betrayal can manifest as "looking the other way" instead of delivering consequences to an executive with a reputation for sexual harassment. Or it can be a failure to support the victim, either by passively avoiding the issue in hopes that someone else will deal with it or actively victim blaming.

In the end, institutional betrayal is toxic for everyone: upstanders, people harmed, and leaders. To the extent that people who cause harm wind up causing more and more harm until they wind up in prison, it's even bad for people who cause harm. A 2023 study found that institutional betrayal was associated with decreased job satisfaction and organizational commitment among employees, as well as increased psychological symptoms among victims. Institutional courage was associated with the opposite.

Institutional betrayal is also bad for the institution itself because this response makes it less likely that people will report problems, thus ensuring there will be more victims in the future. The betrayal becomes a cancer where the organization cannot trust its leaders on any ethical issue. It ultimately does far more harm to the institution than a more courageous response in the first place would have done.

Institutional courage isn't just about a forthright response to problems. It's also about being proactive about preventing it from happening in the first place. Actively creating a culture of consent is crucial. You'd think that we have a shared understanding that sexual assault is both illegal and immoral. I thought so too until I worked at a company where a woman was raped and I overheard several of the young men say, "She was so drunk, what did she expect?" They appeared not to know that having sex with an unconscious woman was rape. When I told them and had a lawyer reiterate the facts, they realized they'd better change their behavior. You may not think that educating your employees about consent is part of your job as a leader, but it is.

Making sure nobody at your company, including you, has unchecked authority can also be a deterrent to physical violence. And remember—power doesn't have to be absolute power for it to create the conditions for violence. In 2017, *The New York Times* published a story about a manager at an auto plant who used his power over shift assignments to coerce a woman to have sex with him. When she refused his advances, he assigned her a shift that started before her child's day care opened and then threatened to fire her if she showed up late. This manager deserved to be fired, but that in itself wouldn't solve the problem. When managers have unchecked power, some of them are likely to abuse it, not just this one guy. Checks and balances make sexual violence less likely to happen. But prevention will never be perfect.

When sexual assault happens despite your efforts to prevent it, how can leaders ensure that they respond with institutional courage? Here are some important things leaders can do:

BIAS   PREJUDICE   BULLYING   ⚡   DISCRIMINATION   HARASSMENT | EVERYONE & ——— PHYSICAL VIOLATIONS |

- Find out if your employees trust your reporting systems
- Educate yourself
- Build trusted reporting systems
- Don't hide behind sham investigations
- Don't silence victims
- Don't pass the trash

Find Out If Your Employees Trust Your Reporting Systems

If you want to know if people in your organization trust their leadership to do the right thing if they report sexual harassment or assault in the workplace, conduct an anonymous survey. Psychologists Jennifer Freyd, Carly Smith, and Alec Smidt have designed surveys that measure employee impressions in these areas and allow institutions to use them for free.[5]

If you launch a survey and discover problems in your organization, you need to address these issues or you'll risk making your employees only feel more cynical and beaten down. Lean on your legal team; consult your top executives. If you can afford it, hire a consultant with expertise in these matters.[6]

Educate Yourself

Learn about sexual assault so that you'll know how to respond effectively when, and if, it takes place on your watch. Make sure you understand that victims often react to violence with silence or muted emotions. Don't get fooled by rape myths that cause too many leaders to expect strong emotions from victims.

You're likelier to get a strong emotional response from the accused, who—upon being held accountable for their behavior—often responds with a behavior pattern Jennifer Freyd calls DARVO. DARVO stands for "Deny, Attack, and Reverse Victim and Offender." In this pattern, the accused will aggressively deny the behavior, attack the individual who confronts them, and reverse the roles of victim and offender, such that they assume the victim role (e.g., the role of "falsely accused") and paint the actual victim as a perpetrator of harm. Ashley Judd has explained how DARVO helped Harvey Weinstein get away with sexual predation for years.

Not everyone who DARVOs is guilty. But it's a reminder not to make a decision about innocence or guilt based on the strength of someone's emotional response. To deepen your empathy and understanding of sexual assault, I recommend these resources:

→ *Know My Name* by Chanel Miller. This memoir will help you understand not only how a compassionate response to sexual assault can help victims heal but also how forcing victims to relive their assaults through the investigative and legal processes can be as traumatic or even more traumatic than the incident itself.

→ *Missoula* by Jon Krakauer. Krakauer uses the lens of a mishandled rape case at the University of Montana to examine how leaders and society at large fail to prevent and respond to sexual violence. This book shows the terrible human toll institutional betrayal takes on both victims and the institution itself. Though set in academia, many of Krakauer's conclusions apply to other workplaces.

→ *Not That Bad: Dispatches from Rape Culture*, edited by Roxane Gay. This book brings a variety of different experiences of sexual assault into focus. Many people struggle the most with labeling sexual assault that doesn't fit the typical rape narrative.

→ *Redefining Rape* by Estelle Freedman is a history of how our understanding of what rape is has evolved over time.

→ The Center for Institutional Courage is a research
and education nonprofit, with a primary focus on
institutional courage as a response to sexual violence
across various kinds of institutions (https://www
.institutionalcourage.org/).

Build Trusted Reporting Systems

The Sarbanes-Oxley Act requires that publicly held companies
maintain a system for employees to report matters that might
have a material impact to the audit committee of the board of
directors. Most large companies rely on a third-party system
that provides an anonymous reporting hotline for this purpose.
However, these systems are not designed with sexual misconduct in mind. Leading institutions are investing in systems to
improve their access to sexual misconduct data, which helps
them manage the risk of undetected sexual misconduct in the
workplace.

A number of reporting systems have emerged in just the last
several years to meet this need. What many of these systems
have in common is that they allow people to report incidents
anonymously.

Anonymity is important because it offers some protection
against the way that victims of sexual assault are often re-
traumatized when they report the crime. These systems don't
automatically punish anyone as a result of an anonymous accu-
sation. They simply trigger an investigation. And they can allow
management to notice any pattern of accusations against one
person. A pattern of accusations doesn't mean a person automatically gets fired or punished. It simply means that there's
more to investigate.

Laurie Girand, an expert in sexual violence reporting systems,
explains why being able to report anonymously is so important: "Every person who makes an allegation to any authority

is accountable to someone. Many codes of conduct state that falsifying a report can result in termination. Corporations are not courtrooms. Employment is a contract, and many employees serve 'at will,' until the company decides it no longer needs them. Both the alleged perpetrator and the target are entitled to a fair investigation, but the target and allies assume the greater risk in reporting, which is why they are owed anonymity."

A reporting system that operates on the principle of safety in numbers is often the only way to get people to report. In *She Said*, Jodi Kantor and Megan Twohey describe how it took months for even one of Harvey Weinstein's many victims to be willing to go on the record. Finally, two of them, actor Ashley Judd and former Weinstein assistant Laura Madden, bravely agreed to speak up. As they were preparing to go to the press, *Variety* and *The Hollywood Reporter* reported that *The New York Times* was about to expose Harvey Weinstein as a serial sexual abuser, and suddenly, with that news, the dam broke. "For months the reporters had been pursuing women," Kantor and Twohey write of themselves, "aching for them to speak. Now they were coming to Jodi and Megan like a river suddenly flowing in the opposite direction."

Not every serial rapist has two Pulitzer Prize–winning investigative reporters working for months to make it safe for victims to come forward. If you had a repeat offender in your workplace, wouldn't you want to know? That's where anonymous reporting systems can help identify and prosecute repeat offenders in the workplace.

Don't Hide Behind Sham Investigations

It's painful enough for victims to have to recount their trauma to even a sensitive investigator, but it retraumatizes a victim when the investigation is inconclusive and a sham.

BIAS   PREJUDICE   BULLYING   ⚡ DISCRIMINATION   HARASSMENT   ┌ EVERYONE & ─── PHYSICAL VIOLATIONS ┐

Cover-Up Posing as Investigation

One time, I had an employee who told me that he had had
sex with a woman who was blackout drunk. I told the
general counsel that he had basically told me he had raped
her, as defined in the state where this happened. However,
the "investigator" the company hired to determine what
happened never talked to me. When I asked to speak
with the investigator, the GC told me I couldn't, because
I "should" not have spoken with the employee. He
aggressively implied I'd broken the law. Then my boss
told me I was spending too much time worrying about
"women's issues." Disgusted, I quit. In retrospect, I wish
I had done more to help the woman find justice. We are
still in touch today. She has overcome the trauma of the
incident and prospered in her career. Both of us share a
deep anger that there seems to be no way to bring the
rapist or the company to justice without retraumatizing her.

By protecting an employee who raped a woman
at work, the company's leaders were demonstrating
institutional betrayal—both immoral and impractical. As
a result, they lost several of their top performers. They
opened themselves up to legal liability. They reinforced
their reputation in the market as a bad place for women to
work at a time when they were growing fast and trying to
recruit new employees. These problems eventually hurt the
company's performance.

Don't Silence Victims

It's often said that the cover-up is worse than the crime. This is
true for several reasons. One, cover-ups are profoundly unjust to

the victims. Two, they perpetuate the underlying conditions that allowed the crime to happen, making further sexual violence in your workplace likelier to occur. Three, cover-ups often cause more problems for an organization than the act of holding perpetrators accountable. That's why it's important to not resort to forced arbitration, payoffs, and NDAs to cover up complaints.

Don't Pass the Trash

Far too often, one company fires a person for sexual harassment or even sexual assault in the office, and then a competing firm hires that person. How do companies avoid "passing the trash" to one another? Making it public that you fired someone for sexual harassment is legally fraught. Firms have been sued for millions of dollars for doing this. But if you fire someone and haven't disclosed the information, and the press finds out, you're likely to find yourself in a PR nightmare. What's the way out of this catch-22 for leaders?

Leaders Drive, Lawyers Advise

Tom Schievelbein, a retired CEO of several large corporations, had a practical solution. When there was irrefutable evidence that sexual harassment or assault had occurred in the office, he sent an internal email explaining why the person was no longer at the company. His lawyers tried to talk him out of doing this, but he reminded the lawyers that he was driving the bus; their job was to point out obstacles and to tell him how to get around them but not to tell him where to go or how to get there.

Sending the email around to employees was important for two reasons. One, it sent a strong message: that kind of behavior would have real consequences. Usually many people knew about the behavior, and it was important to demonstrate that action had been taken. Two, it helped with the "passing the trash" problem. Usually when companies hire someone, they do back-channel reference checks. Since a number of people knew what had happened, the reason someone was fired would come out in the interview process.

If you are hiring someone, be rigorous about asking questions about a history of sexual harassment when checking references. And obviously, don't just call the names the applicants supply. If it's a senior hire, don't just talk to people at the person's level. Find out what the person's former employees have to say. This is a good practice to find out what people are really like, what their reputation is, and how they treat the people they oversee—and whether there is a history of sexual harassment or misconduct.

If you have fired someone and another company does a reference check, push yourself to operate higher than the moral standards required by law. The law does not require disclosure of the person's behavior and may in fact punish disclosure. Yet you can do things to make sure sexual predators don't simply get hired by other companies. Investigate ethical and legal disclosures of internal findings regarding sexual violence.

5. ALCOHOL IN THE WORKPLACE

Ask ten people to think of a sexual encounter with a work colleague they later regretted. Now ask them if alcohol was involved. I bet you'll find that, nine times out of ten, it was. Perpetrators must be held accountable for their actions whether they are drunk or sober. Blaming alcohol rather than the person is an unacceptable abdication of personal responsibility. But that doesn't mean it makes sense to booze it up on the job.

This section may seem strange to you if you are not familiar with the boozy workplace culture I experienced in finance and in tech. I spent most of my career in Silicon Valley, where there is a great deal of alcohol, and often drugs, in the office. The company chef at one place where I worked routinely made hash brownies. In the middle of another office where I worked was a bar stocked with high-end spirits and fine wine. I worked at two different companies that had regular lunchtime kegs. This kind of behavior, while shocking to some, is routine in many industries around the world.

Early in my career, I loved the heavy-drinking culture at many of the companies where I've worked. Looking back on it, though, I don't think the fun of those boozy office parties was even remotely worth the harm that was done by them. Here are some of the things I've seen happen, fueled by alcohol at work events: a rape in the office, a suicide attempt, a marriage destroyed by unwanted sexual advances, a drunk engineer shat himself on a company bus, security called me at home at 3:00 a.m. when they found one of my employees passed out drunk in the office, keyboards and computers ruined by a drunk person's vomit, and a drunk colleague getting hauled off from a company off-site to jail after punching a cop.

It would be denial to say that alcohol in the workplace doesn't greatly increase the likelihood of everything from an unwanted, creepy hug to sexual violence. Drinking at work or at work functions is undeniably risky—for the employees, for their peers, for their boss, and for the company. I don't recommend it. But if you're going to do it anyway, here's how I recommend managing it, depending on your role.

FOR PEOPLE HARMED

If this were a just world, you'd be able to pass out drunk and be safe. The first person who saw you would make sure you were okay, not rape you. If you get drunk, even blackout drunk, this does not give anyone the right to harm you. If you get blackout drunk and are raped, it is the fault of the person who harmed you, full stop.

But even if it's not your fault, you're still the one who gets hurt. So if you love to drink, and/or you work in a culture where drinking to excess is part of how people bond, it's a good idea to think explicitly about how you are going to manage the risks.

I'm not telling you that you should or shouldn't drink. That's your decision. But whatever you decide to do, understand the risks. You may think you're safe with people you work with, but people you know are statistically riskier than strangers. So it behooves you to plan.

If you go out drinking, go with people you trust and have some explicit agreement to keep an eye on one another. Make sure there's a designated driver who also plays the role of designated decider. That way, there's always a sober person to keep you, or at least deter you, from doing anything you'll regret later.

FOR PEOPLE WHO CAUSE HARM

Drinking impairs your judgment, just as it impairs your ability to drive safely. Your friends may be able to take your car keys away, but they can't take your sex drive away. Can you trust yourself not to harm another person when you've been drinking?

Alcohol poses another risk as well. If the person you want to have sex with is drunk, the person may be too impaired to give consent. If you have sex anyway, in most jurisdictions, you are committing rape. What's more, you may be too impaired to judge accurately whether the person has given consent or not. But you are still guilty if you push someone to have sex when the person is too drunk to give consent—just as you are still guilty of drunk driving even if your judgment was so impaired by alcohol that you drove despite your intoxication. So make a plan *before* you go out drinking for how you are going to manage all these risks.

If you're under twenty-four, this is especially important. You're likelier to engage in risky behaviors, and that likelihood is more pronounced when you are with peers or friends.

Follow the advice of Rob Chesnut, former chief ethics officer at Airbnb and author of *Intentional Integrity*. He warns employees, "If you wait to think about how much you are going to drink until you're at the party, you're in trouble. Know your limits and decide how many drinks you can have—one or two—before you go. The worst time to think about how much to drink in a work setting is . . . while you're drinking in a work setting."

BIAS   PREJUDICE   BULLYING   ⚡   DISCRIMINATION   HARASSMENT | EVERYONE & PHYSICAL VIOLATIONS |

FOR LEADERS

I would recommend not allowing alcohol in the workplace at all. Creating a culture of workplace partying is a recipe for everything from awkwardness to disaster. Even workplaces that limit alcohol to special celebrations often find that bad things happen on these occasions.

If you do serve alcohol, remind people to drink responsibly. Don't worry about being the literal buzzkill. Nothing ruins a celebration like a drunk person assaulting a colleague or killing themselves or others in a preventable car accident.

If you want to prevent these sorts of things from happening on your team, it is your job as a leader to calculate the benefits of alcohol as a social lubricant against the risks that too much of it can lead to seriously bad behavior.

Another important thing for leaders to know is that a heavy-drinking culture often creates a hostile work environment for historically disadvantaged people, especially women. Vanessa Kaskiris, who worked in the IT department at UC Berkeley, described "a culture where employees would go out drinking every night, which led to hostile treatment of women if they went, and ostracization if they didn't."

Also, let's not forget people who don't drink, for a variety of reasons. For some, a work culture revolving around alcohol may be uncomfortable because their religion forbids alcohol. Some people have a terrible physical reaction to alcohol and are likely to wind up ill after only a few drinks. And if you have a person struggling with alcoholism or in early recovery or sobriety, such a culture can be more than insensitive; it's dangerous.

Leaders can avoid a lot of problems by not serving alcohol or making explicit policies that limit alcohol consumption at the office. How stringent you make these policies is up to you. Here are some ways I've seen leaders discourage destructive drinking at office events:

→ Don't serve alcohol.
→ Serve alcohol but make sure people have to give a ticket to get a drink and give everyone only one or two tickets.
→ Instruct bartenders to cut people off at two drinks.
→ Let people drink as much as they want but issue warnings. You may think that these warnings are simply common sense, but people lose their common sense when they are drunk. So if you are serving alcohol at work, remind your employees of the following:

  » Don't drink and drive.
  » You are still accountable for the things you do, even when you're too drunk to know what you're doing. You can't read the signs of consent when you're drunk. And "I was too drunk to know what I was doing" is not an excuse for rape any more than it is for drunk driving.
  » Getting drunk in the office or at office parties can be career limiting.
  » Don't have sex with colleagues who are too drunk to give consent no matter where you are—that is rape.

You probably have more important things to do than manage your team's drinking habits. My advice? Keep it simple. Don't serve alcohol at work.

Notes

1. You may be wondering why I feel so strongly that it is wrong to refuse to meet with one gender but not such a big deal to shake hands with one gender. In fact, I believe that if he didn't shake women's hands, it would only be fair if he didn't shake men's hands either. But in this case, the "don't touch if the person doesn't want to be touched" principle seemed more salient. I was initiating the touch, so it was my job to back off in a way that made him feel comfortable. Also, refusing to meet one-on-one disadvantages the people you're not meeting with more than refusing to shake their hand. However, if we'd been onstage and he refused to shake my hand but shook the hands of the men, that would have been problematic, though not as disgusting as having my hand slobbered on.

2. The following resources offer education about emotionally abusive relationships: "10 Signs of an Unhealthy Relationship," One Love Foundation, accessed August 13, 2023, https://www.joinonelove.org/; "Types of Abuse." Love Is Respect, accessed August 13, 2023, https://www.loveisrespect.org/resources/types-of-abuse/?fbclid =IwAR3oCz0WPASoM_tYwwfYbI3SqNxLtCtFo0KHVeifu0eFWknIVoqeOZC sQAk; Anne Pietrangelo and Crystal Raypole, "How to Recognize the Signs of Emotional Abuse," Healthline, July 13, 2023, https://www.healthline.com/health/signs -of-mental-abuse; "What Are the Signs of an Emotionally Abusive Boss?," Eddy Marban Law, December 31, 2018, https://eddymarbanlaw.com/blog/emotionally -abusive-boss/.

3. Per the Rape, Abuse & Incest National Network (RAINN): "Sexual violence is notoriously difficult to measure, and there is no single source of data that provides a complete picture of the crime. On RAINN's website, we have tried to select the most reliable source of statistics for each topic. The primary data source we use is the National Crime Victimization Survey (NCVS), which is an annual study conducted by the Justice Department. To conduct NCVS, researchers interview tens of thousands of Americans each year to learn about crimes that they've experienced. Based on those interviews, the study provides estimates of the total number of crimes, including those that were not reported to police."

4. You can read more about what a sexual assault forensic exam means, how to prepare, and what to avoid doing before you have the exam here: "RAINN: What Is a Sexual Assault Forensic Exam?," RAINN, accessed June 22, 2020, https://www .rainn.org/articles/rape-kit.

5. The Institutional Courage Questionnaire (ICQ) can be accessed at https://dynamic .uoregon.edu/jjf/institutionalbetrayal/icq.html. The Institutional Betrayal Questionnaire (IBQ) can be accessed at https://dynamic.uoregon.edu/jjf/institutionalbetrayal /ibq.html.

6. Many great consultants work in sexual violence prevention and response. The team I know best and admire enormously is that at the Center for Institutional Courage. Their website will orient you to resources for creating change: https://www.institutionalcourage.org/resources-for-changemakers.

CHEAT SHEET

CULTURE
OF CONSENT

If the other person doesn't want
to be touched, don't touch.
If there is any doubt, don't touch.

PHYSICAL VIOLATIONS

Touch + Power,
resulting in everything from an
unwanted hug to violence

TRUSTED
REPORTING SYSTEMS

Make it safe to report
anonymously. Build a fair
investigation process.

11

A Letter to My Younger Self and Her Boss

Using the Toxonomy to Stay Oriented in a Disorienting Situation

My first job out of college was so deeply disorienting that I had to write this book to make sense of it. The problems I experienced felt monolithic, but I can now understand that it was actually six different problems. As I tell the story, I'll use the toxonomy to highlight whether it was bias, prejudice, bullying, discrimination, verbal harassment, or a physical violation. I'll also describe the dynamics between them, which made the whole situation more confusing, and how the management systems that my leaders created and failed to create reinforced these bad dynamics.

The Salary Negotiation

I was thrilled to get my first "real" job after college. I had studied arms control in college, and now that the Berlin Wall had fallen, I was interested in the peace dividend. These were pretty wonky interests, though, so when I got a job with the Soviet Companies Fund investing US pension fund money in Soviet defense factories converting to civilian production, I couldn't believe my luck.

Shortly after I took this job, a friend of mine in a similar job told me she was being paid *four* times more than I was. My friend explained her salary was the market rate, what the guys got paid. I was being dramatically underpaid. My first experience of wage **discrimination**.

BIAS   PREJUDICE   BULLYING   ⚡ | DISCRIMINATION | HARASSMENT   PHYSICAL VIOLATIONS

When I told my boss, Harry, what I'd learned about the market rate for my salary, he denied it, saying, "You're getting paid fairly." When I shared what my friend's salary was, he went on the attack: "She must be sleeping with her boss!" I could tell he didn't really believe what he'd said, and I said so. He was just trying to shut me up—a form of **bullying**. And when I pressed the matter, Harry acted as though he were the victim and I was putting him in an unreasonably difficult position with Robert, the CEO. My first experience with another form of bullying, DARVO (Deny, Attack, Reverse Victim and Offender).

BIAS   PREJUDICE | BULLYING | ⚡ DISCRIMINATION   HARASSMENT   PHYSICAL VIOLATIONS

A legend in our business, Robert was known equally for his success as a contrarian investor and his explosive personality. Harry certainly didn't think I'd talk to Robert myself. He was wrong about that.

I realized that I could not rely on my boss to speak for me. I was going to have to advocate for myself. At the first opportunity, I asked Robert for a meeting and soon found myself facing him in a conference room. He was seated comfortably in an armchair. Something about his big belly and unruly white hair gave him a benevolent appearance, like Santa Claus. He motioned toward a small wooden chair opposite him. At first, he was genial, if patronizing. "You know that our Russian partners call you my secret weapon." He laughed uproariously, and I tried to laugh along, not quite sure what was so funny. It seemed like he was insulting me. "You are a real pistol!" My first experience with **biased** compliment syndrome. Only I didn't know what that was, so I was knocked off-kilter by it. How was I supposed to respond?

BIAS | PREJUDICE BULLYING ⚡ DISCRIMINATION HARASSMENT PHYSICAL VIOLATIONS

Weird as this situation was, I wasn't going to let the way Robert talked to me deter me from talking about what I'd come to talk about. When I raised the issue of my salary, the shift was immediate: Santa Claus was gone. Now he resembled a bird of prey swooping in for the kill. His piercing glare and furrowed gray eyebrows made it clear that he wasn't used to being challenged, especially not by the likes of me. He stared at me unblinkingly for what seemed like several minutes.

"I don't know what makes you think you're underpaid, but I can assure you it wouldn't be fair to the others if we paid you more," he said with a note of finality, and put his hands on the arms of the chair as if he were about to get up. There it was, DARVO, again: denying and going on the attack. Only I didn't know what DARVO was, so I was left feeling unsure of myself. But I had come prepared with data about my peers and average salaries in the industry, and I forced myself to put my evidence forward.

My data just pissed him off. Robert was *really* angry, almost unhinged. He was pale, literally trembling with rage. "If I paid you that much, you'd make more than my daughter makes. I know you don't want to come between me and my daughter." Reversing victim and offender . . .

This non sequitur was so egregious that I didn't even bother pointing out that his daughter was a teacher and that the solution to not paying teachers enough wasn't to lower the salaries of women (but not men) in finance. I didn't dare say anything because the intensity of Robert's self-righteousness was frightening. He was angry and sad that his daughter was underpaid and implied I was trying to come between him and his daughter by asking to be paid fairly myself. The conversation ended abruptly.

I couldn't believe he was that irrational, so I questioned myself. What had I done wrong? What had I failed to understand? Unfortunately, DARVO works, unless you know how to confront it—which I did not. Instead, I tried not to think about the issue of pay **discrimination** anymore.

BIAS   PREJUDICE   BULLYING   ⚡ ⏐ DISCRIMINATION ⏐ HARASSMENT   PHYSICAL VIOLATIONS

An Abuse of Power

Meantime, I was working all the time and increasingly isolated from anyone outside of work. Our team spent most of our time in Moscow collaborating with our Soviet partners. While in Moscow, we lived and worked together in a big house provided to the project by the Soviet Ministry of Defense.

My boss, Harry, and I were frequently traveling together all over Russia and Ukraine all the time, eating most of our meals together. Harry confided to me that he had a serious and chronic medical condition and feared that he might not live much past forty. I started to worry about him. One night, after we'd been up late working on some financial projections, he kissed me—and promptly burst into tears. He told me he was a virgin and deeply afraid that he would die that way. I made sure that he didn't. I thought that since this was consensual, it wasn't any sort of **physical violation**. I didn't understand what an abuse of power this was.

BIAS   PREJUDICE   BULLYING   ⚡   DISCRIMINATION   HARASSMENT | PHYSICAL VIOLATIONS |

When Robert heard about our relationship, he told Harry to inform me that I had to move out of the corporate housing in Moscow. Harry complied, even though he knew it was illegal for Americans to sublet apartments in the USSR. Knowing that Harry was not a good advocate for me, I again talked to Robert myself. "Russia is a sexist society," Robert told me. "I am worried the Soviet government will think we are not using the house appropriately if there are young women living in it." It was **discrimination,** using cultural sensitivity to someone else's **prejudices** as a rationalization.

BIAS | PREJUDICE | BULLYING   ⚡ | DISCRIMINATION | HARASSMENT   PHYSICAL VIOLATIONS

I was almost incapacitated by rage. Robert was putting me in harm's way by making me rent an apartment. Not only did I now have to find an illegal sublet on my own in Soviet Moscow, but the US embassy had recently issued an alert that the metro was considered unsafe for Americans. Since Moscow had no reliable taxi service, I would have to hail down random cars to get to and from work; a friend of mine had recently been forced to jump from a speeding car when the driver she'd hailed decided to make a detour through a deserted park.

Speaking up felt futile, though, so I just put my head down, and I rented an apartment from a babushka needing some extra money, took my chances with transport, and tried not to think about how unfair and dangerous the situation was.

I broke up with Harry. Unfortunately, I was still in love with him, he was still my boss, and we were in a small office together all day every day and late into the night. We often worked eighty-hour weeks, so I rarely saw my friends any longer. I was drinking too much, not sleeping enough, and falling into a depression.

Sleeping with my boss was a big mistake. I own it. Well, half of it. Problem was, I paid for *all* of it. That's what usually happens in such situations. This was an example of how an **abuse of power** (our relationship) can lead to **discrimination** (me being excluded from the major expat perk that the firm offered its American employees working in Moscow). Plus I was now at greater risk of attack on my way to and from work. I was learning something about the **dynamic between abuse, discrimination, and violence.**

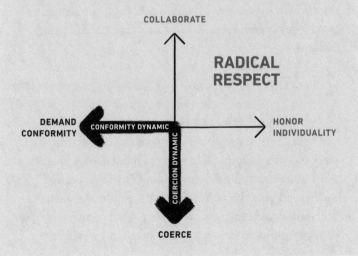

The Chief of Staff

Robert wasn't a super sensitive kind of leader, but even he could see that there was a lot of tension on the team. So he sent Peter, his chief of staff, to provide "adult supervision" in Moscow. Peter said he had a lot of influence with Robert and asked what he could do to improve the situation for us. I told Peter about how dramatically I was underpaid. He responded sympathetically and suggested we discuss it over dinner. I agreed and felt a flicker of hope: perhaps things might work out, after all. A few hours later, he told me that he'd been unable to get a reservation at the restaurant he had in mind, so he'd just bring the food over to my apartment. This felt off to me, but I didn't know how to say no.

Peter arrived with the food, and as we sat down across from each other at the dining table, he once again expressed sympathy for my position. This was a stressful industry, he said. Stress was hard for women. I said I didn't think it was any harder on women than on men. He said he thought it was. He wouldn't want his sister to find herself in my situation. Trying to rebuff this **prejudice**, I said I didn't feel stressed, but I *was* angry about being underpaid.

BIAS [PREJUDICE] BULLYING ⚡ DISCRIMINATION HARASSMENT PHYSICAL VIOLATIONS

Peter nodded, but his tone began to change as he told me that he'd grown up in a country where virtually everyone was underpaid, in ways I couldn't even imagine as an American. I didn't know about DARVO, but I understood what he was doing—trying to make me feel guilty about asking for more money when so many people in the world were so much worse off than I was. I also knew he was being hypocritical since he was making probably twenty times my salary. My peers who were men were making twice my salary, but he would never have given them a guilt trip. Even though I knew all this, his ploy worked. I felt pushy, greedy.

Before I knew what was happening, he had come over to my side of the table and started massaging my shoulders from behind. This was a **physical violation**, but I didn't know how to respond. I just sat there: tense, paralyzed, and creeped out.

BIAS   PREJUDICE   BULLYING   ⚡   DISCRIMINATION   HARASSMENT | PHYSICAL VIOLATIONS |

People often criticize women for not immediately leaving situations such as this. But this was one of the top guys in the company. He had what seemed like unlimited power over me. He was also in my apartment. Where was I going to go?

It only took Peter about thirty seconds—an extremely long and uncomfortable thirty seconds—to reach over my shoulder and touch my breast. *That* spurred me into action. I jumped up, grabbed my keys, opened the door to my apartment, and ran down the stairs out into the street. I looked over my shoulder to make sure he wasn't following. As I strode along in the cold Moscow night air, I laughed to myself, thinking how foolish he must feel all by himself in my apartment. I marveled at how much safer I felt alone at night on the streets of Moscow than in my own home with an executive at the company where I worked.

Needless to say, the raise didn't happen. But one good thing did happen. Peter was, I think, deeply embarrassed about having been abandoned in my apartment. He took the next flight out, declaring that Moscow was too cold for him.

Which Ballerina?

The next time Robert came to Russia, he told my colleagues and me about going to the Bolshoi Ballet with some of our company's Soviet partners.

"So, the ballet is finally over, and Vladimir leans over and whispers, 'Robert, do you like ballerinas?'"

Robert mimicked how he felt taken aback by the question and said, "Sure."

"But, Robert," the Russian factory director leer-whispered, "*which* ballerina?"

Robert looked around at us—three young men and me—with raised, wildly bushy eyebrows. "He was offering to deliver the ballerina of my choice to my hotel room!"

The young men were impressed. I was horrified. Surely this was a measure of immorality, not power?

Robert seemed to think he'd done enough by not availing himself of the offer. Robert is no hero in this story, but I do know he and my colleagues shared my belief that human trafficking was immoral. Yet nobody said a damn word—including me. Robert turned the whole thing into a "funny" anecdote, as if laughing at the situation made the whole thing not quite real. This is how denial, the silence of the bystander, works.

In retrospect, it would've been much better if I'd spoken up at Robert's story about the ballerinas. A common way that denial reinforces a default to silence is to whisper, "Oh, don't exaggerate. It's not that bad." That is dangerous. I had read the unabridged *Gulag Archipelago*, 1,400 pages outlining precisely how bad things could get. But, I told myself, that explanation of atrocities was a book, not real life. It was written way back in 1973. Now it was 1991. Surely we had moved on from that. *Nope!*

Yes, it's not a good idea to exaggerate how bad things are. And it's an even worse idea to ignore blatantly immoral behavior. You don't want to be the boy who cried wolf. But it's even riskier to be the boy who pretended the wolf wasn't there when it was clearly stalking you or people close to you.

Most of the onus was on Robert as the CEO to exercise his responsibility as a leader and to confront our partner directly, rather than making a joke of this to his young employees. But it was also my job, and also the job of my peers to be upstanders, to intervene in some way, not to default to silence. When we failed to do that, we failed to stand up for what we believed in, for the better world we believed we were there to help create, and we failed ourselves—failed to become the good people we aspired to be.

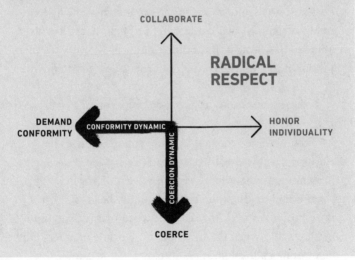

Harassing Harry and Frotting Fred

Since Peter didn't work out, Robert sent Fred, one of his close friends, to manage our team. This was a good thing because it meant Harry and I didn't have to travel alone together any longer. Fred also decided that I would now work for Steve, not for Harry. Also a good thing. When I told Fred how little I was paid, he'd gotten me a raise. I was now being paid twice as much—so only 50 percent below market. Progress, if not ideal. He became a trusted mentor.

One evening, I was sitting in the lobby of a hotel where we were staying on a business trip, reading the newspaper. Harry walked by and snatched the paper from my hands, announcing, "Directors read before analysts." He'd taken to petty acts all the time. Consensual relationships in which one person has positional power over another (e.g., one person is the boss of the other) often become psychologically abusive, especially after they end. My breakup with Harry was no exception. If he'd been my peer, this would have been bullying. But since he had been my boss and was senior to me in the organization, he had an unfair advantage that made it hard to fight back. It crossed a line to harassment. But I didn't have this framework then. I thought this was just what I got for sleeping with my boss.

BIAS   PREJUDICE   BULLYING   ⚡   DISCRIMINATION | HARASSMENT | PHYSICAL VIOLATIONS

Fred observed the incident and followed me to the elevator. "He was really nasty back there," Fred said, with just enough sympathy to make my tears of anger well up. I was counting by prime numbers in my head to control my emotions, a trick that I had learned from a high school math teacher when I'd asked her how prime numbers might be of practical benefit in real life.

Fred held out his arms for a hug. Partly because I trusted him and partly because a hug would prevent him from seeing me cry, I walked into his arms. Next thing I knew, he was grinding his erect penis into me. Mercifully, the elevator door opened; I ducked under his arm and darted out. I've rarely felt so alone or under siege. But I put the whole thing out of my mind.[1] I felt I didn't have a "real" **physical violation** to complain about since he hadn't pursued me off the elevator and tried to rape me.

BIAS   PREJUDICE   BULLYING   ⚡ DISCRIMINATION   HARASSMENT   [PHYSICAL VIOLATIONS]

Did I talk to my friends or family about what had happened? I did not. I feared that the situation with Harry would come back to bite me. I was afraid that people would say that Fred and Peter knew about Harry and would speculate that if I'd dated Harry, I must be open to dating other coworkers. Yet I also knew these absurd insinuations would somehow work, like Robert's gaslighting me about my salary. It was a fight I was unlikely to win.

I was afraid that if I talked to others, not only would my character be questioned, so would my competence. One of the first things that people say to women reporting sexual misconduct is "Make sure your performance is beyond reproach." Despite how I was being treated, I had done good work. But, let's face it, almost nobody could do their best work when being treated that way. I was no exception. I was not doing my very best work. But rather than acknowledging that I would hardly be "playing the victim" if I attributed some of that to my circumstances, I blamed myself.

The Upstander

A few weeks after this, Robert came to Moscow with
Emmett, who was a partner at the firm. I noticed that
Emmett was reading a worn copy of *Pride and Prejudice*.
Seeing him reading one of my favorite novels made me
decide to open up and try to have a conversation with him.

We bonded over fiction and moved on to reality.
Emmett agreed with me that my salary was still unfair.
He also told me he was horrified that I had been thrown
out of the company housing. "Seems like Harry should've
been the one to go," he muttered. He told me he'd already
brought it up with Robert, but to no avail. Even though
his intervention didn't improve my pay or my housing, it
meant a lot. He'd validated my sense of injustice. Emmett
was a real lifeline. I'd routinely been awakened at 3:00 a.m.
by all the thoughts and anger I'd repressed all day long:
Was *I* the one being irrational, or were these men I was
working with the irrational ones? Knowing that someone
saw things the way I did helped me sleep through the
night.

The Exit Option

Finally, I decided my best option was to get the hell out of
there and find a new job. Emmett introduced me to people
at a different firm. They offered me a job—at a market
salary. I gave notice.

Two things happened that surprised me. First, when I
told my friend, the one who had initially told me what my
salary should be, about my new job, *her* boss called me up
and chastised me for not telling him I was looking. I had
felt more trapped than I was. Second, Robert wanted to
talk to me when he heard I was quitting.

Once again, Robert reacted angrily, calling me disloyal.

And once again, I found myself speechless. What I wanted to say was, "What in the hell did you give me to be loyal to? You treated human trafficking as though it's a joke, you underpaid me, you yelled at me when I asked for a raise, and you created an environment in which it was safe for your executives to grab my boob and grind their dicks into me on the elevator but not safe for me to report it!"

I didn't say any of that—in part because it was so deeply ingrained in me not to use those sorts of words, especially not at work. I could imagine all too well the kind of self-righteous shaming I'd get from Robert if I accurately described what had happened. Fred and Peter would not be held accountable.

Anticipation of that kind of shaming silenced me about the real issues. I simply said, "Robert, they are paying me twice what you paid me."

"So it's all about the money for you, is it?" Robert replied as though he thought he could **bully** me into not quitting. As if his own career in finance hadn't been motivated by the desire to make money. As if I were some sort of gold digger expecting to earn a market salary.

BIAS   PREJUDICE   [BULLYING]⚡   DISCRIMINATION   HARASSMENT   PHYSICAL VIOLATIONS

In my next job, I was able to do my best work. I created a business that was on a $100-million-per-year run rate within two years. I believe that better working conditions were critical to that success. If Robert had created a Radically Respectful rather than a Brutally Ineffective work culture, it might have been one of the best investments he ever made. This is a universe-through-a-grain-of-sand way of explaining why diverse, well-functioning teams are as good for business as they are for justice.

And there is more to the story here. Years later at Fred's funeral, I heard Robert joke about Fred's "pecker problem." I actually think that Fred needed help, and Robert's denial was a form of codependence. Many who read drafts of this book warned me that any mention of "sex addiction" would likely let people like Fred off the hook too easily. But it is my feeling that Fred had a problem he was ashamed of. If that were the case, Robert would've been a better friend to acknowledge it and help him than to retreat to jokes and denial. That would have been kinder to Fred, and it also would have been a hell of a lot better for me if Fred had gotten help for his compulsive behavior.

Advice to My Younger Self

If I could go back in time, here's what I'd tell my younger self.

1. Document
   Write this shit down! Keeping a journal will help dispel some of the gaslighting. Stop working so much that you don't have time to write in your journal, which was always a source of solace. Don't abandon that just when you need it most.

2. Build solidarity
   Good job building solidarity with friends outside of work, and learning about market salaries! And good job building solidarity with Emmett.

But don't get so busy at work that you neglect your friends. Don't isolate yourself or feel afraid to talk to your friends and family. You need solidarity. Pick your head up; don't put it down. It's time to work less and take care of yourself more. You are not going to get rewarded for your hard work, no matter how well you do in this job.

If you'd spent more time with your friends and less time at work, when you were contemplating having an affair with your boss, they would no doubt have warned you, *NO NO NO!* Writing this now is kind of like watching one of those horror movies where you're yelling at the screen, *Don't go down into that basement!* I know you really believe that his positional power over you didn't matter. You thought that since you cared about him it didn't matter that he was your boss. I wish you hadn't had to learn the hard way why not to sleep with your boss. . . . But cut yourself some slack. You were young, alone in Moscow, and working all the time.

3. Locate the exit nearest you
   Ask your friend if her company is hiring *before* raising the salary issue with Harry or Robert. It's always a good idea to know what one's BATNA (best alternative to a negotiated agreement) is *before* a negotiation.

   You are not as trapped as you feel. If you're working so hard in a job you hate that you don't have time to look for other jobs, ask friends or family if they can float you for a few months, and quit even before you've found another job. That is not asking for charity. It is asking for an investment in you.

   As the story progressed, the tone of this advice would shift from "Don't forget to quit!" to "GET OUT!"

4. Talk directly with the person who caused you harm
Good for you for realizing that you needed to go to Robert
directly, that your boss was not a good advocate for you.
Yes, in theory, it might've been better if you'd gone into
the conversation with a job offer in your back pocket. But
I get it why you didn't have the energy to go get another
job offer; the one you had kept you plenty busy. And the
job market for Americans in Moscow in 1991 was not
robust. Getting this job had felt like a miracle. I admire the
boldness with Robert. I just wish you'd had a job offer in
hand so you could've quit sooner.

   I know this exchange left you feeling not only off-kilter
but also weak for feeling off-kilter. Cut yourself some
slack. Of course you felt off-kilter. That doesn't mean
you're weak. Almost anyone in your shoes would've felt
that way. Take the time to document what happened,
continue building solidarity with friends by talking about
it, and explore other job opportunities. You'll feel like
you're on more solid ground.

5. Report to HR
You were right that reporting Harry, Peter, and Fred to HR
would likely have gotten you fired. Robert was the firm's
founder, CEO, and majority shareholder. Fred was his
good friend, and Peter was his chief of staff. HR was in his
pocket. He had given you every reason to think HR would
not be open to any report of their behavior. There were no
checks on his power.

   But, if you had another offer, that wouldn't have
mattered. And reporting to HR would have created a
record that could have been helpful in a lawsuit, since
HR was unlikely to respond in the way they were legally
required to. And it would have helped in writing this

story. Wouldn't you like to have seen how HR would've responded?

6. Take legal action
   Yes, this is not a fair fight. You have no money. Robert has not one but two private jets. You are working in Russia, and calling the States is expensive and difficult. But a law firm would take the case on commission. And your father is a lawyer. You are not helpless. In fact, you have privilege, and you can use it to make the world a little more fair.

7. Tell your story publicly
   Better late than never! This was 1991, well before #MeToo. It was inconceivable to you that anyone would listen. But I do wish now you'd written all this down then. It would be really interesting to read.

Advice to a Younger Harry

Sleeping with your employees is an abuse of power. You must quit this job and get another one now that you've slept with her.

Much later, Harry told me that he had wanted to hire me not because he really thought they needed an analyst but because he wanted to date me. And he'd pitched Robert on the idea by telling him what a low salary I would accept.

Oh, Harry! You could have simply asked me out. I was lonely, knowing few people in Moscow. I would have happily gone on a date with you. And then I would've gotten a job working with my friend. That would've been so much easier for everyone. If you want to date someone, date them. If you want to hire someone, hire them.

Advice to a Younger Robert

Create some checks and balances at your company so that someone will tell you the truth about your behavior.

- Ask your CFO to benchmark salaries and come up with a transparent pay scale rather than paying people as little as you could possibly get away with.
- Find a good therapist. You have some anger management issues, among others.
- You are probably saying, "How was I supposed to know what Peter and Fred were doing?" The problem was that there was nobody safe for her to tell because you had unchecked authority at the firm.
- Conduct a proper exit interview with her to learn from your mistakes.
- Create a culture of consent.
- Put in place a "no dating in your chain of command" rule and enforce it.
- Allow Kim to stay where it is safe, make Harry move out of the housing, and strip him of his management responsibilities. Or simply fire him.
- Put a trusted reporting mechanism in place.

I'd like to think some young people today would feel safe responding differently if they experienced what I did in my first job. It still wouldn't be easy, though. These things still happen, and they are still hard to respond to. I do think that taking legal action and telling the story publicly are courses of action more open to people today than they were in 1990. But those are both hard rows to hoe, even today.

If you are in a swirl of discrimination, abuse, and physical violations—whether these problems have their roots in gender, race, sexual orientation, religion, regional biases, class, or other biases that plague humanity—you have my compassion and my solidarity. I hope that reading my story can help you find compassion for yourself—and figure out how to respond in a way that gets you to a safer, better place so that you can use your talents to build a better life for yourself and a better world for others.

I also like to think that a young manager today would do better than my boss did and better than his boss did. However, as I learned when I was CEO, being a good person is not enough. Leaders must design systems to prevent these things from happening, and to make it likelier that employees can pull a kind of fairness "kanban cord"[2] about the bias, prejudice, bullying, discrimination, harassment, and physical violations that may be happening on your team, despite your best efforts to prevent them.

Notes

1. To those who haven't been in my situation, and even to those who have, my response may seem inexplicable. Yet repressing awareness of what is happening is a common psychological response to being betrayed by someone you trust. Psychologist Jennifer Freyd writes about this beautifully in her book *Blind to Betrayal*. (purple flag!)

2. A kanban cord can be pulled by any worker to stop an assembly line when a flaw is noticed so that the flaw can be immediately addressed instead of getting baked into the product. Imagine a car being assembled. It's much cheaper to stop the assembly line and remove a faulty brake pad right away than to finish assembling the whole car and then take it back apart to fix the brake pad—and far, far better to stop the line and fix the brake pad than to ship the car with the faulty brake pad and risk killing your customer.

12

Put Some Wins on the Board

Have you ever worked somewhere where everything felt more or less right? Where your boss was fair and reasonable, your colleagues respectful, and the atmosphere conducive to doing your best work? Where there were real efforts to prevent bias, prejudice, bullying, discrimination, harassment, physical violations—and a response of institutional courage when they did happen? What was it like? Even if you've never had the experience, dream a little. What *would* it be like?

People often ask me, "What company is getting this right?" No single company or organization is perfect. But many have great practices that I've mentioned in this book. All of us can learn to do better. While none of us have experienced utopia, most of us have had many glimpses of what a radically respectful workplace could be like. Let's bring those glimpses into focus.

Let me share one anecdote about a job I had shortly after the experience described in the previous chapter. This was the moment when I realized that things could be different at work.

Not Doing It for the Data

I was a consultant, working at a steel mill. One of my tasks was to get some data from the mill's sole database administrator. (This was 1995.) He kept telling me tomorrow and tomorrow and tomorrow. Then one night, he showed up at my hotel with the data, insisting he come up to my room to give it to me. "I'm not doing it for the data," I told him.

The next day, I told my boss the story, proud of my clever quip. I had learned to distance myself from this kind of behavior by pretending it was just a funny anecdote.[1] Of course, it was also seriously infuriating in the moment, doubly so as the incident also resurrected past traumas. He did not treat it like a funny anecdote. He took it seriously. He offered to fire the client. When I said I was comfortable continuing to work there, he reported the incident to the mill's CEO, and there were consequences for the database administrator. That was the first time I realized that I wasn't on my own in fighting sexual harassment, that I was working for a company that demonstrated institutional courage. It felt as though someone came along and picked up a burden I hadn't been aware I was carrying. That was more motivating than any bonus plan could possibly have been.

Here's another example. The first few years I spent working at Google were the closest thing to Radical Respect that I had ever experienced in my career. It's important to acknowledge that not everyone had a radically respectful experience at Google even in the early days. Since then, the company has made some decisions that feel really wrong to me. Things were and are not perfect at Google.

But I had a great experience, and I'd like to share it. If we are going to move toward Radical Respect without succumbing to cynicism and despair, we need to celebrate the wins. So I'd like to end with a description of my experience at Google in 2004 and the lessons I learned from it.

Radical Respect Is More Successful—and More Fun

In an environment where I felt secure, comfortable, and on an equal footing with my colleagues, I was able to do some of the best work of my life. I brought everything I had to that job. My team and I delivered on my promise to "defy the law of large numbers." We increased our revenue ten times while actually shrinking costs. We built an extremely profitable, fast-growing business. And we had a lot of fun doing it, building relationships that have endured to this day. I loved my work and my team; we accomplished a great deal together.

Radical Respect Demands a Conscious Design

The work environment at Google was no accident. SVP for business operations Shona Brown had optimized its organizational design to maximize effectiveness and innovation. That design yielded two great benefits: unstoppable business results *and* a more reasonable working environment. There were two key principles: Optimize for Collaboration and Honor Individuality. Like all people, Shona is human and imperfect. But she did damn good work designing Google's management systems for fairness and success.

Optimize for Collaboration, Not Coercion

Shona believed that in the modern economy, command-and-control management just doesn't work that well. Bureaucracy is inefficient and kills innovation. Her insight was that top-down leadership, where worker bees are told what to do and how to think, stifles productivity and creativity. But you still need a hierarchy. Early on, Google's founders had experimented with getting rid of managers altogether. That didn't work.

Shona's insight was that while dominance hierarchies are bad for innovation, a collaboration hierarchy can work. There was still an organizational chart with a CEO, VPs, directors, managers, and so on. But in this model, leaders at all levels were subject to real checks and balances that were baked into the company's management systems, processes, and organizational design.

The idea was to strip managers of traditional sources of power, such as hiring, promotion, and salary decisions. This authority was given instead to teams, which were likelier to make better decisions. No leader at the company, not even the CEO, could hire people without putting them through a hiring process or promote people without putting them through a promotion process. Managers couldn't just pay bonuses or decide salaries unilaterally.

Nobody could coerce employees to do something they didn't want to do. I'll never forget watching an argument between one of the three most senior leaders at the company and a group of engineers working on a project. The executive proposed one approach. The team had a different idea. The executive couldn't convince them, so he suggested taking three or four of the hundreds of engineers working on the project to do a small Skunk Works proof of concept for his idea. The team demurred. "If this were an ordinary company, I'd make you all do it my way!" exclaimed the executive. "I just want to try this idea out."

The team explained again why the executive's idea wouldn't work and why it would be disruptive to have even three or four people pursuing it. He allowed himself to be overruled. This kind of behavior requires a high level of trust going both ways. That's what a good system does: it allows trust to thrive. Across the board, processes at Google optimized for collaboration and discouraged coercion. When performance reviews came around, managers were rated by their employees as well as vice versa. When people did behave badly at Google, they usually got extremely quick and clear feedback from their peers and their manager. And when the person behaving badly was the manager? Even before the manager's boss found out about and corrected this behavior, team members would abandon the manager. Google made it easy for employees to switch teams without their manager's approval. Having a bully for a boss was an asshole tax that Google felt nobody should have to pay.

The purpose of the management hierarchy was twofold: one, to ensure accountability; two, to provide a coaching and mentoring service to help employees grow. Managers were held accountable, but they were not given much "control" to get things done. They had to rely on building real relationships with each of their employees and on inspiring or persuading people to get things done.

The management structures at Google discouraged a command and control, "tell people what to do" kind of leadership. In fact, using managerial authority to coerce others without allowing them to challenge you was one of the few ways a manager could get fired. Instead, everyone at Google was expected to work collaboratively, and ideas came from any and all directions.

Honor Individuality, Don't Demand Conformity

Shona also believed that diverse teams are more innovative. Therefore, it was important to respect the individuality of *all* employees. The CEO would exhort employees, "Be loud! Challenge me! If I'm wrong, I want to know." It wasn't enough for the CEO to respect the individuality of the employees; the employees had to respect one another as well. Respecting individuality didn't mean letting people say whatever they wanted about anything. It didn't mean giving one person's ignorance and another's expertise equal weight. It also didn't mean that one had to allow for endless debate and argument. It did mean, though, truly listening to everyone without bias or prejudice. It meant remaining open to different points of view, as well as different and unexpected ways of being.

One of the most visible people at the company often wore large rabbit ears. Anyone who dismissed this person's skills because of the unusual choice in headgear would've been frowned upon. At most companies, the employee in rabbit ears would have been ignored or mocked because our brains often automatically censor or dismiss the unexpected. But Google was disciplined about making sure different points of view got heard and not allowing job titles or sartorial choices to be the filter for what got heard and what didn't.

Google went beyond merely tolerating differences between people. Instead, it took measures to create a culture that was not just open to disagreement and debate but actually made it a *duty* to dissent.

Those early days at Google showed me that when individuals feel encouraged to bring their whole selves to work—when they feel confident they will be heard rather than shut down if they speak up—they do better work, and they work better together. Productivity increases, innovation flourishes, and things are much more fair. Everyone is happier. It becomes a virtuous cycle.

How many other people have experienced that kind of Radical Respect? Recently, I posted on social media, "Did you ever have a job where there was almost no workplace injustice—minimal bias, no prejudice, no bullying, no discrimination, no harassment, no sexual assault? If so, will you tell me your story??"

I expected the vast majority of the responses to be negative. And some were: "You mean has anyone worked solely for and with robots?" or "Nope. The ACTUAL unicorn in the startup world lol." But 53 percent of the responses—more than half!—were affirmative, and my follow-up phone conversations with several of these strangers convinced me that I am not alone. Here are some things people told me:

- "I think I work there. I'm very happy at my workplace."
- "This is true of my experience with my first employer of ten years, as a corporate consultant, no less. The key was the hiring criteria: smart and nice. This was a culture that really valued kindness."
- "Got one now . . . I am trusted—that's at the center of it, I think. To be trusted is so motivating."
- "I have a story. It was in Michigan, which, given current news cycle, might seem hard to believe but it had it all—transgender employees, promotions while pregnant. It was my best tech job ever, and many of us are still friends."

- "I had such an experience. They're ranked as Canada's number one place to work. Learned a lot about how a work environment can be / what's possible. Experimentation over perfection. Curiosity over assumptions. Kindness over ego."

A PROCESS, NOT A DESTINATION

Here is the key thing to remember about Radical Respect. It's a process, not a destination. There's no natural stopping point. *You have to keep striving to achieve it*—monthly, weekly, even daily, hourly. Think of your workplace as being at the top of a steep hill. You have a spectacular view, but you have to climb that hill every day to enjoy it. Or think of it as a building. If you hire good engineers and workers, use quality materials, and build a strong foundation, your building will last longer than if you don't. But even a well-made building can quickly become uninhabitable if you don't clean and maintain it.

Life is change. If you don't revisit and buttress the safeguards in place to make sure that coercion and conformity aren't creeping into the way people work together, then workplace injustice and the inefficiency that accompanies it will take over your culture. The aspects of human nature we are least proud of will always be pulling us away from efforts to collaborate and toward the instinct to coerce; away from respecting individuality and toward demanding conformity. Daily attention is needed to resist these forces and keep your workplace just.

And as organizations grow, the efforts to safeguard against bias, prejudice, bullying, discrimination, harassment, and physical violations need to get more and more robust. If you are a leader in a workplace, it's your job to do the same. If you are an upstander, it's your job to intervene in some way when you notice workplace injustice. In an ideal world, which this is not, your intervention speaks truth to power and holds leaders accountable. If you are harmed in your workplace, it's your job to choose the response that protects you first and foremost, and helps others if you can. And if you've caused harm, it's your job to acknowledge what you've done and make amends. Ignorance is no excuse. Good intentions are better than bad intentions, but not enough. We all need to get proactive about intending not to harm others.

EVERYONE HAS A ROLE TO PLAY

I hope that by this point you have a couple of ideas of things you can do, today, that will help you create the kind of workplace where everyone can do the best work of their lives and build the best relationships of their career.

I hope that if you notice bias, prejudice, or bullying directed at you or someone else, you'll know what to say and respond to bias with an "I" statement, prejudice with an "it" statement, and bullying with a "you" statement.

I hope if you're a leader you'll make a just workplace likelier by establishing bias disrupters; by clarifying where the line is between one person's right to hold a prejudiced belief, but not to impose it on others; and by making sure there are real consequences for bullying. I hope you'll apply checks and balances and measure what matters in your management process, and communicate a clear culture of consent.

If you're harmed by discrimination, harassment, or physical violations, I hope you'll have a better idea of how to document what is happening in a way that dispels gaslighting, to build solidarity, and to locate the exit nearest you. I hope you'll come away with a better understanding of the risks and benefits of reporting to HR, having a direct conversation with the person who harmed you, taking legal action, and telling your story.

And if you've caused harm, I hope you'll have better ideas about how you can become part of the solution by becoming more aware, acknowledging the harm you did, accepting the consequences, making amends, apologizing, and changing.

LOVE AND JOY

Creating a kick-ass work environment where you can take a step in the direction of your dreams and love the people around you is joyful. If you're approaching this with dread, back the truck up and figure out a different approach.

As the poet Toi Derricotte wrote, "Joy is an act of resistance." If you're a leader, resist the temptation to control and coerce; instead, design systems that ensure a working environment where everyone can do the best work of their lives and build the best relationships of their careers. When you approach this design with joy, you're far likelier to succeed. And when you're speaking truth to power, try to do it with love. Remember the person you're speaking truth to is also human.

In a commencement address to Wellesley's class of 2018, Tracy K. Smith, the twenty-second poet laureate of the United States, offered a beautiful reminder that to achieve our ideals, we need to bring love and joy to the work.

> We tend to avoid that word [love] when we talk about politics, about demographics and policy, employing in its place a term like "tolerance." But tolerance is meager. Tolerance means I will make space for you beside me on some kind of imaginary national bus, then slide back over so you don't get too much of what I never stopped thinking is mine. . . . Tolerance requires no

cognitive shift. . . . But Love is a radical shift. Love tells me that your needs must be as important to me as mine are; that I can only truly honor and protect myself by honoring and protecting you. . . . [Love] assures me that giving you what you need is a way of ministering to myself, to the Us that you and I together make. . . .

[I]n order to embrace Love, I must move past fear, past a fixation on my own claim to power or authority.

I believe we do our best work when we love our work, the results of our work, and the people with whom we work. I do not believe that work must be drudgery we are forced to do.

We can look forward to the work we do to create more radically respectful workplaces with excitement instead of the deep dread too many people bring to this task. We can laugh at our own biases when they are disrupted, rather than getting defensive. We can relish the new clarity of our thinking when our prejudices are challenged. We can enjoy kinder, gentler relationships when we learn to stop bullying and start caring for one another. This doesn't have to be a food fight. It can be a delicious smorgasbord.

IT'S SIMPLE, EVEN IF IT'S NOT EASY

When the problems seem insurmountable, return to these two core ideas: First, honor the individuality of each of your colleagues. Don't demand that they conform to some preconceived idea you might have of who they "ought" to be. Second, collaborate with your colleagues. Don't try to dominate or coerce them.

Honor individuality, don't demand conformity. Optimize for collaboration, not coercion. That's all it takes to create Radical Respect!

Note

1. For a more serious (and funny) treatment of this tendency to distance ourselves
   from pain using humor, watch *Nanette* by Hannah Gadsby.

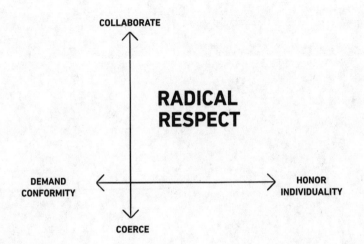

Acknowledgments

Writing a book is an act of collaboration, not a solitary endeavor. The fact that only my name is on the cover of this book reflects a myth that belies the reality. Many people collaborated in writing this book and launching it into the world.

My process is not a linear one, to say the least, and that can be frustrating—at times infuriating, I'm told—to my collaborators. I am deeply grateful to them for sticking with me throughout hundreds of thousands of words written and deleted, for giant changes made after the last minute, and for allowing me to do a major edit for this paperback edition.

First, my family, both the family I was born into and the family my husband, Andy, and I created.

My father wins the award for reading this book the most times—he read *six* different drafts. His enthusiasm kept me going when I wondered if I should give up. He gave me a lot to think about for each version, as well as detailed copy edits. As we were going through the final copy edits, my father was battling cancer and extreme fatigue from his treatments. Yet still he caught more mistakes than anyone. Words cannot express my admiration and gratitude. We lost him before the book came out, but he lives on in every page.

My mother wins the award for the best response to the absurdly sexist rules of the tennis court. Her willingness to challenge a system in a way that allowed her to keep playing and me to understand from an early age how messed up it was was invaluable. She, my brother, and my sister, all read this book multiple times. Their comments and thoughts made it immeasurably better.

My husband, Andy, read almost as many drafts as my father (not that it was a contest!). My life got immeasurably more joyful the day I met Andy. I am grateful to his parents, for raising such an enlightened man, and to his siblings. Shortly after we met, Andy invited me to spend time with Eleanor, Tom, and Lana. That was the moment I knew: these were people I needed in my life. Andy has often credited his aunts for teaching him to be a real feminist, and for that, I'm grateful. My husband's uncle Jim Ottaway read an early draft of this book and offered incredible insight.

Andy and our children made it possible for me to finish this book despite quarantine and homeschooling during Covid. They allowed me to retreat to the shed in the backyard and blew the trumpet when it was time for me to come in for dinner—which they made while I wrote and deleted words.

Our children's very existence is the inspiration to make the world more just. They contributed their common sense, put up with my absences and notable stress levels, and had a lot of good thoughts as to whether the subtitle should be *Get It Done* or *Get Sh*t Done* or *Don't Take Sh*t, Get Sh*t Done*. Though in the end we abandoned all those subtitles, it was fun to think this through with them.

I could never have managed to write this book without our adopted family member, Rosy Garcia. When we were separated from Rosy by quarantine, we all missed her terribly and were thrilled when she could return.

Tim Bartlett, the editor (a.k.a. the boss) of this book, flew to California and perched on the landing between two rooms to help me begin to create order out of the chaos of my shitty first draft. And then he patiently edited and edited and edited as I wrote and abandoned draft after draft. It kept getting better, and I can promise him that if I could think in a more efficient way, I'd do it, but this is the only way I seem to be able to work. Thank you, Tim, for putting up with me! And a huge thanks to the folks at St. Martin's Press who worked with Tim and me to bring this book to life. After reading an early version of the book, Alice Pfeifer sent me one of the most encouraging notes I've ever gotten, just when I needed it most. She kept Tim and me on track and made sure we made it to the finish line, more or less on time. Jennifer Fernandez, Jennifer Simington, and Alan Bradshaw gave this book the copyediting love it badly needed—twice! They improved literally every sentence. Laura Clark's enthusiasm for this project and guidance on how to reach each of its different audiences has always pushed me to clarify my thinking, and to have fun doing it. Gabi Gantz's sense of humor and wisdom keep publicity real—and keeping BS out of PR is indeed a rare and refreshing gift. Danielle Prielipp's drive and organization and spark make marketing fun. Ellis Levine made legal review a pleasure. And deep gratitude goes to my agent, Howard Yoon, who helped me refine the idea for this book when it was still pretty inchoate and who was unafraid to wade into a truly shitty first draft and tell me what was worth thinking more about and what was worth discarding. I also want to extend my deepest gratitude to the team at Radical Candor: Brandi Neal, Nick Ditmore, Jason Rosoff, Amy Sandler, and Nora Wilcox. Each of them read this book and gave me invaluable insights. They also gave me the greatest gift of all: time. They did all the work of managing the company so I could just write. The candor coaches also read and commented on various drafts of this book, making it better each time. Huge thanks to Melissa Andrada, Becca Barish, Aaron Dimmock, Joe Dunn, Bina Martin, Farrah Mitra, Mike Pugh, and Stephanie Usry.

I think in images, but I am no designer and cannot draw worth a damn, so collaboration is essential. Nick Ditmore was my constant companion throughout this book. He drew and redrew every graphic in this book hundreds of times, and each iteration helped me clarify my thinking.

I did not want to be limited by my lived experience here.

A number of people offered their expertise and their life experiences to broaden my perspective. First, Laura Eldridge, a women's health writer and activist, started talking to me about this project in November 2017. She assigned me reading each week. When I started writing, I was woefully ignorant of most of the writers who eventually influenced this book. She read what I wrote each week. When I threw away an eighty-thousand-word draft and started over, she didn't seem even a little alarmed. She just kept reading, and we talked every Friday until the last version.

When I first started writing, the head of the wellness program at the Second City, Becca Barish, offered me some Radical Candor: "The way your generation feels about the word *girl* is the way my generation feels about pronouns. You cannot write this book without taking sexual orientation and gender identity into account." She was correct, and it's hard not to feel ashamed that she had to tell me. But shame is not a productive emotion. Becca, as well as Chris Bartlett, the executive director at William Way LGBT Community Center, both read this book to be my heteronormative bias busters.

Chairman Mom founder Sarah Lacy also offered me some Radical Candor: I was too locked in my perspective as a privileged White woman. But she didn't just offer criticism; she offered help. She did a thorough edit of the book. And, knowing she shares White privilege, she also introduced me to Breeze Harper, cofounder of Critical Diversity Solutions.

Breeze became my bias buster extraordinaire and also one of my favorite people. For over a year, Breeze read and reread drafts I sent her, gave me articles and books to read, and was endlessly generous and fun to work with as she helped me confront problems I'd introduced into my manuscript. Breeze was so helpful that she inspired me to seek out other bias busters as well. I got invaluable insights for this book from Heather Caruso, assistant dean for equity, diversity, and inclusion at

UCLA Anderson School of Management, Jennifer M. Gómez, assistant professor of psychology at Boston University, Allyson Hobbs, professor of history at Stanford University, Annie Jean-Baptiste, head of product inclusion at Google, and Danae Sterental, founder of HereWe and lecturer at Stanford University for courses, including Equity by Design. I am so deeply grateful to each of them!

One of the most important goals of this book is to give actionable advice to leaders. I wrote first from my own experience, about things I'd done that worked and things I wished I'd done. But would other leaders find the advice I was giving helpful? Would they put any of these suggestions into practice? I wanted to make sure I was keeping it real. So I turned to two of the most brilliant operating leaders I know. Shona Brown, the former SVP of business operations at Google, and Jared Smith, cofounder of Qualtrics, were both incredibly generous with their time. Shona read as I wrote, giving me advice every few weeks over the years I spent writing this book. And Jared devoured a later draft of the book; we spent an hour per chapter going over his comments and having lively conversations.

Because I wrote and rewrote *Radical Respect* several times, it was invaluable to bring in new editors to read it fresh. Naval Postgraduate School historian Dr. Zach Shore helped me work through some of the early ideas for this book, walking and talking. He also read an early version and was able to cut through a lot of clutter and offer a much cleaner way to think about its structure, as well as smoothing out the language in some rough patches. Will Dana, former managing editor at *Rolling Stone*, provided invaluable insight as he edited two different versions of the manuscript. He pushed me hard as a writer, and I learned so much from him. He was also endlessly patient with me on calls that invariably happened in airport waiting areas.

Then, as we entered quarantine, Alice Truax, a *New Yorker* editor who had been invaluable to *Radical Candor*, took both me and the manuscript in hand. When I had talked to her about this project early on, it was Alice who flagged my own denial for me. And as she read, Alice attended to every word in every sentence, while at the same time nudging me (always with great kindness) toward several major revelations about myself. I had thought I'd understood my denial, but Alice helped me recognize that I had much further to go. *Radical Respect* is a much better book, and I am a happier person, thanks to Alice.

As Alice and I were editing, Lisa Schievelbein, founding executive director of the Center for Institutional Courage, read with an eye to my citations. Not only does Lisa have a keen eye for both structure and detail within the text, her knowledge of psychological research is encyclopedic. I have rarely seen anyone who knows how to get shit done faster and more joyfully than Lisa.

So many other people read and edited this book: Aileen Lee, Allison Kluger, Ann Poletti, Anne Libera, April Underwood, Barbara Chai, Beth Ann Kaminkow, Bethany Crystal, Caroline Reitz, Christa Quarles, Christine Howard, Clea Sarnquist, Dambisa Moyo, Dan Pink, Darren Walker, Deborah Gruenfeld, Diane Chaleff, Elizabeth Kim, Ellen Konar, Ellen Ray, Emily Procter, Esther Dyson, Evan Cohen, Françoise Brougher, Frank Yeary, Heather Caruso, Jane Penner, Jason Li, Jim Collier, Joanna Strober, John Maeda, Jorge Arteaga, Joshua Cohen, Julia Austin, Hope Blackley, Kamini Ramani, Kelly Leonard, Lauren Yeary, Leyla Seka, Lisa Krupicka, Meghan Olivia Warner, Mekka Okereke, Michael Schrage, Moira Paz, Moises Naim, Natalie Ray, Olga Narvskaia, Peter Reinhardt, Riya Berry, Ruchi Sanghvi, Russ Laraway, Ryan Smith, Sanjay Khare, Sarah Kunst, Scott O'Neil, Sheryl Sandberg, Steve Diamond, Sukhinder Singh Cassidy, Susan Fowler Rigetti, Tamar Nisbett, and Tiffani Lee were all generous with their time and radically candid with their praise and criticism. So grateful to each of them!

Thank you to the folks I met on Twitter/X who shared their stories of Radical Respect with me: Indu Khosla, Joshua Lewis, Miche Priest, Alexandria Procter, "RunningDin," Andrew Prasatya, Sunder Sarangan, Pierre Babineau, Jen Ross, Brandon Belvin, Maulik, Mika Blundell, Betty Carroll, and Tuli Skaist.

How could I incorporate comments from so many people? Google Docs was built for just that. It may seem silly to mention the people who made the tool I used to write this book. But specifically, I want to thank Alan Warren and Jude Flannery. When Alan and Jude and I worked together at Juice Software, we talked a lot about collaboration and document-centric chat. We didn't manage to make this idea a reality at Juice, but then Google hired us, and they made it happen there. Though they have both left, the Google Docs team just keeps making the product better. This is a little object lesson in the miracle that is human collaboration. A spark of an idea flares and sputters out, only to be reignited in a different context, and then someone else carries the torch forward. While we are on the topic of infrastructure, my husband, Andy, also gets some more credit. He came up with the idea of the she-shed in the backyard. Writing a book about gender injustice in one's bedroom is not ideal. Many thanks to Mike Turkington and Alex Cordrey for building me a room of my own, so necessary for a writer.

That is almost 2,500 words of thanks, and I know I've forgotten people whom I care about. To whomever that is, blame my faulty brain, but know that I love you and I thank you.

Notes

Epigraph
Lorde, Audre. *Sister Outsider: Essays and Speeches*. Berkeley, CA: Crossing Press, 1984.

Introduction: We Can Fix Problems Only When We Are Willing to Notice Them
Appiah, Kwame Anthony. "The Case for Capitalizing the B in Black." *The Atlantic*, June 18, 2020. https://www.theatlantic .com/ideas/archive/2020/06/time-to-capitalize-blackand-white /613159/.
Calderón, Dolores. "Locating the Foundations of Epistemologies of Ignorance in Education Ideology and Practice." In *Epistemologies of Ignorance in Education*, edited by Erik Malewski and Nathalia Jaramillo. Charlotte, NC: Information Age, 2011.
McGoey, Linsey. *The Unknowers: How Strategic Ignorance Rules the World*. London: Zed Books, 2019.
"Racial Disparities Are Widespread in California." Public Policy Institute of California, February 6, 2023. https://www.ppic.org/blog /racial-disparities-are-widespread-in-california/.
Scott, Kim. *Just Work: Get Sh*t Done, Fast & Fair*. New York: St. Martin's Press, 2021.
Scott, Kim. *Radical Candor: Be a Kick-Ass Boss Without Losing Your Humanity*. New York: St. Martin's Press, 2017.
Tongue, Denzel. "Opinion: How Systemic Racism Shows Up in California—and Why We Must End It." *California Health Report: Solutions for Health Equity,* June 18, 2020. https://www .calhealthreport.org/2020/06/18/opinion-how-systemic-racism -shows-up-in-california-and-why-we-must-end-it/.
Weiss, Fredric Larry. *Freud: Knowing and Not Wanting to Know*. New York: St. Martin's Press, 1990.

1: A Framework for Success

Muhammad, Khadijah. "How We're Failing at Respecting the Black Woman." *Joshua's Truth*, June 17, 2020. https://joshuastruth.com /2020/06/17/how-were-failing-at-respecting-the-black-woman/.

Porter, Michael E. "The Five Competitive Forces That Shape Strategy." *PubMed* 86, no. 1 (January 1, 2008): 78–93, 137.

Scott, Kim. *Radical Candor: Be a Kick-Ass Boss Without Losing Your Humanity*. New York: St. Martin's Press, 2017.

Workplace Bullying Institute. "2021 WBI U.S. Workplace Bullying Survey." Accessed August 13, 2023. https://workplacebullying.org /2021-wbi-survey/.

2: How Leaders Can Foster a Culture of Respect

Benjamin, Ruha. *Race After Technology: Abolitionist Tools for the New Jim Code*. Oxford: Polity, 2019.

Center for Institutional Courage. "Knowledge Base and Research Priorities." Accessed August 13, 2023. https://www .institutionalcourage.org/knowledge-base-and-research-priorities.

Correll, Shelley J., and Caroline Simard. "Research: Vague Feedback Is Holding Women Back." *Harvard Business Review*, April 29, 2016. https://hbr.org/2016/04/research-vague-feedback-is-holding -women-back?mod=article_inline.

Duhigg, Charles. *Smarter Faster Better: The Transformative Power of Real Productivity*. New York: Random House, 2016.

Duhigg, Charles. "What Google Learned from Its Quest to Build the Perfect Team." *New York Times*, February 25, 2016. https://www .nytimes.com/2016/02/28/magazine/what-google-learned-from-its -quest-to-build-the-perfect-team.html.

Edmondson, Amy, and Kim Scott. "Follow These 4 Steps to Create Psychological Safety in Your Teams." *Fast Company*, November 22, 2022. https://www.fastcompany.com/90814937/follow-these -4-steps-to-create-psychological-safety-in-your-teams.

"First Amendment Freedom of Speech in the Workplace: Can Employees Say Anything They Want?" HRdirect, October 13, 2022. https://www.hrdirect.com/can-employees-exercise-complete -freedom-of-speech-in-the-workplace.

Freire Institute. "Concepts Used by Paulo Freire." Accessed August 13, 2023. https://freire.org/concepts-used-by-paulo-freire.

Garden, Charlotte. "Was It Something I Said? Legal Protections for Employee Speech." Economic Policy Institute, May 5, 2022. https://www.epi.org/unequalpower/publications/free-speech-in-the-workplace/.

Goldberg, Lewis R. "The Structure of Phenotypic Personality Traits." *American Psychologist* 48, no. 1 (1993): 26–34.

Goodwin, Renee D., and Ian H. Gotlib. "Gender Differences in Depression: The Role of Personality Factors." *Psychiatry Research* 126, no. 2 (2004): 135–42.

Ingraham, Christopher. "Rich Guys Are Most Likely to Have No Idea What They're Talking About, Study Suggests." *Washington Post*, April 26, 2019. https://www.washingtonpost.com/business/2019/04/26/rich-guys-are-most-likely-have-no-idea-what-theyre-talking-about-study-finds/.

Jerrim, John, Phil Parker, and Dominique Shure. "Bullshitters. Who Are They and What Do We Know About Their Lives?" Social Science Research Network, April 2019. https://papers.ssrn.com/sol3/papers.cfm?abstract_id=3390272.

Jordan, Vernon E., and Annette Gordon-Reed. *Vernon Can Read! A Memoir*. New York: PublicAffairs, 2008.

Kurter, Heidi Lynne. "Is Micromanaging a Form of Bullying? Here Are 3 Things You Should Know." *Forbes*, June 29, 2021. https://www.forbes.com/sites/heidilynnekurter/2021/06/29/is-micromanaging-a-form-of-bullying-here-are-3-things-you-should-know/?sh=57f38d864467.

Lipton, Mark. *Mean Men: The Perversion of America's Self-Made Man*. New York: Voussoir Press, 2017.

Lyons, Daniel. *STFU: The Power of Keeping Your Mouth Shut in an Endlessly Noisy World*. New York: Henry Holt, 2023.

Mayden, Jason (@curbsideministries). Accessed August 13, 2023. https://www.instagram.com/explore/tags/curbsideministries/?hl=en.

Mayden, Jason (@jasonmayden). "Are You an Accomplice or an Ally?" Instagram video. Accessed August 13, 2023. https://www.instagram.com/jasonmayden/tv/B2Z9zIQHwlV/?hl=nb.

Moule, Jean. "Understanding Unconscious Bias and Unintentional Racism." *Phi Delta Kappan* 90, no. 5 (2009): 320–6.

Rabasca Roepe, Lisa. "Barriers for Black Professionals." Society for Human Resource Management, February 6, 2021. https://www

.shrm.org/hr-today/news/all-things-work/pages/racism-corporate
-america.aspx.

Snyder, Kieran. "The Abrasiveness Trap: High-Achieving Men and
Women Are Described Differently in Reviews." *Fortune*, August
26, 2014. https://fortune.com/2014/08/26/performance-review
-gender-bias/.

Steele, Claude M. *Whistling Vivaldi: And Other Clues to How Stereotypes Affect Us*. New York: W. W. Norton, 2010.

Torres, Monica. "Black Employees Face Backlash from White
Managers When They Self-Promote at Work." HuffPost, February 10, 2023. https://www.msn.com/en-us/lifestyle/career/black
-employees-face-backlash-from-white-managers-when-they-self
-promote-at-work/ar-AA17kkA7.

Woolley, Anita Williams, Christopher F. Chabris, Alex Pentland,
Nada Hashmi, and Thomas W. Malone. "Evidence for a Collec-
tive Intelligence Factor in the Performance of Human Groups."
Science 330, no. 6004 (October 29, 2010): 686–8.

Workplace Bullying Institute. "2021 WBI U.S. Workplace Bullying
Survey." Accessed August 13, 2023. https://workplacebullying.org
/2021-wbi-survey/.

3: Be an Upstander, Not a Silent Bystander

Cole, Teju. "The White-Savior Industrial Complex." *The Atlantic*,
March 21, 2012. https://www.theatlantic.com/international
/archive/2012/03/the-white-savior-industrial-complex/254843/.

Fosha, Diana. *The Transforming Power of Affect: A Model for Accel-
erated Change*. New York: Basic Books, 2000.

Foss, Sonja K., and Cindy L. Griffin. "Beyond Persuasion: A Proposal
for an Invitational Rhetoric." *Communication Monographs* 62,
no. 1 (2009): 2–18.

Haidt, Jonathan, and Tobias Rose-Stockwell. "The Dark Psychology
of Social Networks." *The Atlantic*, December 2019. https://
www.theatlantic.com/magazine/archive/2019/12/social-media
-democracy/600763/.

"Justice Ruth Bader Ginsburg on the Legacy of Justice Scalia." Aspen
Community Programs video, 1:11:46. August 1, 2017. https://
www.aspeninstitute.org/videos/justice-ruth-bader-ginsburg-legacy
-justice-scalia/.

Kaufman, Scott Barry. "Are You a Moral Grandstander?" *Scientific American*, October 28, 2019. https://blogs.scientificamerican.com/beautiful-minds/are-you-a-moral-grandstander/.

Lewis, John. "John Lewis' 2016 Commencement Address at Washington University in St. Louis." Accessed August 13, 2023. https://source.wustl.edu/2016/05/john-lewis-2016-commencement-address-washington-university-st-louis/.

O'Donnell, Riia. "How Atlassian Got Rid of the 'Brilliant Jerk': A Q&A with Bek Chee, Global Head of Talent." HR Dive, July 24, 2019. https://www.hrdive.com/news/how-atlassian-got-rid-of-the-brilliant-jerk-a-qa-with-bek-chee-global/559168/.

Resnick, Brian. "Moral Grandstanding Is Making an Argument Just to Boost Your Status. It's Everywhere." Vox, November 27, 2019. https://www.vox.com/science-and-health/2019/11/27/20983814/moral-grandstanding-psychology.

Right to Be. Accessed August 13, 2023. https://righttobe.org/.

Rogers, Carl R., and Richard Evans Farson. *Active Listening*. Bristol, UK: Mockingbird Press, 2021.

Saslow, Eli. *Rising out of Hatred: The Awakening of a Former White Nationalist*. New York: Doubleday, 2018.

"'Snack Man' Talks About Heroic Act on Subway." YouTube video, 2:57. Posted by Anderson, May 18, 2012. https://www.youtube.com/watch?v=b58mzz7mQpg.

Tangney, June Price, and Ronda L. Dearing. *Shame and Guilt*. New York: Guilford Press, 2002.

Tappin, Ben M., and Ryan T. McKay. "The Illusion of Moral Superiority." *Social Psychological and Personality Science* 8, no. 6 (2016): 623–31.

Wanga, Caroline. "Authenticity: Who You Are Is Non-Negotiable." YouTube video, 37:16. Posted by Management Leadership for Tomorrow, April 29, 2020. https://www.youtube.com/watch?v=HAIiqOG4KBU.

Washington, Jamie. "Woke Olympics: Navigating a Culture of Social Justice Arrogance in the Context of Higher Education." YouTube video, 1:28:47. Posted by National Conference on Race & Ethnicity, September 26, 2019. https://www.youtube.com/watch?v=0B_qPHYJsDY.

Wiesel, Elie. *Night*. New York: Hill and Wang, 2006.

4: What to Say When You Don't Know What to Say

Blair, Elaine. "The Power of Enraged Women." *New York Times*, September 27, 2018. https://www.nytimes.com/2018/09/27/books /review/rebecca-traister-good-and-mad-soraya-chemaly-rage -becomes-her.html.

Brown, Brené. *Daring Greatly: How the Courage to Be Vulnerable Transforms the Way We Live, Love, Parent, and Lead.* New York: Avery, 2012.

Chemaly, Soraya. *Rage Becomes Her: The Power of Women's Anger.* New York: Atria Books, 2018.

Cuddy, Amy. "Your Body Language May Shape Who You Are." You-Tube video, 21:02. Posted by TED. October 1, 2012. https://www .youtube.com/watch?v=Ks-_Mh1QhMc.

Elsesser, Kim. "Power Posing Is Back: Amy Cuddy Successfully Re-futes Criticism." *Forbes*, April 3, 2018. https://www.forbes.com /sites/kimelsesser/2018/04/03/power-posing-is-back-amy-cuddy -successfully-refutes-criticism/?sh=643cbe843b8e.

Grohol, John M. "15 Common Defense Mechanisms." Psych Central, April 28, 2022. https://psychcentral.com/health/common-defense -mechanisms.

Johnson, Rian, dir. *Glass Onion*. Los Gatos, CA: Netflix, 2022. 141 min. https://www.netflix.com/title/81458416.

Lorde, Audre. *Your Silence Will Not Protect You: Essays*. London: Silver Press, 2017.

Manne, Kate. *Down Girl: The Logic of Misogyny*. Oxford: Oxford University Press, 2018.

Mayden, Jason (@curbsideministries). Accessed August 13, 2023. https://www.instagram.com/explore/tags/curbsideministries/?hl =en.

Mayden, Jason (@jasonmayden). "Are You an Accomplice or an Ally?" Instagram video. Accessed August 13, 2023. https://www .instagram.com/jasonmayden/tv/B2Z9zIQHwlV/?hl=nb.

Morrison, Toni. "A Humanist View." Portland State University's Oregon Public Speakers Collection, May 30, 1975. https://www .mackenzian.com/wp-content/uploads/2014/07/Transcript _PortlandState_TMorrison.pdf.

Murray, Charles. *The Emerging British Underclass*. London: Institute of Economic Affairs, 1990.

Obama, Michelle. "First Lady Michelle Obama's Full Speech at the 2016 Democratic National Convention." YouTube video, 14:45. Posted by *PBS NewsHour,* July 25, 2016. https://www.youtube .com/watch?v=4ZNWYqDU948.

PACER's National Bullying Prevention Center. "Conflict vs. Bullying: What's the Difference?" Accessed August 13, 2023. https://www .pacer.org/bullying/info/questions-answered/conflict-vs-bullying.asp.

Rankine, Claudia. *Citizen: An American Lyric.* Minneapolis: Graywolf Press, 2014.

Scott, Kim. *Radical Candor: Be a Kick-Ass Boss Without Losing Your Humanity.* New York: St. Martin's Press, 2017.

Simon and Garfunkel. "The Sound of Silence." *Wednesday Morning, 3 A.M.* Columbia/Legacy, 2001, compact disc.

Sutton, Robert I. *The No Asshole Rule: Building a Civilized Workplace and Surviving One That Isn't.* New York: Grand Central Publishing, 2007.

Traister, Rebecca. *Good and Mad: The Revolutionary Power of Women's Anger.* New York: Simon & Schuster, 2018.

Travis, Dnika J., Jennifer Thorpe-Moscon, and Courtney McCluney. "Emotional Tax: How Black Women and Men Pay More at Work and How Leaders Can Take Action." Catalyst: Workplaces That Work for Women, October 11, 2016. https://www.catalyst.org /research/emotional-tax-how-black-women-and-men-pay-more-at -work-and-how-leaders-can-take-action/.

West, Lindy. *Shrill.* New York: Hachette Books, 2017.

Williams, Paula Stone. "I've Lived as a Man & a Woman—Here's What I Learned." YouTube video, 15:24. Posted by TEDx Talks, December 19, 2017. https://www.youtube.com/watch?v =lrYx7HaUlMY.

5: Be Part of the Solution, Not Part of the Problem

Davies, Robertson. *The Manticore.* New York: Penguin Classics, 2006.

De Beauvoir, Simone. *The Second Sex.* New York: Knopf Doubleday, 2012.

DiAngelo, Robin. *White Fragility: Why It's So Hard for White People to Talk About Racism.* Boston: Beacon Press, 2018.

Dweck, Carol S. *Mindset: The New Psychology of Success.* New York: Random House, 2006.

Eddy, Mary Baker. *Science and Health with Key to the Scriptures*. Boston: The Christian Science Board of Directors, 1994.

Elsesser, Kim. "Power Posing Is Back: Amy Cuddy Successfully Refutes Criticism." *Forbes*, April 3, 2018. https://www.forbes.com /sites/kimelsesser/2018/04/03/power-posing-is-back-amy-cuddy -successfully-refutes-criticism/?sh=643cbe843b8e.

Ewing, Rachel. "'That's Crazy': Why You Might Want to Rethink That Word in Your Vocabulary." *Penn Medicine News*, September 27, 2018. https://www.pennmedicine.org/news/news-blog/2018 /september/that-crazy-why-you-might-want-to-rethink-that-word -in-your-vocabulary.

Higginbotham, Evelyn Brooks. "African-American Women's History and the Metalanguage of Race." *Signs* 17, no. 2 (Winter 1992): 251–74.

Horne, Annalee Flower. "How 'Good Intent' Undermines Diversity and Inclusion." *The Bias*, September 26, 2017. https://thebias.com/2017 /09/26/how-good-intent-undermines-diversity-and-inclusion/.

Iñiguez, Santiago. *In an Ideal Business: How the Ideas of 10 Female Philosophers Bring Value into the Workplace*. New York: Springer, 2020.

Kahneman, Daniel. *Thinking, Fast and Slow*. New York: Farrar, Straus and Giroux, 2013.

Maimon, Moshe Ben. *The Guide to the Perplexed: A New Translation*. Stanford, CA: Stanford University Press, 2023.

Mill, John Stuart. *On Liberty*. New York: Dover Publications, 2002.

Morrison, Toni. *Playing in the Dark: Whiteness and the Literary Imagination*. New York: Vintage, 1993.

Mulligan, Brenden. "Everything I Hate About Justin Caldbeck's Statement." Medium, June 24, 2017. https://brendenmulligan .com/everything-i-hate-about-justin-caldbecks-statement -11b6c9cea07e.

Rose, Todd. *The End of Average: How We Succeed in a World That Values Sameness*. New York: HarperOne, 2016.

Ross, Lee. "The Intuitive Psychologist and His Shortcomings: Distortions in the Attribution Process." *Advances in Experimental Social Psychology* 10 (1977): 173–220.

Ruttenberg, Danya. *On Repentance and Repair: Making Amends in an Unapologetic World*. Boston: Beacon Press, 2022.

Thoreau, Henry David. *Walden*. Boston: Beacon Press, 2004.

West, Lindy. *Shrill*. New York: Hachette Books, 2017.

6: Design Principles for Radical Respect

Covey, Stephen. *Trust and Inspire: How Truly Great Leaders Unleash Greatness in Others*. New York: Simon & Schuster, 2022.

Google. "re:Work." Accessed August 13, 2023. https://rework .withgoogle.com/print/guides/5721312655835136/.

Grantham-Philips, Wyatte, Geoff Mulvihill, and the Associated Press. "Fortune 100 Companies Are Getting Swarmed by Republican AGs Using the Supreme Court Affirmative Action as a Lever into the Workplace." *Forbes*, July 15, 2023. https://fortune.com/2023 /07/15/affirmative-action-13-republican-attorney-general-letter -corporate-ceos-fortune-100/.

Harvard Law School Forum on Corporate Governance. "Preparing for Potential Updates to HCM & Board Diversity Disclosure Requirements." Accessed August 13, 2023. https://corpgov.law .harvard.edu/2021/10/18/preparing-for-potential-updates-to-hcm -board-diversity-disclosure-requirements/.

Rock, David, and Heidi Grant. "Why Diverse Teams Are Smarter." *Harvard Business Review*, November 4, 2016. https://hbr.org /2016/11/why-diverse-teams-are-smarter.

Sutton, Robert. "Teams as a Double-Edged Sword." *Bob Sutton Work Matters*, October 15, 2006. https://bobsutton.typepad.com /my_weblog/2006/10/teams_as_a_doub.html.

Swisher, Kara. "Hitting the Glass Ceiling, Suddenly, at Pinterest." *New York Times*, August 14, 2020. https://www.nytimes.com /2020/08/14/opinion/pinterest-discrimination-women.html.

Zheng, Lily. "How to Effectively—and Legally—Use Racial Data for DEI." *Harvard Business Review*, July 24, 2023. https://hbr.org /2023/07/how-to-effectively-and-legally-use-racial-data-for-dei?ab =hero-subleft-3.

7: Apply Design Principles to Management Systems

Bahcall, Safi. *Loonshots: How to Nurture the Crazy Ideas That Win Wars, Cure Diseases, and Transform Industries*. New York: St. Martin's Press, 2019.

"BBC Gender Pay Gap Report 2019." Accessed August 13, 2023. http://downloads.bbc.co.uk/aboutthebbc/reports/reports/gender -pay-gap-2019.pdf.

"Canvas by Instructure." Canvas. Accessed August 13, 2023. https:// www.instructure.com/canvas?domain=canvas/.

Cooney, Samantha. "Microsoft Won't Make Women Settle Sexual Harassment Cases Privately Anymore. Here's Why That Matters." *Time*, December 19, 2017. https://time.com/5071726/microsoft -sexual-harassment-forced-arbitration/.

Dickey, Megan Rose. "Google Ends Forced Arbitration for Employees." TechCrunch, February 21, 2019. https://techcrunch.com/2019/02 /21/google-ends-forced-arbitration-for-employees/.

Edmondson, Amy C. *The Fearless Organization: Creating Psycho- logical Safety in the Workplace for Learning, Innovation, and Growth*. Hoboken, NJ: Wiley, 2018.

Farrow, Ronan. *Catch and Kill: Lies, Spies, and a Conspiracy to Protect Predators*. New York: Little, Brown, 2019.

Fowler, Susan. "I Wrote the Uber Memo. This Is How to End Sexual Harassment." *New York Times*, April 12, 2018. https://www .nytimes.com/2018/04/12/opinion/metoo-susan-fowler-forced -arbitration.html.

Goldberg, Emma, and Sarah Kessler. "New Laws Force Honesty About Pay. Companies Are Catching Up." *New York Times*, October 29, 2022. https://www.nytimes.com/2022/10/29/business /nyc-us-salary-transparency.html.

Goldin, Claudia, and Cecilia Rouse. "Orchestrating Impartiality: The Impact of 'Blind' Auditions on Female Musicians." *American Eco- nomic Review* 90, no. 4 (September 2000): 715–41.

Gruenfeld, Deborah H., and Larissa Z. Tiedens. "Organizational Preferences and Their Consequences." In *Handbook of Social Psychology*, edited by S. T. Fiske, D. T. Gilbert, and G. Lindzey. Hoboken, NJ: John Wiley & Sons, 2010.

Harvard Law School Forum on Corporate Governance. "Preparing for Potential Updates to HCM & Board Diversity Disclosure Requirements." Accessed August 13, 2023. https://corpgov.law .harvard.edu/2021/10/18/preparing-for-potential-updates-to-hcm -board-diversity-disclosure-requirements/.

Huang, Jess, Alexis Krivkovich, Irina Starikova, Lareina Yee, and Delia Zanoschi. "Women in the Workplace 2019." McKinsey & Company, October 2019. https://www.mckinsey.com/~ /media/McKinsey/Featured%20Insights/Gender%20Equality /Women%20in%20the%20Workplace%202019/Women-in-the -workplace-2019.ashx.

James, Melissa. "Culture Fit vs. Culture Add: Why One Term Actually Hurts Diversity." *OV Blog*, May 9, 2018. https:// openviewpartners.com/blog/culture-fit-vs-culture-add/.

Johnson, Stefanie K., David R. Hekman, and Elsa T. Chan. "If There's Only One Woman in Your Candidate Pool, There's Statistically No Chance She'll Be Hired." *Harvard Business Review*, April 26, 2016. https://hbr.org/2016/04/if-theres-only-one -woman-in-your-candidate-pool-theres-statistically-no-chance -shell-be-hired.

Kahneman, Daniel. *Thinking, Fast and Slow*. New York: Farrar, Straus and Giroux, 2013.

Kantor, Jodi, and Megan Twohey. *She Said: Breaking the Sexual Harassment Story That Helped Ignite a Movement*. New York: Penguin, 2019.

Kaufman, Wendy. "How One College Is Closing the Computer Science Gender Gap." NPR, May 1, 2013. https://www.npr.org /sections/alltechconsidered/2013/05/01/178810710/How-One -College-Is-Closing-The-Tech-Gender-Gap.

Larson, Erik. "3 Best Practices for High Performance Decision-Making Teams." *Forbes*, March 23, 2017. https://www.forbes .com/sites/eriklarson/2017/03/23/3-best-practices-for-high -performance-decision-making-teams.

Lewis, Michael. *The Undoing Project: A Friendship That Changed Our Minds*. London: Penguin Books, 2017.

Mayer, Kathryn. "One Benefit of Pay Transparency? More Productive Workers." Society for Human Resource Management, April 25, 2023. https://www.shrm.org/resourcesandtools/hr-topics /compensation/pages/pay-transparency-may-result-in-more -productive-workers.aspx.

Miller, Bennett, dir. *Moneyball*. Culver City, CA: Sony Pictures, 2011. 133 min.

Miller, Stephen. "Black Workers Still Earn Less Than Their White Counterparts." Society for Human Resource Management, June 11, 2020. https://www.shrm.org/resourcesandtools/hr-topics /compensation/pages/racial-wage-gaps-persistence-poses-challenge .aspx.

Moyo, Dambisa. *How Boards Work: And How They Can Work Better in a Chaotic World*. New York: Basic Books, 2021.

National Partnership for Women and Families. "Quantifying America's Gender Wage Gap by Race/Ethnicity." Accessed August 13, 2023. https://nationalpartnership.org/wp-content/uploads/2023/02 /quantifying-americas-gender-wage-gap.pdf.

National Women's Law Center. "It's Time to Pay Black Women What They're Owed." Accessed August 13, 2023. https://nwlc.org /resource/black-womens-equal-pay-day-factsheet/.

Revoir, Paul. "BBC GET HUMPH: Radio 4 Today Host John Humphrys and Jon Sopel Slammed by Bosses for Joking About the Gender Pay Gap." *The Sun*, January 11, 2018. https://www .thesun.co.uk/tvandshowbiz/5322720/bbc-gender-pay-gap-jokes -john-humphrys-jon-sopel/.

Steele, Claude M. *Whistling Vivaldi: And Other Clues to How Stereotypes Affect Us*. New York: W. W. Norton, 2010.

Swisher, Kara. "Here I Am to Talk Gender Exclusion." Accessed August 13, 2023. https://www.pscp.tv/w/1OdKrWeDwwvGX.

Tarr, Tanya. "By the Numbers: What Pay Inequality Looks Like for Women in Tech." *Forbes*, April 4, 2018. https://www.forbes.com /sites/tanyatarr/2018/04/04/by-the-numbers-what-pay-inequality -looks-like-for-women-in-tech/#75a3511960b1.

Textio. Accessed August 13, 2023. https://textio.com/.

"Timeline: How the BBC Gender Pay Story Has Unfolded." BBC, June 29, 2018. https://www.bbc.com/news/entertainment-arts -42833551.

Tommasini, Anthony. "To Make Orchestras More Diverse, End Blind Auditions." *New York Times*, July 16, 2020. https://www.nytimes .com/2020/07/16/arts/music/blind-auditions-orchestras-race.html.

Wagner, Kurt. "Facebook Followed Uber and Google and Is Ending Forced Arbitration for Sexual Harassment Cases." Vox, November 9, 2018. https://www.vox.com/2018/11/9/18081520/facebook -forced-arbitration-change-sexual-harassment-uber-google.

Wakabayashi, Daisuke. "Uber Eliminates Forced Arbitration for Sexual Misconduct Claims." *New York Times*, May 15, 2018. https://www.nytimes.com/2018/05/15/technology/uber-sex-misconduct.html.

Wilkie, Dana. "How DE&I Evolved in the C-Suite." Society for Human Resource Management. Accessed August 13, 2023. https://www.shrm.org/executive/resources/articles/pages/evolving-executive-dei-diversity-c-suite.aspx.

Woo, Erin. "A Tech Whistle-Blower Helps Others Speak Out." *New York Times*, November 24, 2021. https://www.nytimes.com/2021/11/24/technology/pinterest-whistle-blower-ifeoma-ozoma.html.

8: Create Virtuous Cycles, Prevent Vicious Cycles

Eyre, Richard. "In the Spirit of Ibsen." *The Guardian*, September 20, 2013. https://www.theguardian.com/stage/2013/sep/20/richard-eyre-spirit-ibsen-ghosts.

Hill, Evan, Ainara Tiefenthäler, Christiaan Triebert, Drew Jordan, Haley Willis, and Robin Stein. "How George Floyd Was Killed in Police Custody." *New York Times*, May 31, 2020. https://www.nytimes.com/2020/05/31/us/george-floyd-investigation.html.

Manne, Kate. *Down Girl: The Logic of Misogyny*. Oxford: Oxford University Press, 2018.

Miller, Chanel. *Know My Name: A Memoir*. New York: Viking, 2019.

Newkirk, Vann R., II. "The Myth of Reverse Racism." *The Atlantic*, August 5, 2017. https://www.theatlantic.com/education/archive/2017/08/myth-of-reverse-racism/535689/.

"Pyramid of Hate." Anti-Defamation League. Accessed August 13, 2023. https://www.adl.org/sites/default/files/documents/pyramid-of-hate.pdf.

Theoharis, Jeanne. "Martin Luther King Jr.'s Challenge to His Liberal Allies." Black Perspectives, February 22, 2021. https://www.aaihs.org/martin-luther-king-jr-s-challenge-to-his-liberal-allies/.

9: Speak Truth to Power Without Blowing Up Your Career

Benner, Katie. "Women in Tech Speak Frankly on Culture of Harassment." *New York Times*, June 30, 2017. https://www.nytimes.com/2017/06/30/technology/women-entrepreneurs-speak-out-sexual-harassment.html.

Bennett, Jessica. "I'll Share My Salary Information If You Share
    Yours." *New York Times*, January 9, 2020. https://www.nytimes
    .com/2020/01/09/style/women-salary-transparency.html.

Bhuiyan, Johana. "Uber Has Agreed to Settle a Class Action Discrim-
    ination Suit for $10 Million." Vox, March 27, 2018. https://www
    .vox.com/2018/3/27/17170154/uber-discrimination-lawsuit-10
    -million.

Brougher, Françoise. "The Pinterest Paradox: Cupcakes and Toxicity."
    Medium, August 11, 2020. https://medium.com/digital-diplomacy
    /the-pinterest-paradox-cupcakes-and-toxicity-57ed6bd76960.

"Computer Science at Colgate University." Accessed August 13,
    2023. https://www.collegefactual.com/colleges/colgate-university
    /academic-life/academic-majors/computer-information-sciences
    /computer-science/computer-science/.

Fowler, Susan. "I Wrote the Uber Memo. This Is How to End Sexual
    Harassment." *New York Times*, April 12, 2018. https://www
    .nytimes.com/2018/04/12/opinion/metoo-susan-fowler-forced
    -arbitration.html.

Frankl, Viktor E. *Man's Search for Meaning*. London: Rider, 2011.

Griffith, Erin. "Pinterest's Ben Silbermann Steps Down as Chief Exec-
    utive." *New York Times*, June 28, 2022. https://www.nytimes.com
    /2022/06/28/business/pinterest-ben-silbermann.html.

MeToo. Accessed August 13, 2023. https://metoomvmt.org/.

Mueller, Aaron, Zach Wood-Doughty, Silvio Amir, Mark Dredze, and
    Alicia Lynn Nobles. "Demographic Representation and Collective
    Storytelling in the Me Too Twitter Hashtag Activism Movement."
    Proceedings of the ACM on Human-Computer Interaction, April
    2021.

National Women's Law Center. "Lilly Ledbetter Fair Pay Act." Ac-
    cessed August 13, 2023. https://nwlc.org/resource/lilly-ledbetter
    -fair-pay-act/.

Okereke, Mekka. "The Difficulty Anchor." *Mekka Tech*, August 9,
    2018. https://mekka-tech.com/posts/2018-08-09-the-difficulty
    -anchor/.

Respers France, Lisa. "How Jessica Chastain Got Octavia Spencer
    Five Times the Pay." CNN, January 26, 2018. https://www.cnn
    .com/2018/01/26/entertainment/octavia-spencer-jessica-chastain
    -pay/index.html.

Schwab, Katharine. "Discrimination Charges at Pinterest Reveal a
  Hidden Silicon Valley Hiring Problem." *Fast Company*, July 2,
  2020. https://www.fastcompany.com/90523292/discrimination
  -charges-at-pinterest-reveal-a-hidden-silicon-valley-hiring-problem.
Sutton, Robert. *The Asshole Survival Guide: How to Deal with People
  Who Treat You Like Dirt*. Boston: Mariner Books, 2017.
Thompson, Clive. *Coders: The Making of a New Tribe and the Re-
  making of the World*. New York: Penguin, 2019.
Woo, Erin. "A Tech Whistle-Blower Helps Others Speak Out." *New
  York Times*, November 24, 2021. https://www.nytimes.com/2021
  /11/24/technology/pinterest-whistle-blower-ifeoma-ozoma.html.

10: Reinforce a Culture of Consent

Bargh, John A., Paula Raymond, John B. Pryor, and Fritz Strack.
  "Attractiveness of the Underling: An Automatic Power → Sex
  Association and Its Consequences for Sexual Harassment and
  Aggression." *Journal of Personality and Social Psychology* 68, no.
  5 (1995): 768–81.
"Betrayal and Courage in the Age of #MeToo." YouTube video,
  1:16:03. Posted by CASBS, February 12, 2019. https://www
  .youtube.com/watch?v=dRxyVMzyTG0.
Center for Institutional Courage. "The Call to Courage." Accessed
  August 13, 2023. https://www.institutionalcourage.org/the-call-to
  -courage.
Chesnut, Robert. *Intentional Integrity: How Smart Companies Can
  Lead an Ethical Revolution—and Why That's Good for All of Us*.
  London: Pan Books, 2021.
Chira, Susan, and Catrin Einhorn. "How Tough Is It to Change a
  Culture of Harassment? Ask Women at Ford." *New York Times*,
  December 19, 2017. https://www.nytimes.com/interactive/2017
  /12/19/us/ford-chicago-sexual-harassment.html.
Enrich, David, and Rachel Abrams. "McDonald's Sues Former
  C.E.O., Accusing Him of Lying and Fraud." *New York Times*,
  August 10, 2020. https://www.nytimes.com/2020/08/10/business
  /mcdonalds-ceo-steve-easterbrook.html.
Freedman, Estelle. *Redefining Rape: Sexual Violence in the Era of
  Suffrage and Segregation*. Boston: Harvard University Press,
  2015.

Freyd, Jennifer J. "What Is DARVO?" Accessed August 13, 2023. https://dynamic.uoregon.edu/jjf/defineDARVO.html.

Freyd, Jennifer J., and Alec M. Smidt. "So You Want to Address Sexual Harassment and Assault in Your Organization? *Training* Is Not Enough; *Education* Is Necessary." *Journal of Trauma & Dissociation* 20, no. 5 (September 12, 2019): 489–94.

Gassam Asare, Janice. "Stop Asking Black People If You Can Touch Their Hair." *Forbes*, January 8, 2020. https://www.forbes.com/sites/janicegassam/2020/01/08/stop-asking-black-people-if-you-can-touch-their-hair/?sh=369321e150a7.

Gay, Roxane. *Not That Bad: Dispatches from Rape Culture*. New York: Harper Perennial, 2018.

Haddon, Heather. "McDonald's Fires CEO Steve Easterbrook over Relationship with Employee." *Wall Street Journal*, November 4, 2019. https://www.wsj.com/articles/mcdonalds-fires-ceo-steve-easterbrook-over-relationship-with-employee-11572816660.

Kantor, Jodi, and Megan Twohey. *She Said: Breaking the Sexual Harassment Story That Helped Ignite a Movement*. New York: Penguin, 2019.

Keltner, Dacher, Deborah H. Gruenfeld, and Cameron Anderson. "Power, Approach, and Inhibition." *Psychological Review* 110, no. 2 (2003): 265–84.

Krakauer, John. *Missoula: Rape and the Justice System in a College Town*. New York: Doubleday, 2015.

Loofbourow, Lili. "The Myth of the Male Bumbler." *The Week*, November 15, 2017. https://theweek.com/articles/737056/myth-male-bumbler.

MeToo. Accessed August 13, 2023. https://metoomvmt.org/resources/.

"#MeToo with Ashley Judd, Ronan Farrow, and Tarana Burke." Ted Talk video, 36:20. April 2018. https://www.ted.com/talks/worklife_with_adam_grant_metoo_with_ashley_judd_ronan_farrow_and_tarana_burke?language=en.

Miller, Chanel. *Know My Name: A Memoir*. New York: Viking, 2019.

No More Global Directory. Accessed August 13, 2023. https://nomoredirectory.org.

Norris, Floyd. "A Crime So Large It Changed the Law." *New York Times*, July 14, 2005. https://www.nytimes.com/2005/07/14/business/a-crime-so-large-it-changed-the-law.html.

"Power and Sex." Eindhoven University of Technology. Accessed August 13, 2023. https://rauterberg.employee.id.tue.nl/presentations/MAO-KISSINGER_files/v3_document.htm.

RAINN. "National Sexual Assault Hotline: Confidential 24/7 Support." Accessed August 13, 2023. https://www.rainn.org/resources.

RAINN. "Scope of the Problem: Statistics." Accessed August 13, 2023. https://www.rainn.org/statistics/scope-problem/.

Sanders, Jayneen. "8 Reasons NOT to Call Your Child's Genitals 'Pet' Names." HuffPost, January 9, 2017. https://www.huffpost.com/entry/8-reasons-not-to-call-your-childs-genitals-pet-names_b_58743186e4b0eb9e49bfbec3?guccounter=1.

Smidt, Alec M., Alexis A. Adams-Clark, and Jennifer J. Freyd. "Institutional Courage Buffers Against Institutional Betrayal, Protects Employee Health, and Fosters Organizational Commitment Following Workplace Sexual Harassment." *PLOS ONE*, January 25, 2023.

"Systemic Sexism in UC Berkeley's IT Department." Katz Banks Kumin. Accessed August 13, 2023. https://katzbanks.com/news/systemic-sexism-uc-berkeleys-it-department/.

Willoughby, Teena, Marie Good, Paul J. C. Adachi, Chloe Hamza, and Royette Tavernier. "Examining the Link Between Adolescent Brain Development and Risk Taking from a Social-Developmental Perspective." *Brain and Cognition* 83, no. 3 (December 2013): 315–23.

Yaffe-Bellany, David. "McDonald's Fires C.E.O. Steve Easterbrook After Relationship with Employee." *New York Times*, November 3, 2019. https://www.nytimes.com/2019/11/03/business/mcdonalds-ceo-fired-steve-easterbrook.html.

11: A Letter to My Younger Self and Her Boss

Austen, Jane. *Pride and Prejudice*. New York: Penguin Books, 2002.

Freyd, Jennifer J. "What Is DARVO?" Accessed August 13, 2023. https://dynamic.uoregon.edu/jjf/defineDARVO.html.

Freyd, Jennifer J., and Pamela Birrell. *Blind to Betrayal: Why We Fool Ourselves We Aren't Being Fooled*. Milwaukee: Trade Paper Press, 2013.

Solzhenitsyn, Aleksandr. *The Gulag Archipelago, 1918–1956: An Experiment in Literary Investigation*. New York: Basic Books, 1997.

12: Put Some Wins on the Board

Derricotte, Toi. "From the Telly Cycle." Rattle, December 12, 2009. https://www.rattle.com/from-the-telly-cycle-by-toi-derricotte/.

Gadsby, Hannah, dir. *Nanette*. Los Gatos, CA: Netflix, 2018. 69 min. https://www.netflix.com/title/80233611.

Gruenfeld, Deborah H., and Larissa Z. Tiedens. "Organizational Preferences and Their Consequences." In *Handbook of Social Psychology*, edited by S. T. Fiske, D. T. Gilbert, and G. Lindzey. Hoboken, NJ: John Wiley & Sons, 2010.

"Tracy K. Smith Delivers Wellesley's 2018 Commencement Address." YouTube video, 29:04. Posted by Wellesley College, June 20, 2018. https://www.youtube.com/watch?v=1QO2iavTAJY.

Index

abuse, 225, 227, 317.
  See also abuse-of-
    power relationships
abuse-of-power
  relationships, 255,
    269–73, 301–3,
    315–16
  harassment and, 308
  leaders and, 270–73
  people causing harm
    and, 271–73
  people harmed and,
    273–74
  physical violations and,
    309
  sexual harassment and,
    309
accountability
  CEOs and, 198
  leaders and, 161–62,
    282
  managers and, 322
action, 3
active listening, 74.
  See also invitational
    rhetoric
Adams, Ernest, 65
affirmative action, 2023
  Supreme Court
    ruling on, 163
airtime, self-monitoring,
    54
alcohol, 254–55, 291–95
  consent and, 255
  leaders and, 294–95
  people harmed and,
    292
  people who cause harm
    and, 293
amends, making, 127–53,
    327
Anahita, Sine, 133, *133*

Anderson, Steve, 70–71
anger. *See also* rage
  "angry Black woman"
    stereotype, 56
  power and, *153*
  women and, 56,
    118–19
Anti-Defamation League,
    226
anti-Semitism, 164, 210
apologies, 128, 327
  vs. justification, 152
  knowing how not
    to apologize, 143,
    150–52
  knowing how to
    apologize, 143,
    148–50
  as substitute for fixing
    the problem, 152
  that are not apologies,
    150–51
  understanding what
    you're apologizing
    for, 127–28
Appiah, Kwame Anthony,
    5–6n2
assholes, 158, 171
  "temporary" vs.
    "certified," 106
Association, guilt by, 88
Atlassian, 47
Avedaño, Ingrid, 245
awareness, 3, 127–53,
    317n1

backhanded praise, 60
bad-loss behavior, 201
Bahcall, Safi, 179
Banks, Aerica Shimizu,
    250
Basecamp, 226

BATNA (best alternative
  to a negotiated
  agreement), 239, 313
BBC, pay disparities at,
    180–82
Beane, Billy, 214–15
Beauvoir, Simone de, 138
beliefs. *See also* prejudice
  differing, 73–75
  prejudiced, 137–38.
    see also prejudice
  questioning, 136–40
Benjamin, Ruha, 35
betrayal, 276
  institutional, 282–83,
    288
bias, 1–4, 13, *25*, 167,
    171, 228, 241, *253*,
    298, 300, 317, 328.
    *See also specific
    forms of bias*
  abuse and, 225, 227
  awareness of, 129–36
  bias busters, 130–31,
    136, *153*
  biased compliment
    syndrome, 300
  bias quantifiers, *216*
  "bias think," 214–15
  challenging biased
    comparisons in
    hiring committees,
    206, 208
  class bias, 97, 317
  coaching and, 188–89,
    216
  compensation and,
    175–76, 180–82, *216*
  conformity and, 12
  decision-making and,
    162–64
  defining, 14

bias (*continued*)
  disambiguation and,
    14–18
  discrimination and, 12,
    217, 225, 227, 228
  disruption of, 29–38,
    62, 94–95, 97, 326
  effective responses
    to, 83
  efforts to safeguard
    against, 325–26
  exiting and, *216*
  firing decisions and,
    193
  forced arbitration and,
    216
  framework for success,
    19–20
  gender bias, 13, *225*,
    226–27, 317
  global effects of,
    214–15
  harassment and, 228
  heteronormativity bias,
    94
  hiring and, *216*
  holding up a mirror
    to, *90*
  intervention in, 63–89
  "I" statements and,
    94–96, 114, *126*,
    326
  "it" statements and, 94
  in job descriptions,
    210–11
  management systems
    and, 12, 175–76
  market bias, 177,
    178–79
  masquerading as
    feedback, 114, more?
  mentoring and, *216*
  NDAS and, *216*
  negotiation bias,
    177–78
  organizational design
    and, *216*
  performance
    management and,
    216
  performance review
    system and, 57

physical violations and,
    227
power systems and, 12
prevention of, 4, 26–28
promotion and,
    166–70, 185, 186
quantifying, 163
racial bias, 13, 225,
    226–27, 250, 317
    (*see also* racism)
regional bias, 97
religious bias, 317
responding to, 91
seniority bias, 177
sexual orientation bias,
    96, 317
shared commitment to
    build stamina, 31,
    35–36
shared norms and, 31,
    33–35
shared vocabulary for
    speaking up, 31,
    32–33
unconscious, 12, 66–68,
    95, 162–64, 166–70,
    206
upstanders and, 69–71
violence and, 218–20,
    222, 224, 225,
    226–27
"you" statements (or
    questions) and, 94
binary language, 134
#BLM (Black Lives
    Matter) movement,
    2, 251
bloviating
  blocking, 53–54
  shutting down, 46,
    50–54
Brougher, Françoise,
    248–51, 252
Brown, Brené, 110
Brown, Michael, murder
    of, 2
Brown, Shona, 320–23
Brutal Ineffectiveness,
    164, 170–72, *171*,
    217, 227, 311
BS, shutting down, 46,
    50–54

building solidarity, *253*,
    312–13
  asking for help, 236–37
  asking for information,
    235–36
  finding a "difficulty
    anchor," 237–39
bullying, 2–4, 12–13, *25*,
    26–28, 171, 225,
    228, *253*, 298, 299,
    311, 317, 322, 328
  career consequences,
    46–48
  compensation
    consequences, 46–48
  vs. conflict, 109
  consequences for, 23,
    46–48, 62, 106, 171,
    326
  conversation
    consequences, 46
  creating consequences
    for, 46–48, 62
  DARVO and, 299, 300
  defining, 14–15
  delaying and, 78–79, *90*
  delegating and, 78, *90*
  directing and, 76–77, *90*
  disambiguation and,
    14–18
  distracting and, 77–78,
    90
  documentation of, 76,
    79, *90*
  dominance and, 22
  effective responses
    to, 83
  efforts to safeguard
    against, 325–26
  framework for success,
    21–23
  how not to be mistaken
    for a jerk, 140–42
  ignoring, 105
  intervention in, 63–89
  "I" statements and,
    105
  masquerading as
    feedback, 114, more?
  prevention of, 45–50
  responding to, 91
  upstanders and, 76–79

violence and, 218–20,
222, 225
vulnerability and,
109–10
ways to intervene,
76–79
"you" statements (or
questions) and,
76–77, 105–9, 114,
126, 326
Burke, Tarana, 251, 278
bystander effect, 65
bystanders, silent, 63–89

California
NDAs in, 195–96,
250–51
Silenced No More Act,
195–96, 250–51
state law on transparent
compensation in, 176
calling in, vs. calling out,
84
Center for Institutional
Courage, 286
CEOs. See also leaders
accountability and, 198
good intentions are not
enough for, 198–200
harassment and, 197
change, 128, 325, 327
Chastain, Jessica, 235–36
cheat sheet, 297
checks and balances, 200,
216, 283, 316, 326
Chemaly, Soraya, 118
Chesnut, Rob, 293
choices, proactive, 92
Christian Science Church,
137
Citigroup, 50–51
clarifying your thinking,
75
class bias, 97, 317
Clifford Chance, 187–88
climate change, 197
clumsy curiosity, allowing
for, 121, 122–23
coaching, 173
bias and, 188–89, 216
design principles and,
186–93

gender and, 188
at Google, 322
informal, 188–89
meeting for lunch,
189–90
mentoring and, 188–89
venues for, 188, 190
coercion, 9, 10–11, 10,
12, 89, 165, 171,
303, 307, 325, 329
Coercion Dynamic,
218–20, 218, 219,
222–29, 222, 227,
303, 307, 329
discouraging, 322, 328
gender bias and,
223–24
self-righteous shaming
and, 80–81, 81, 84
Cohen, Evan, 187–88,
189
Cole, Teju, 86
Colgate University,
238–39
collaboration, 11, 12,
165, 171, 218–20,
218, 219, 222–24,
222, 227, 303, 307,
329
collaboration
hierarchies, 321
vs. conformity, 328
at Google, 322
optimizing for, 9,
10–11, 10, 80, 89,
320–21, 322, 328
Colorado, 176
command and control,
vs. teamwork, 161,
320–21
common ground, finding,
75
communication
measured at the
listener's ear, 143,
146–48
company policy. See also
HR; management
systems
designing a principled
compensation
system, 175–77

"it" statements and,
43, 44
prejudice and, 99–100
upholding culture of
consent, 99–100
compensation, 173
benchmarking salaries,
316
bias and, 174–76,
180–82, 216
cutting pay data with
demographics, 175,
177–80
demographics and,
174–75
designing a principled
compensation
system, 175–77
design principles and,
175–82
disparities in, 174–80,
180–82, 198–99,
299–301, 304–6,
310, 315
federal law and, 182
gender and, 174,
180–82
managers and, 175–76
pay gap analysis,
177–80
pay parity, 197
race and, 174
salary negotiation,
298–99
salary ranges and, 176
state law on transparent
compensation, 176
transparency and, 176,
178–79, 316
wage discrimination,
299–301, 304–6,
310, 315
competition, 171
"competition pods,"
267–68
Conflict, vs. bullying,
109
conformity, 9, 11, 12, 89,
171
to average, 140
bias and, 12
vs. collaboration, 328

conformity (*continued*)
  Conformity Dynamic, 218–21, *218*, *219*, 224–29, *303*, *307*, *329*
  demand for, *165*, *171*, 218–20, *218*, *219*, 222–24, *222*, 227, *303*, *307*, 323–24, 325, 328, *329*
  gender bias and, 220
  politeness and, 219–20
confrontation, cost/benefit analysis, 240–43
Connecticut, 176
conscious design, Radical Respect and, 320
consent, *297*
  abuse-of-power relationships and, 255, 269–73
  alcohol and, 254–55
  consensual touch between peers, 255, 266
  drugs and, 255
  enforcing the rules, 270–71
  fostering, 26–62
  giving people a chance to learn, 259–61
  hookups and, 267–69
  leaders and, 256–61, 266
  leading by example, 270
  overcommunicating, 257–58
  people harmed and, 262–63
  people who cause harm and, 263–64
  policy upholding, 266–67
  reinforcing a, 254–97
  reporting consent violations to HR, 267–68
  sexual assault and, 274–90
  unwanted touch and, 255–61

  upstanders and, 261–62, 267–68
  violence and, 255, 274–90
consequences
  accepting, 128, 327
  for bullying, 23, 46–48, 62, 106, 171, 326
  for harassment, 171
conversations
  when you may want to have deeper, 73–75 (*see also* speaking up)
  conversation starters about prejudice, 42–44
Copaken, Deborah, 279
"corporate citizenship," 206
Correll, Shelley, 58
country club management, 165
Craig, Daniel, 114
credibility, earning, 122–23
Critical Diversity Solutions, 60
Cuddy, Amy, 103–4, 124, 125n1, 140–42
culture add, vs. culture fit, 11, 206, 208
culture of consent. *See* consent

DARVO ("Deny, Attack, and Reverse Victim and Offender"), 284–85, 299, 300, 304
Davies, Robertson, 136
decision-making
  bias and, 162–64
  unbiased, 162–64
  unilateral, 183–86, *216*
default to silence, resisting, 110–17, 118–19, 306–7
defensiveness, managing, 130, 132–33
degrading, avoiding, 139, *153*

delaying, bullying and, 78–79, *90*
delegating, bullying and, 78, *90*
Del Toro Lopez, Roxana, 245
demographics
  overrepresentation and, 210–11
  pay data and, 175, 177–80
  psychological safety and, 188
  résumés and, 212–13
  underrepresentation and, 210–11
denial, 3, 163
Derricotte, Toi, 327
design principles
  applying to management systems, 173–216
  checks and balances, 160
  leaders and, 317
  management systems and, 4
  measuring what matters, 160, 162–64
  proactively designed management systems, 164–70
  for radical respect, 157–72
  what good design looks like, 159–64
detachment, upstanders and, 65
dialogue, importance of, 75
dichotomizing, avoiding, 139, *153*
directing, bullying and, 76–77, *90*
disambiguation, 14–18
discomfort, being explicit if it helps, 279–80
discrete incidents, vs. dynamics, 224–27
discrimination, 2, 4, 13, *59*, 171, 174, 241, 298, 299, 301,

302, 317. *See also specific forms of discrimination*
abuse-of-power relationships and, 303
bias and, 12, 217, 225, 227, 228
documentation of, 231, 232–34, *253*, 326
efforts to safeguard against, 325–26
fighting, *253*
forced arbitration and, 196
gender discrimination, 56, 57, 59, 65–66, 224, 248–51
intentionality and, 163
perpetuation of, 249
protecting yourself from, 229–53
racial discrimination, 56, 57, 59, 65–66, 92–93, 220, 224, 225, 226
reporting to HR, 231, 243–46, 314–15, 326
sexual discrimination, 244–45
taking legal action, 231, 247–51, 315
telling your story publicly, 315
wage discrimination, 299–301, 304–6, 310, 315
disempowering employees, 161
dissent, 323
distracting, bullying and, 77–78
distraction, racism and, 92–93
diversity, measuring progress toward, 163–64
diversity candidates, 203–4
diversity, disclosure laws mandating, 163

documentation, 312, 326
of bullying, 76, 79, *90*
contemporaneous records, 234
of discrimination, 231, 232–34, *253*, 326
of harassment, 231, 232–34, *253*, 326
dominance, 12
bullying and, 22
dominance hierarchies, 157, 321
downplaying, 111, 115
drugs, consent and, 255
dynamics, 218, 298–303
Coercion Dynamic, 218–20, *218, 219*, 222–29, *222, 227*, *303, 307, 329*
Conformity Dynamic, 218–20, *218, 219*, 220–21, 224–29, *303, 307, 329*
vs. discrete incidents, 224–27
systemic injustice and, 224
vicious cycles and, 227–29

Eddy, Mary Baker, 137
Edmondson, Amy, 56, 192
emotions. *See also* anger; rage
privileged, 151
weaponization of, 151
in the workplace, 118–19, 120
employees
bias in firing decisions, 193
disempowering, 161
employee life cycle, 173
"empowering," 160–61
frustrated by injustice, 241
tracking why people quit, 193, 194–95
equity, 174, 182
ESG (environmental, social, and governance) factors, 197

essentializing, 264–65
Eustace, Alan, 211–12
exclusion, 166
excuses
making, 111, 115
vs. solutions, 211–12
exiting, 173, 310–11, 313, 326
bias and, 193, *216*
bias in firing decisions, 193
design principles and, 193–97
exit interviews, 245, 316
tracking why people quit, 193, 194–95
expectations, tempering, 140
expressing yourself, 74–75. *See also* telling your story

Facebook, 196, 240–41
fairness, 87
false coherence, questioning, 130, 131–32
false harmony, 165
Farrow, Ronan, 195
Fawcett Society, 181
federal law, compensation and, 182
feedback, 134, 322
as atomic building block of management, 55
avoiding tainted, 55, 57–58
backhanded praise, 60
from direct reports, 55–56
disallowing feedback fails, 55–60
giving, 1–2
questioning, 111, 114–15
racist compliment syndrome, 60
soliciting, 55–56, 121–22
upstanders and, 64

feeling shame, vs. being shamed, 82
fighting fire with fire, 81
finger-pointers, 50
firing decisions, bias and, 12, 193
fixed mindset, 143–44
Floyd, George, 226–27
forced arbitration, 289
  bias and, *216*
  eliminating, 173, 195, 196–97
forgiveness, demanding, 152
Foss, Sonja, 74
Fowler Rigetti, Susan, 196, 244–45, 252
Frankl, Victor, 92, 240
Freedman, Estelle, 285
Freud, Sigmund, 2
Freyd, Jennifer, 27–28, 284, 317n1
fundamental attribution error, avoiding, 139

gaslighting, 87, 275–76, 312, 326
Gay, Roxane, 285
gender, 57, 69. *See also* gender bias; gender discrimination
  coaching and, 188
  compensation and, 174
  Conformity Dynamic and, 220–21
  mentoring and, 188
  prejudice and, 137–38 (*see also* gender discrimination)
  promotion and, 184, 185
  race and, 251–52
  venues and, 191–92
gender bias, 66–68, 71–72, 94, 96, 98, 120, 137–38, 225, 226–27, 317
  coercion and, 223–24
  compensation and, 180–82
  conformity and, 220
  discrimination and, 224

hiring and, 206–7
  pay disparity and, 198–99
  promotion and, 166–70, 185
  violence and, 224
gender discrimination, 56, 57, 59, 65–66, 184, 185, 198–99, 224, 245, 248–51
gender diversity, 197, 211–12
gender identity bias, 96–97
gender roles, 72–73
gender violence, 226–27. *See also* sexual violence
genocide, 226
Girand, Laurie, 286–87
Ginsburg, Ruth Bader, 75
Glassdoor, reviews on, 213
Google, 36–38, 51, 53, 196, 211–12, 220, 237, 319–24
  coaching at, 322
  collaboration at, 322
  managers at, 320–22
  mentoring at, 322
  Radical Respect at, 319–24
  teams at, 321–22
  trust at, 322
Google Meet, 54
Gracie, Carrie, 181
Griffin, Cindy, 74
groping, 279–80
growth mindset, 143–45
guidance, giving, 1–2
guilt be association, 88
guilt be inaction, 88

harassment, 2, 4, 12–13, 174, 200–201, 217, 228, 229–31, 240–41, 317, 319
  abuse-of-power relationships and, 308, 309
  bias and, 228
  CEOs and, 197

consequences for, 171
  documentation of, 231, 232–34, *253*, 326
  don't pass the trash, 289, 290
  efforts to safeguard against, 325–26
  fighting, *253*
  forced arbitration and, 196
  protecting yourself from, 229–53
  race and, 230
  reporting to HR, 231, 243–46, 314–15, 326
  sexual harassment (*see* sexual harassment)
  taking legal action, 231, 247–51, 315
  telling your story publicly, 315
  verbal harassment, 298
  violence and, 218–20, 222
harm, acknowledging, 327
harmony, false, 165
Harper, Breeze, 60, 134–35
Harvey Mudd, 211–12
heteronormativity bias, 94
hierarchies, 157
  collaboration hierarchies, 321
  dominance hierarchies, 321
  management hierarchies, 322
Hired magazine, 174
hiring, 162–64, 173, 202–4
  asking about history of sexual assault, 290
  bias and, 12, *216*
  casting a wider net, 203–4
  challenging biased comparisons, 206, 208
  checking references, 290

design principles and, 202–15

gender bias and, 206–7

hiring committees, 204–6

job descriptions and, 203, 210–11

making candidates comfortable, 214

making sure everybody gets the message, 204

measuring what matters in, 209–10

monitoring the numbers, 204

quotas and, 210

racial bias and, 207

women on hiring panels, 204

hiring criteria, explicit, 206, 207–8

hiring panels, women on, 204

historically marginalized groups, 61n1

The Hollywood Reporter, 287

Holocaust, 226

homophobia, 69

hookups, 267–69

Horne, Annalee Flower, 146

Houston Rockets, 208, 209

how not to be mistaken for a jerk, 140–43

HR, 159, 198, 244–45

reporting consent violations to, 267–68

reporting discrimination and harassment to, 231, 243–46, *253*, 314–15, 326

reporting sexual assault to, 278–79

humor, using, 121, 123–24

Ibsen, Henrik Johan, 217

ignorance, 3, 163

impact, focusing on, 143, 145–46

inaction, guilt by, 87

Incredible Hulk, 82, 84–85

individuality

honoring, 9, 11, 89, 218–20, *218, 219, 222, 227, 303, 307,* 320, 323–24, 328, *329*

respecting, *165, 171,* 325

individuals, vs. teams, 161

injustice, 241

dynamics and, 224

employees frustrated by, 241

intervening against, 325–27

systemic injustice, 164, 171, 224, 251

Instagram Curbside Ministries, 119

instincts, trusting your, 111, 116–17

institutional betrayal, 282–83, 288

institutional courage, 27–28, 319

intentional choices, 92

intentionality, discrimination and, 163

intentions, 143, 145–46, 165, 326

assuming good, 145–46

intervention, 63–89

in bullying, 76–79

against injustice, 325–27

with "I" statements, 69

with "it" statements, 69

leaders win and, 88–89

with "you" statements (or questions), 69

intolerance, 69

racial intolerance, 69

regional intolerance, 69

religious intolerance, 69. *see also* anti-Semitism

invitational rhetoric, 74

"I" statements, 23

bullying and, 105

responding to bias with, 19–20, 23–24, *25,* 32, 69, 94–96, 114, *126,* 326

Ithaca, New York, 176

"it" statements

bias and, 94

company policy and, 43, 44

intervention with, 69

responding to prejudice with, 20–21, 23–24, *25,* 42–44, 99–104, 114, *126,* 326

Ive, Jony, 53

Ivy League schools

quotas of Jews and, 164

James, Melissa, 208

Jean-Baptiste, Annie, 53

Jersey City, New Jersey, 176

Jezebel, 149

Jim Crow South, 170

job descriptions, 203

bias in, 210–11

Jordan, Vernon, 60

joy, 327–28

Judd, Ashley, 280–81, 285, 287

justification, vs. apologies, 152. *See also* excuses

Kahneman, Daniel, 129–32, 207–8

Kalanick, Travis, 170

"kanban cord," 317, 317n2

Kantor, Jodi, 195, 287

Kaskiris, Vanessa, 294

King, Martin Luther Jr., 220

Kissinger, Henry, 281

Kleiner Perkins, 70–71

knight in shining armor, 82, 85–86

"knowing without knowing," 2

Krakauer, Jon, 285

Kunst, Sarah, 230

Language, sensitive,
    146–48
Laraway, Russ, 140–42
lawyers
    advisory role of,
        289–90
    hiring, 247, 252n2
    sexual assault and
        sexual harassment
        and, 289–90
leaders, 4, 12, 157
    abuse-of-power
        relationships and,
        270–73
    accountability and,
        161–62, 282–84
    alcohol and, 294–95
    consent and, 256–61,
        266
    consequences for
        bullying and, 23
    culture of consent and,
        256–61, 266
    in denial, 163
    design principles and,
        317
    educating yourself
        about sexual assault,
        284–85
    failures of, 200–202
    institutional betrayal
        and, 282–83
    institutional courage
        and, 282–84
    leading by example, 270
    listening with
        compassion, 275–76
    promotion and, 182–83
    Radical Respect
        framework for, 62
    responsibilities of,
        26–28
    sexual assault and,
        289–90
    upstanders and, 88–89
    violence and, 275–76,
        281, 282–90
Ledbetter, Lilly, 248
Lee, Aileen, 70–71
legal action, taking, 231,
    247–51, 253, 315,
    327

Lewis, John, 63
Lewis, Michael, 208, 209
Libera, Anne, 123
Lilly Ledbetter Fair Pay
    Act, 248
Lin, Jeremy, 208, 209
listening with compassion,
    275–76
Lorde, Audre, 91
love, 327–28
Lyons, Dan, 52

Madden, Laura, 287
Maimonides, 127
male ego, protecting, 111
management hierarchies,
    322
management systems,
    326
    applying design
        principles to,
        173–216
    bias and, 3, 12
    bullying and, 3
    design principles and, 4,
        157–72
    leaders' responsibility
        for designing fair, 216
    prejudice and, 3
managers
    absentee, 55, 58–59
    accountability and, 322
    bias and, 55, 58–59,
        175–76
    compensation and,
        175–76
    at Google, 320–22
    hiring and, 205–6
    responsibilities of, 59
    tyrannical, 161
    unilateral managerial
        decisions, 183–86
Manne, Kate, 113
market bias, addressing,
    177, 178–79
Maryland, 176
Math of the
    Overrepresented, 166
Mayden, Jason, 31, 119
McClure, Dave, 230
McDonald's, 270–71
McGoey, Linsey, 2–3

measurements, 163–64
Medina, Ana, 245
mediocracy, 171
mentoring, 173
    bias and, 216
    coaching and, 188–89
    design principles and,
        186–93
    gender and, 188
    at Google, 322
    informal, 188–89
    meeting for lunch,
        189–90
    venues for, 188, 190
mentors, asking for help
    from, 236–37
meritocracy, 171
#MeToo movement, 230,
    244–45, 251–52,
    274, 278
microaggressions
    disambiguation and,
        14–18
    downplaying, 115
micromanaging, avoiding,
    55, 58
Microsoft, 196
Microsoft Teams, 54
Mill, John Stuart, 127
Miller, Chanel, 226, 274,
    285
Mills, Charles, 3
"mirror-tocracy," 165
misogyny, 224, 225
mistakes, acknowledging
    publicly, 128
Moneyball, 214–15
moral grandstanding, 82,
    83–84
Morey, Daryl, 208, 209
Morrison, Toni, 92–93,
    138
Moyo, Dambisa, 197
Murphy, Matt, 70–71
Murray, Charles, 101–2
Musk, Elon, 170
MySpace, 251

name-calling, 50
National Sexual Assault
    Hotline, 277
Nazi Germany, 210

negotiation bias,
    addressing, 177–78
Nevada, 176
New York City, New
    York, 176
The New York Times, 287
New York Times, 283
NO MORE Global
    Directory, 278
nonbinary employees, 57
nonbinary language, 134
nondisclosure agreements
    (NDAs), 201, 248,
    289
    bias and, *216*
    in California, 195–96,
        250–51
    eliminating, 173,
        195–96
norms, consciously
    designed, 12

Oakland As, 214–15
Obama, Michelle, 124
observers, 4
Obvious Exclusion,
    164–66, *165*
"office housework"
    tasks, 69
Okereke, Mekka, 237
O'Neil, Scott, 214
OpenTable, 202–4
Optimize for
    Collaboration, 320–21
organizational design, 173
    bias and, *216*
    design principles and,
        197–202
organizations,
    homogenous, 161–62,
    211
Ostrom, Tom, 58
Overgeneralization,
    avoiding, 264–65
overrepresentation, 164,
    210–11
Ozoma, Ifeoma, 195,
    250–51

PACER, 109
"passing the trash," 289,
    290

pay data, cutting by
    demographic, 175,
    177–80
pay disparity, 174–76
    at the BBC, 180–82
    gender bias and,
        198–99
pay gap analysis, 177–80
payoffs, 289
pay parity, 197
Payscale, 177
pay transparency. *See*
    compensation
peer reviews, 46–47
people causing harm
    abuse-of-power
        relationships and,
        271–73
    talking directly with,
        314, 326–27
people harmed, 4, 87
    abuse-of-power
        relationships and,
        273–74
    alcohol and, 292
    consent and, 262–63
    finding support and
        solidarity, 277–78
    how to choose a
        response, 91
    Radical Respect
        framework for, *126*
    responsibilities of,
        92–125
    violence and, 277–81
people who cause harm,
    4, 327. *See also*
    consequences
    alcohol and, 293
    consent and, 263–64
    culture of consent and,
        263–64
    Radical Respect
        framework for,
        153
    responsibilities of,
        127–53
    violence and, 281
"perfcrastination," 184
performance indicators,
    developing and
    strengthening, 163

performance management,
    173
    bias and, *216*
    designing a principled
        performance
        management system,
        183–86
    design principles and,
        182–86
performance management
    systems, 46–47,
    183–86
performance reviews,
    46–47, 322
    bias and, 57
    linguistic analysis of,
        183, 186
persistence, 130, 133–34
personal agency,
    maintaining, 4
Philadelphia 76ers, 214
physical contact, consent
    and, 254–97
physical violations, 2, 4,
    12, 13, 218–20, *297*,
    298, 302, 305, 306,
    317. *See also* sexual
    assault; unwanted
    touch
    abuse-of-power
        relationships and,
        309
    bias and, 227
    efforts to safeguard
        against, 325–26
    fighting, *253*
Pinterest, 248–51, *252*
Politeness, conformity
    and, 219–20
polite racism, 220
political bias, 97
positional power, 13
positive target
    identification, 121
"postural feedback," 104,
    141
power
    abuse-of-power
        relationships, 255,
        269–73, 301–3, 308,
        309, 315–16
    anger and, *153*

power (*continued*)
bias and, 12
to exclude, *253*
to intimidated, *253*
physical, 13
power dynamics, 171.
see also dynamics
power systems, 12
sex and, 281
touch and, *297*
power systems, bias and,
12
prejudice, 1–4, 13, *25*,
26–28, 171, 228,
241, *253*, 298, 302,
304, 317, 328. *See
also specific forms of
prejudice*
company policy and,
99–100
conversation starter
about, 42–44
creating space for
conversation, 40–45,
62
deeper conversations
about, 73–75
defining, 14
degradation and, *153*
disambiguation and,
14–18
dichotomizing and,
153
effective responses
to, 83
efforts to safeguard
against, 325–26
framework for success,
20–21
gender and, 137–38
holding up a shield
to, *90*
intervention in, 63–89
"it" statements and,
99–104, 114, *126*,
326
masquerading as
feedback, 114
prevention of, 39–45
questioning, 136–40
as rationalization, 302
responding to, 91

vs. unconscious bias,
97–98
upstanders and, 71–73
prevention, 26–28
proactive choices, 92
"progressive"
organizations, 12
Project Aristotle, 51
promotion, 162–64
bias and, 12, 166–70,
184–85, 186
gender and, 184, 185
leaders and, 182–83
under-promoting,
182–83
promotion data, 183,
184–86
promotion gap, 184–85
promotion
recommendations,
183, 186
race and, 184
sexual behavior and,
281
unconscious bias and,
166–70
promotion data,
measuring what
matters in, 183,
184–86
promotion gap, 184–85
promotion
recommendations,
linguistic analysis of,
183, 186
protecting yourself from
discrimination and
harassment, 229–53,
253
building solidarity, 231
documentation, 231,
232–34, *253*
locating nearest exit,
231, 239–40
reporting to HR, *253*
taking legal action, 231,
247–51, *253*
talking directly with the
person, 231, 240–43,
253
telling your story
publicly, 231, 251–53

psychological safety
culture of, *56*
demographics and,
188
team success and,
192–93
public companies,
obligation for
transparency and,
197–98
Putin, Vladimir, 170
Pythagoras, 139

Qualtrics, 205
Quarles, Christa, 202–4
quotas, 163–64, 210

race, 57. *See also* racial
discrimination
compensation and,
174
Conformity Dynamic
and, 220, 221
gender and, 251–52
promotion and, 184
racial bias, 96, 207,
225, 226–27, 250,
317
racial intolerance, 69
racial violence, 226–27
sexual harassment and,
230
venues and, 190–91
racial discrimination, 56,
57, 59, 224, 225,
226, 245
distraction and, 92–93
polite, 220
racist compliment
syndrome, 60
standing up to, 65–66
racism, 56, 57, 59, 224,
225, 226. *See also*
racial discrimination
distraction and, 92–93
polite, 220
standing up to,
65–66
racist compliment
syndrome, 60
Radical Candor, 1–2,
3, 59

Radical Respect, 157,
218–20, *218*, *219*,
222, 227, *303*, *307*,
329. *See also* Radical
Respect framework
conscious design and,
320
cultivating, 225–26
culture of, 64
defining, 9–11, *10*
at Google, 319–24
honoring individuality,
11
optimize for
collaboration, not
coercion, 10–11, *10*
as process, not
destination, 325–26
rarity of, 12
success and, 320–21
what gets in the way of,
12–13
who is responsible for?
24–25
Radical Respect
framework
for leaders, *62*
for people who cause
harm, *153*
for upstanders, *90*
rage, 110, 118–20
RAINN, the Rape, Abuse
& Incest National
Network, 278, 296n3
Rankine, Claudia, 91
rape, 284–86, 288. *See
also* sexual assault
rape crisis centers, 278
rape myths, 284
references, checking, 290
referrals, 211
regional bias, 97
regional intolerance, 69
relationships, protecting,
111, 115–16
religious bias, 317
religious intolerance,
69. *See also* anti-
Semitism
reporting systems
anonymity and,
286–87, 297

building trusted,
286–87, 297, 316
employee trust in, 284,
316
reporting
discrimination and
harassment to HR,
326
reputations, 213
fear of risking, 111,
116–17
good, 122
responses
to bias, 83
to bullying, 83
choosing, 92–125
for people harmed, 91
to prejudice, 83
to sexual violence,
92–125
responsibilities, 24–25
of leaders, 26–28
of managers, 59
of people who cause
harm, 127–53
résumés
anonymizing, 203
breakdown of, 210–13
demographics and,
212–13
retribution, fear of, 111,
116, 117
Right To Be, 76
Rogerian arguments, 74
Rogers, Carl, 74
roles, 4, 24–25
Rose, Todd, 140
Ruinous Empathy, 113–14
Ruinous Himpathy,
113–14
rules
avoiding demand for,
264, 265–66
Ruttenberg, Danya, 127

salaries. *See also*
compensation
benchmarking, 316
salary negotiation,
298–99
state law and salary
ranges, 176

Sandberg, Sheryl, 37
Sanghvi, Ruchi, 240–41
Sarbanes Oxley Act, 286
Saslow, Eli, 75
Scalia, Antonin, 75
Schievelbein, Tom,
289–90
Scott, Kim
"Letter to My Younger
Self and Her Boss,"
298–317
*Radical Candor: Be
a Kickass Boss
Without Losing Your
Humanity*, 1–3, 12,
112, 113, 215n1
"search and destroy"
approach, 162
self-monitoring, 54
self-righteous shaming,
80–87, *81*
coercion and, 84
flavors of, 82–87
Incredible Hulk, 82,
84–85
knight in shining armor,
82, 85–86
moral grandstanding,
82, 83–84
social media and,
80–81, 83
White savior complex,
82, 86
seniority bias, addressing,
177, 179–80
sex, power and, 281
sex addiction, 312
sexism, 56, 57, 59,
65–66, 224. *See also*
gender bias; gender
discrimination;
sexual discrimination
sexual assault, 228,
251, 255, 274–90,
296n3
accountability for false
reporting, 286–87
advocates and, 278
avoiding silencing of
victims, 288–89
being explicit if it helps,
277, 278–80

sexual assault (*continued*)
  building trusted
    reporting systems,
    286–87
  choosing your response,
    277
  cover-ups, 288–89
  don't pass the trash,
    289, 290
  educating yourself
    about, 284–85
  employee trust in
    reporting systems,
    284–85
  evidence of, 278
  finding support and
    solidarity, 277–78
  forced arbitration and,
    289
  forensic exams and, 278
  institutional betrayal
    and, 288
  leaders and, 289–90
  NDAs and, 289
  payoffs and, 289
  rape myths, 284
  recovering from,
    280–81
  reporting to HR,
    278–79
  sham investigations,
    287–88
  victims of, 277–81,
    284–90
sexual discrimination,
  244–45. *See also*
  gender discrimination
sexual harassment,
  200–201, 217, 230,
  244–45, 319
  abuse-of-power
    relationships and, 309
  don't pass the trash,
    289, 290
  forced arbitration and,
    196
  race and, 230
  reporting to HR, 314–15
sexual misconduct data,
  286
sexual orientation bias,
  96, 317

sexual violence. *See* sexual
  assault
shame, feeling shame vs.
  being shamed, 82.
  see also shaming
shaming
  ineffectiveness and, 95
  intentions in, 81
  self-righteous, 80–87,
  81
  sham investigations,
    287–88
  shared identity,
    upstanders and, 66
  sharing the load,
    upstanders and, 66
Shore, Zach, 135
"should," avoiding saying,
  135, 143, 148
silence
  avoiding silencing of
    victims, 288–89
  breaking silence and
    rage cycle, 110,
    118–19
  resisting default to
    silence, 306–7
  silent bystanders,
    63–89
Silenced No More Act,
  195–96, 250–51
Skills, assessing, 206–7
"small things,"
  aggregation of, 130,
  132
Smidt, Alec, 284
Smith, Jared, 205
Smith Carly, 284
"Snack Man," 77
Snyder, Kieran, 57
social media, 80–81, 83,
  147. *See also specific
  platforms*
solidarity
  across differences,
    65–66
  building, 123, 231,
    235–39, *253,*
    312–13, 326
  finding, 277–78
  solace from, 273
  upstanders and, 65–66

solutions
  being part of, 127–53
  vs. excuses, 211–12
South Africa, under
  apartheid, 170
Soviet Companies Fund,
  298–316
speaking up. *See also*
  telling your story
  ROI on, 96–97
  speaking truth to
    power, 5, 229–53
  talking directly with
    people causing harm,
    314, 326–27
speech, violence and,
  226
Spencer, Octavia, 235–36
Stalinism, 171
state law, salary ranges
  and, 176
Steele, Claude, 58
stereotyping, 264–65
Stevenson, Matthew, 75
strategic ignorance, 3
strength in numbers,
  upstanders and,
  64–65
success
  frameworks for, 18–24
  success stories, 3,
    318–29
Supreme Court
  2023 ruling on
    affirmative action,
    163
  Ledbetter and, 248
Sutton, Bob, 106, 240
Swisher, Kara, 165,
  181–82
systematically advantaged
  groups, 55, 61n1,
  165–66
systematically
  disadvantaged
  groups, 55, 61n1,
  119, 165–66.
  See also historically
  marginalized groups
  attrition and, 194–95
  promotion gap and,
    184–85

systemic injustice, 164, 171, 224, 251
systems, consciously designed, 12

talking directly with people causing harm, 314, 326–27
teams
　cohesion of, 161
　command and control vs. teamwork, 161, 320–21
　diverse, 323–24
　empowered, 161
　at Google, 321–22
　high-functioning, 161
　homogenous, 161, 171, 184 (see also conformity)
　vs. individuals, 161
　subpar, 164
　team outcomes, 56
　team success and psychological safety, 192–93
　teamwork, 46–47, 161, 320–21
Tech Connection, 208
telling your story, 277, 280–81
　being explicit if it helps, 277, 278–80
　publicly, 231, 251–53, 253, 315, 327
Textio, 184
Thomas, David, 59
Thoreau, Henry David, 137
360 review process, 46–47
Tolerance, 327–28
touch
　power and, 297
　unwanted, 255–61
"toxonomy," 12–13, 14–18, 298–317
Traister, Rebecca, 118–19
transparency
　compensation and, 176, 316

public companies and, 197–98
transphobia, 69
trust
　at Google, 322
　vulnerability and, 110
turnabout is not fair play, 121
Turner, Brock, 274
Twitter/X, 170
Twohey, Megan, 195, 287

Uber, 196, 244–45
unconscious bias
　vs. prejudice, 97–98
　unconscious bias training, 206
under-promoting, 182–83
underrepresentation, 164, 210–11
unilateral managerial decisions, avoiding, 183–86
unwanted touch, 255–61
upstanders, 4, 63–90, 223, 252, 253, 310
　advantages of, 64–69
　bias and, 69–71
　bullying and, 76–79
　consent and, 261–62, 267–68
　cultivating, 110, 120–24
　detachment and, 65
　feedback and, 64
　leaders and, 88–89
　listening with compassion, 275–76
　prejudice and, 71–73
　productive intervention by, 87–88
　Radical Respect framework for, 90
　responsibilities of, 63–89
　shared identity and, 66
　sharing the load and, 66
　solidarity across differences and, 65–66
　strength in numbers and, 64–65
　violence and, 274–76
Urbaniak, Kasia, 23

Van der Swaagh, Seth, 53
Variety, 287
venues
　gender and, 191–92
　race and, 190–91
　that exclude, 188, 190
verbal harassment, 298
vicious cycles
　avoiding, 32
　Coercion Dynamic and, 227–29
　Conformity Dynamic and, 227–29
　dynamics and, 227–29
　preventing, 217–28
violence, 2, 12, 13, 218–20, 255, 303
　avoiding silencing of victims, 288–89
　bias and, 222, 224, 225, 226–27
　building trusted reporting systems, 286–87
　bullying and, 222, 225
　consent and, 274–90
　educating yourself about, 284–85
　employee trust in reporting systems, 284
　gender bias and, 224
　harassment and, 222
　interrupting, 274–75
　leaders and, 275–76, 281, 282–90
　"looking the other way," 283
　people harmed and, 277–81
　people who cause harm and, 281
　sexual violence, 228, 251
　sham investigations, 287–88
　speech and, 226
　upstanders and, 274–76
virtuous cycles, 53, 217–28
voice, giving the quiet a, 53
vulnerability, bullying and, 109–10

wages. *See* compensation
Walsh, Bill, 27
Wanga, Caroline, 121–22
wanting to be nice, 111, 112–13
Washington, Jamie, 84
Weinstein, Harvey, 285, 287
Weinstein Company, 170, 171
West, Lindy, 110, 123–24, 148–50
what to say when you don't know what to say, 91–126
White privilege, 86
White savior complex, 82, 86
White supremacy, 86

White Women's Tears, 151
Wiesel, Elie, 63
Williams, Paula Stone, 96
women. *See also* gender
  anger and, 118–19
  "angry Black woman" stereotype, 56
  vs. "girls," 29–30, 36–38
  as software engineers, 211–12
  White Women's Tears, 151
Woolley, Anita, 51
working environments
  creating respectful, collaborative, 5
  "toxic," 12–13

"unfair," 12–13
  workplace culture, 4
Workplace Bullying Institute survey, 45

Yeary, Frank, 50–51
Yeary, Lauren, 238–39
yelling, 50
"you" statements (or questions)
  bias and, 94
  responding to bullying with, 21–24, *25*, 69, 76–77, 105–9, 114, *126*, 326

Zoom, 54
Zuckerberg, Mark, 240–41

About the Author

E. Mackey

Kim Scott is the author of *Radical Respect* and *Radical Candor*. Kim was a CEO coach at Dropbox, Qualtrics, Twitter, and other tech companies. She was a member of the faculty at Apple University and before that led AdSense, YouTube, and Double-Click teams at Google. Kim learned the most valuable but painful management lessons as cofounder and CEO of two failed start-ups. She shares what she's learned from failures and successes alike at the executive education company she cofounded and on the acclaimed management podcast she cohosts.

The *New York Times* bestseller
that's become a cultural touchstone
and essential for every workplace

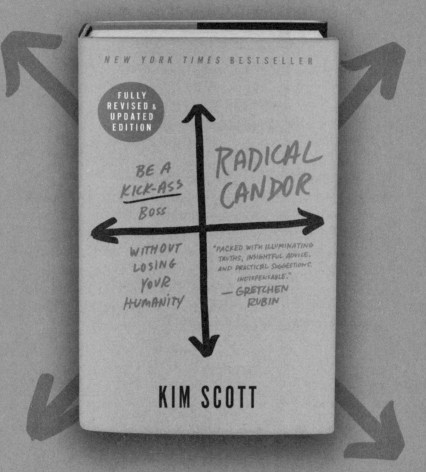

NEW YORK TIMES BESTSELLER

FULLY
REVISED &
UPDATED
EDITION

BE A
KICK-ASS
BOSS

RADICAL
CANDOR

WITHOUT
LOSING
YOUR
HUMANITY

"PACKED WITH ILLUMINATING
TRUTHS, INSIGHTFUL ADVICE,
AND PRACTICAL SUGGESTIONS.
INDISPENSABLE."
— GRETCHEN
RUBIN

KIM SCOTT

"If you manage people—whether it be one person
or a thousand—you need *Radical Candor*. Now."

—Daniel H. Pink, author of the *New York Times* bestseller *Drive*

ST. MARTIN'S PRESS